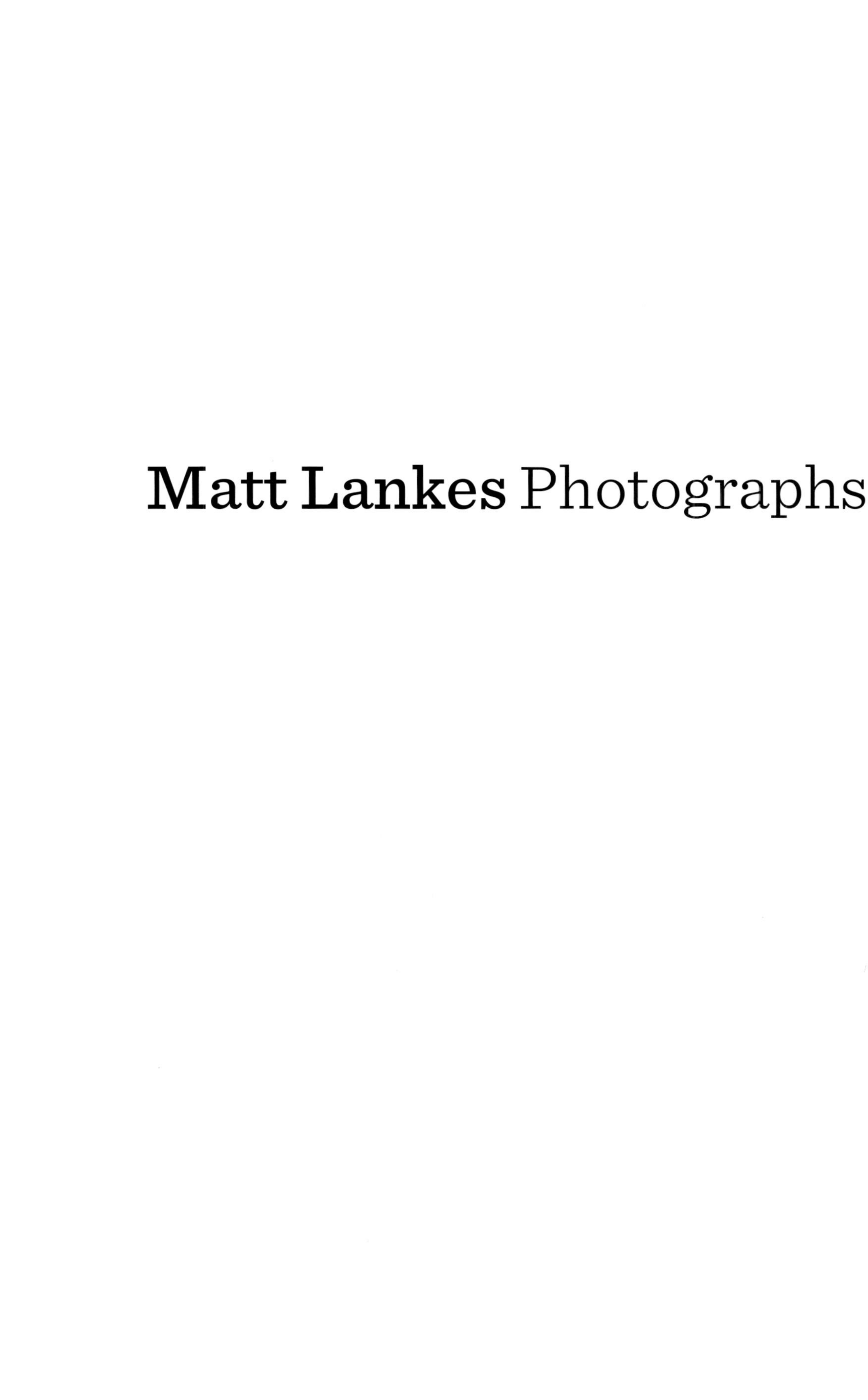

Matt Lankes Photographs

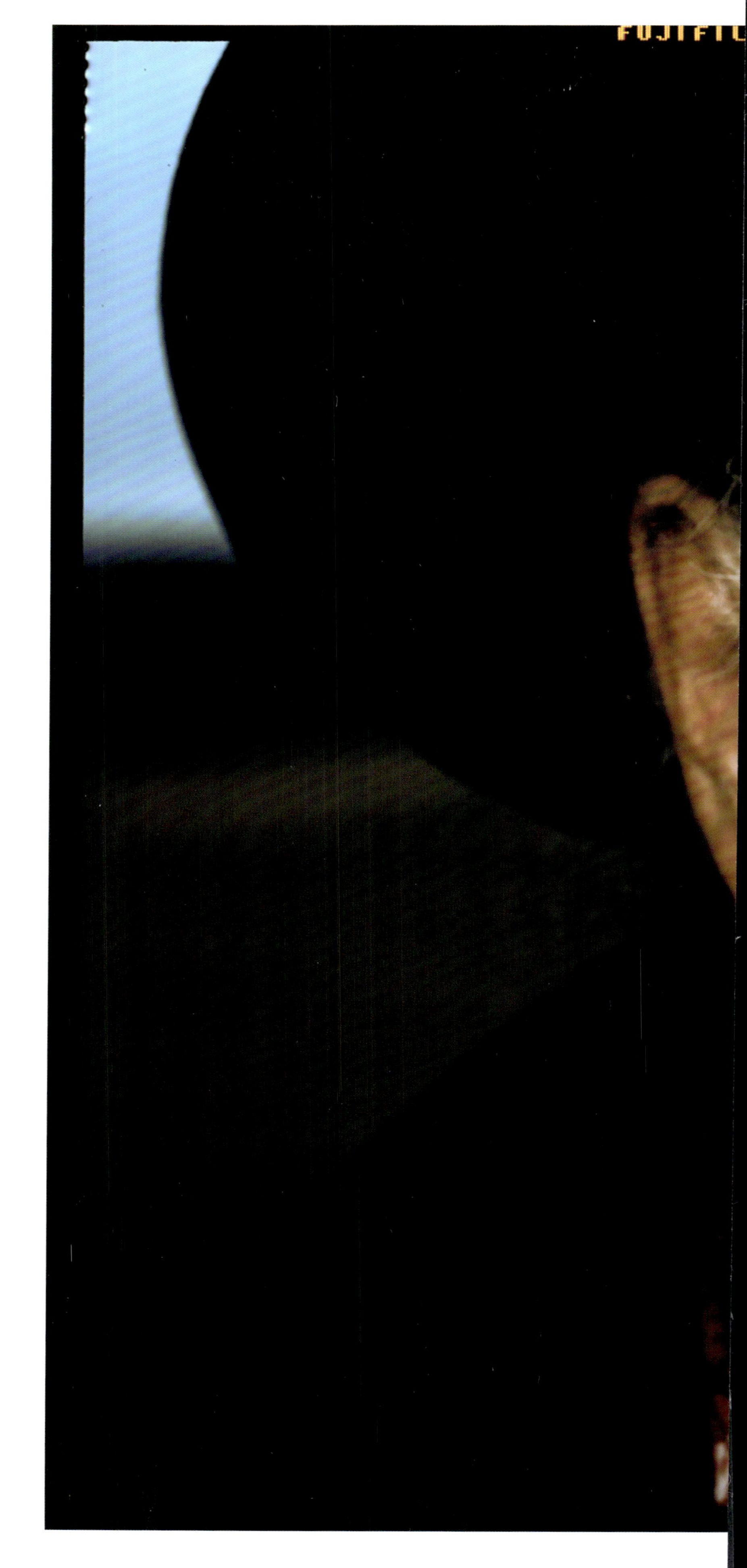

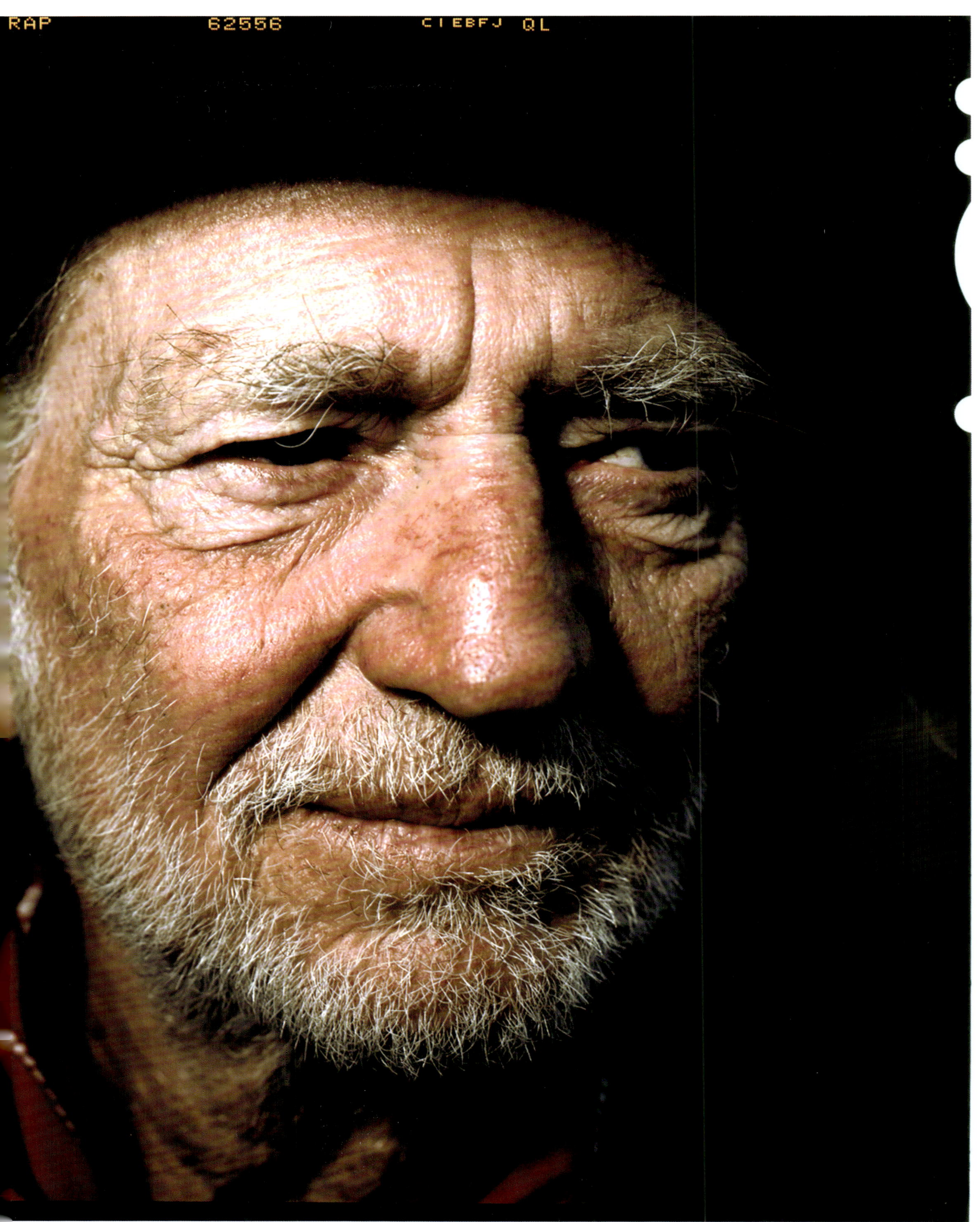
RAP
62556
CIEBFJ QL

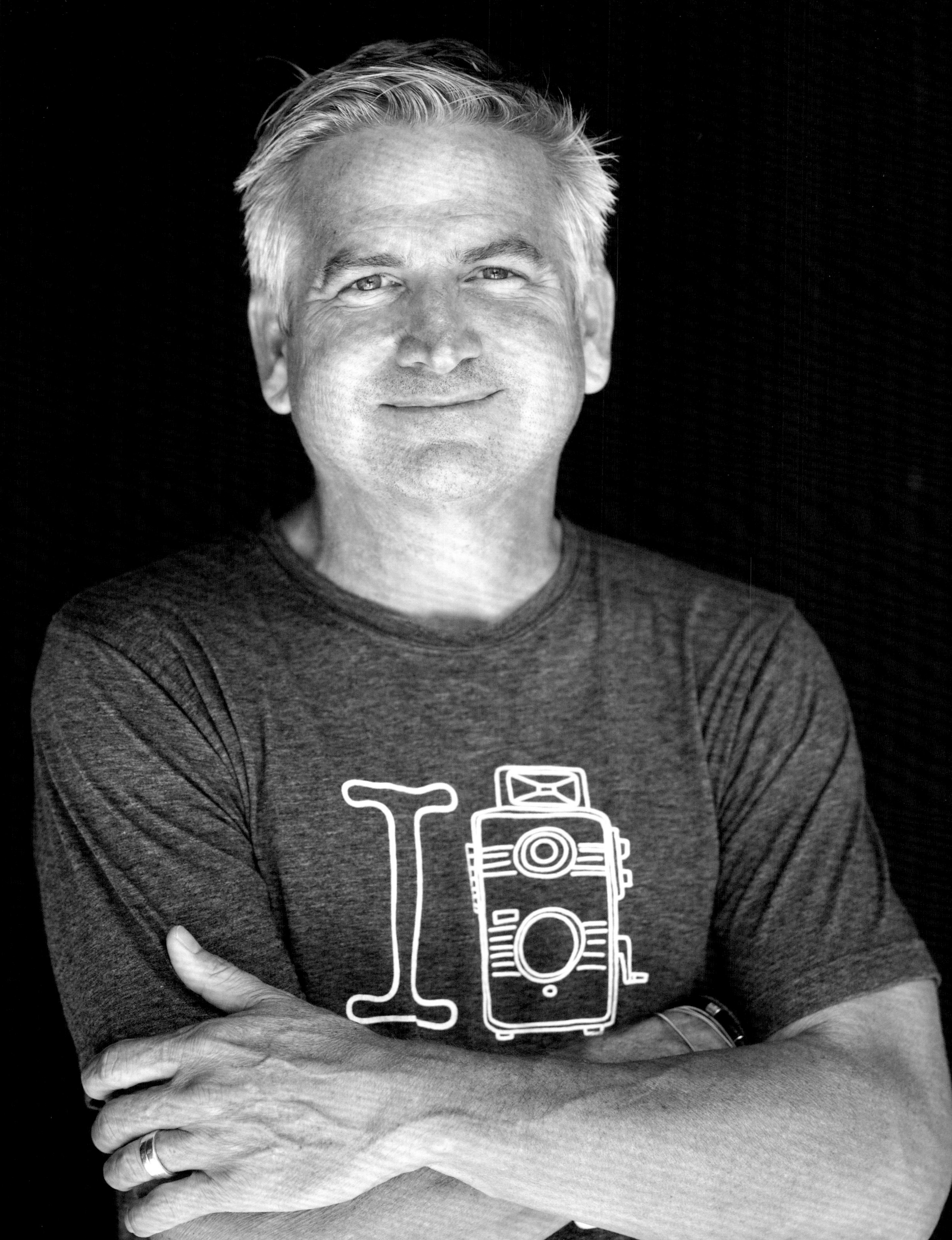
I

Matt Lankes
Photographs

Foreword by Ellar Coltrane

Introduction by Michael O'Brien

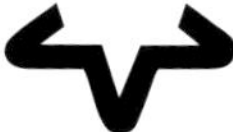

UNIVERSITY OF TEXAS PRESS

Foreword by Ellar Coltrane

Matt taught me to use my first camera and gave me the wonderful gift of documentation of myself over the years.

The annual return to the black velvet sheet and the cumbersome 4x5 antique camera of Matt's portrait station could be likened to a spiritual or meditative practice and in retrospect was a valuable device of reflection in my development as a child.

I was invited to simply exist and project my most relevant self-image.

I know I'm not alone in that I will cherish his work and what I see in the eyes of his subjects for the rest of my days.

Matt, your legacy and attention to glimmers of the internal landscapes of your subjects will never be forgotten.

I love you.

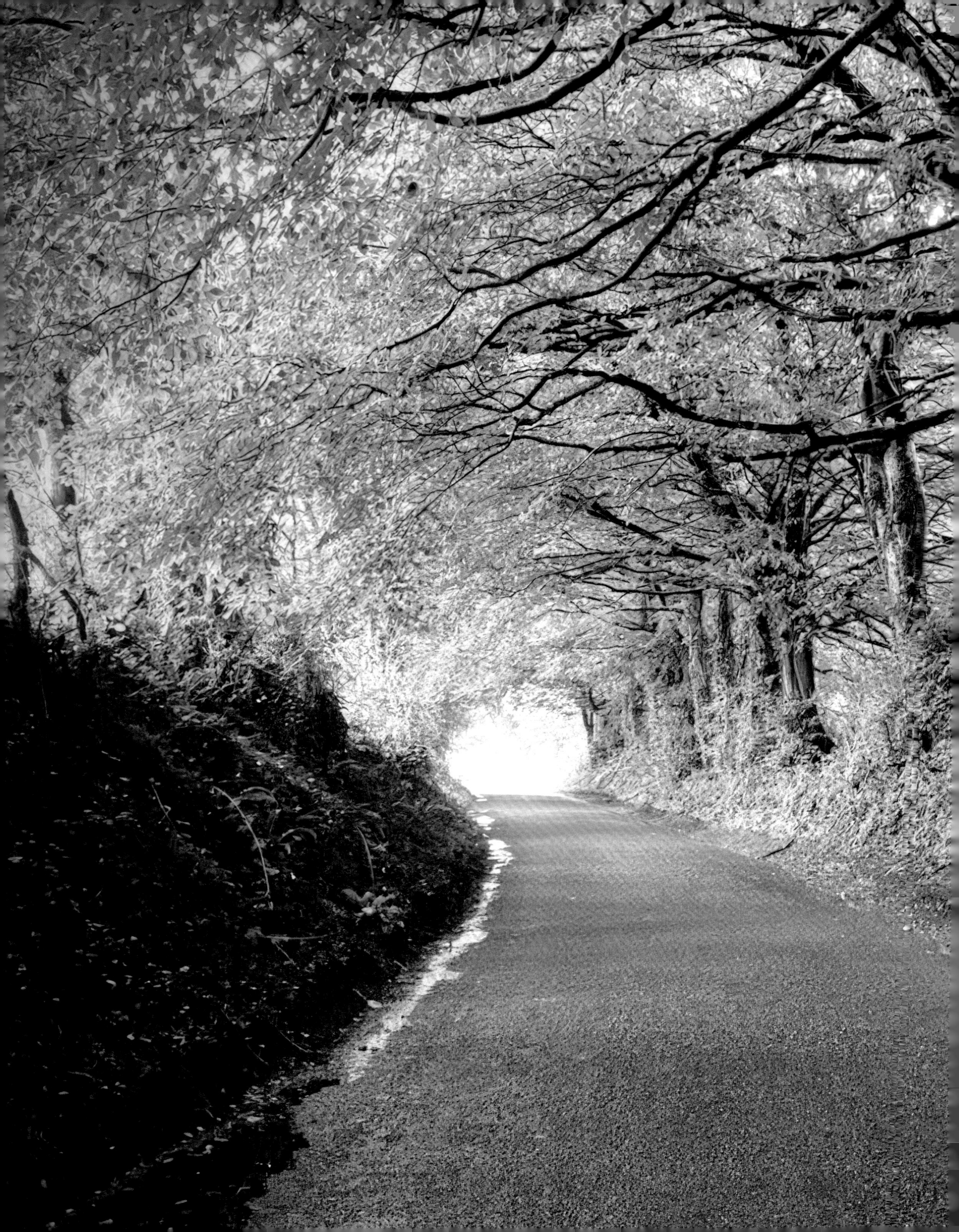

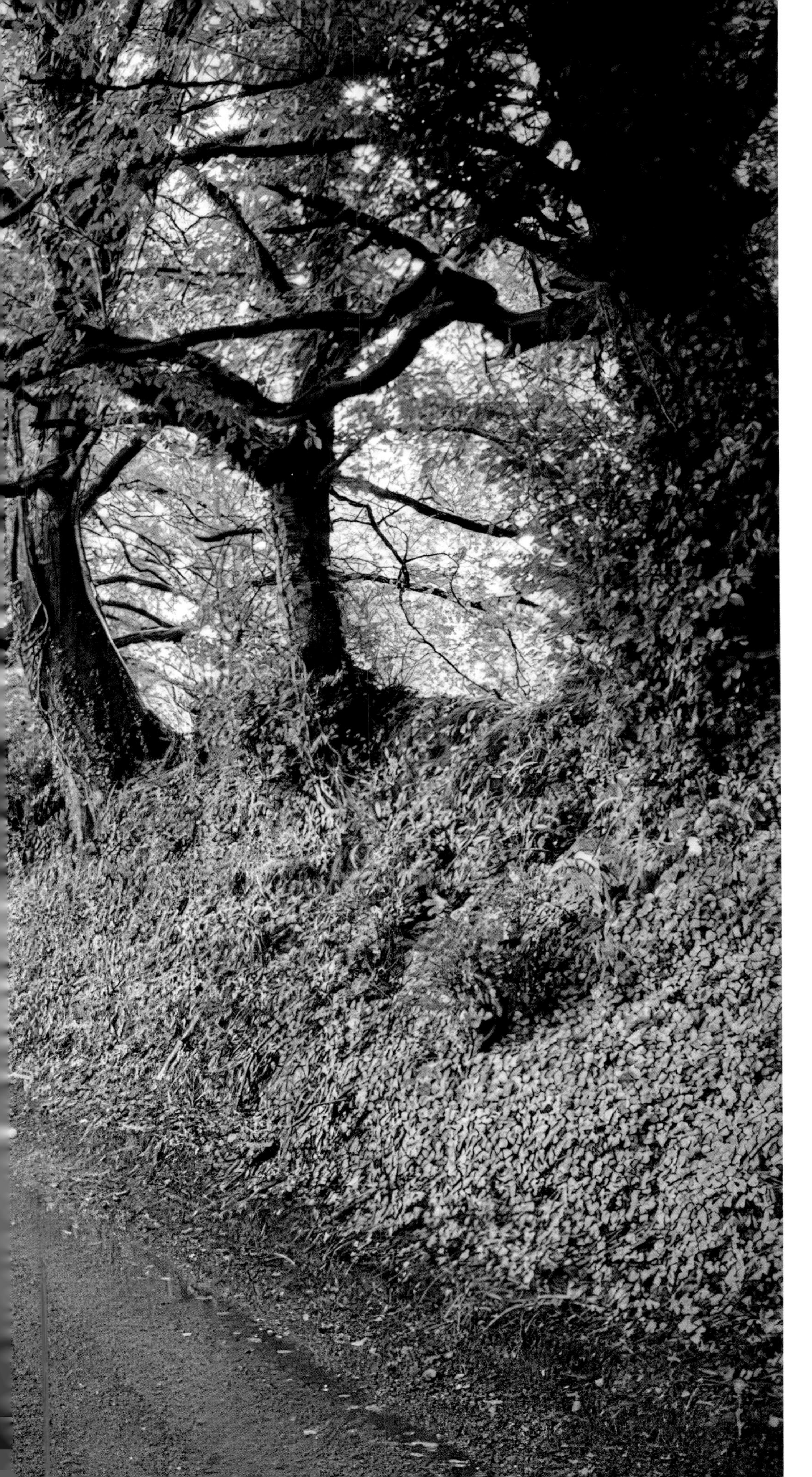

Matt Lankes: A Photographic Life

by Michael O'Brien

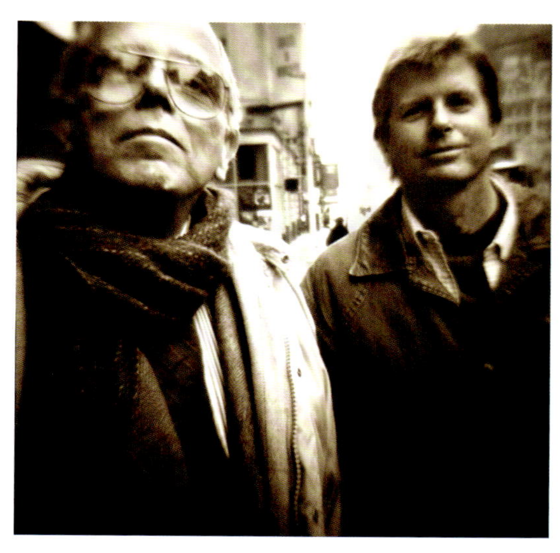

Above: ***John** Loengard and **Michael** O'Brien, in New York City.*
*Opposite: Polaroid of **Matt** and **Willie** Nelson at Luck Ranch.*

Many have taken photographs, but few have found as much pure joy in the craft as Matt Lankes. For more than forty years, photography has been his singular calling—an occupation that continued to inspire him every day.

Matt's father, Tom Lankes, was a news photographer for the *Austin American-Statesman*. Watching him work, Matt absorbed the rhythms of a photographer's life. These early exposures left an indelible imprint.

His mother, a copy editor at the University of Texas, also shaped Matt's path. With her gift for storytelling and gentle encouragement, she nurtured his creative spirit from the beginning.

In high school, Matt found a second home in the darkroom at Austin High. With a camera and film supplied by his dad, he eagerly captured the world around him—often volunteering to photograph classmates' fledgling rock bands. Music became his second passion.

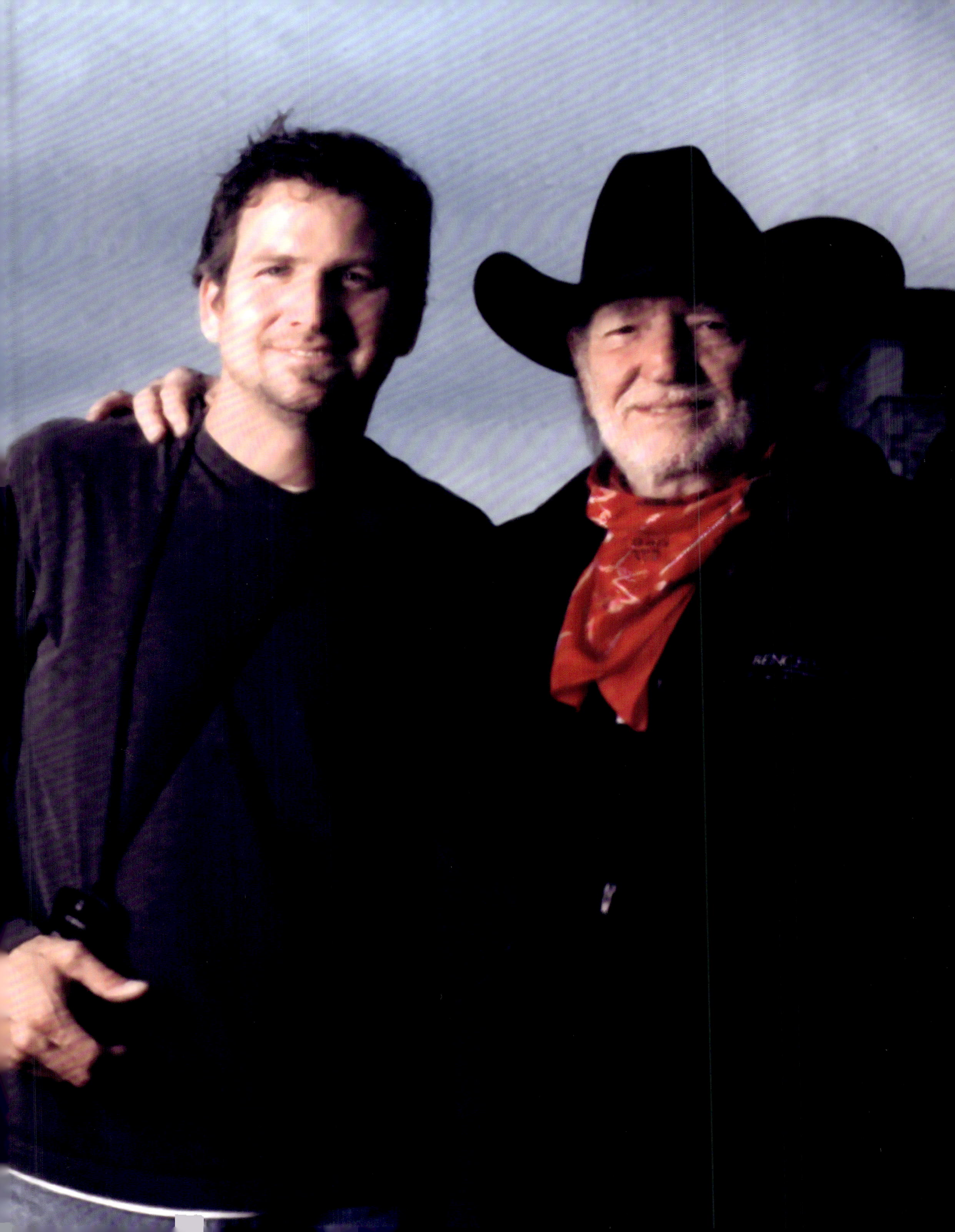

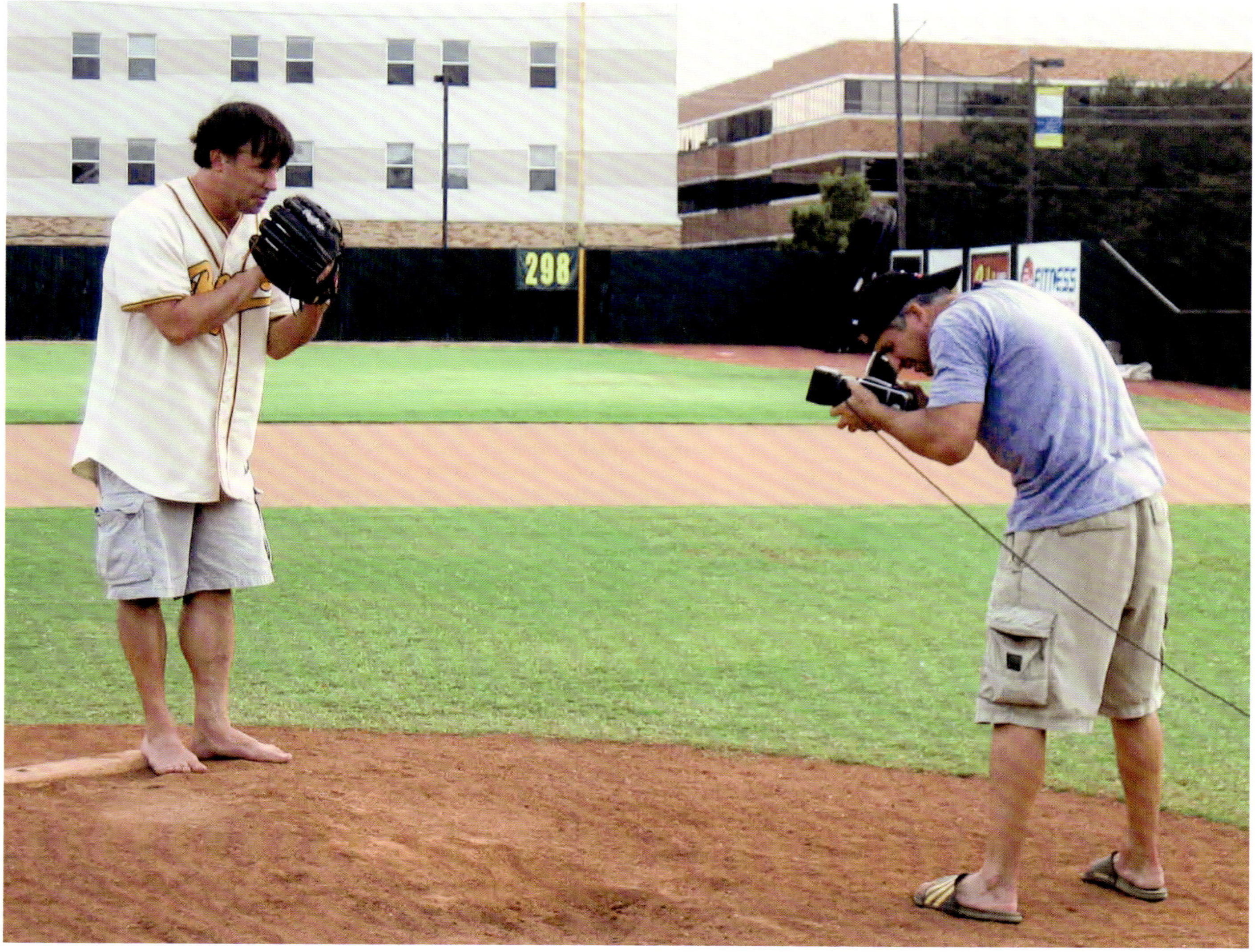

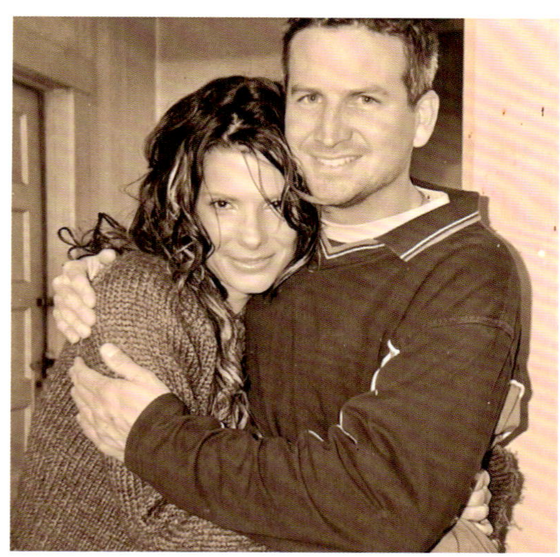

Top: ***Matt*** *photographing* ***Richard*** *Linklater. Above:* ***Sandra*** *Bullock and* ***Matt*** *on the set of* Hope Floats.

In the fall of 1990, just three credit hours shy of graduating from St. Edward's University in Austin, Matt set out to build his own photographic career. He quickly realized that school, and his early studio work, didn't suit his kinetic nature. He thrived in the field, chasing moments rather than staging them. Determined to stay busy, he assisted both local photographers and visiting professionals. Quick, intuitive, and charismatic, Matt became indispensable on set.

At the same time, he pursued his own work—photographing musicians, actors, artists, friends, and family. He had an innate understanding of light, favoring natural illumination over artificial strobes. His approach was instinctual; he could find a photograph almost anywhere. His emotional intelligence—his charm, humor, and empathy—put people at ease, allowing him to capture their essence.

His portfolio grew to include striking portraits of his children, Nicholas and Sinéad, and cultural icons like Willie Nelson, Billy Joe Shaver, Patricia Arquette, Ethan Hawke, Bob Schneider, Kat Edmonson, and many others. In every face, you see the warmth of Matt's connection—and the quiet joy he felt behind the camera.

In 2004, Matt joined the production of *Boyhood,* Richard Linklater's 12-year coming-of-age film. Matt's sister, Cathleen Sutherland—one of the film's producers—brought him on as a behind-the-scenes still photographer.

Below: ***Glen*** *Powell and* ***Matt*** *at the premiere of* Hit Man. *Bottom:* ***Ellar*** *Coltrane, star of* Boyhood, *and* ***Matt***.

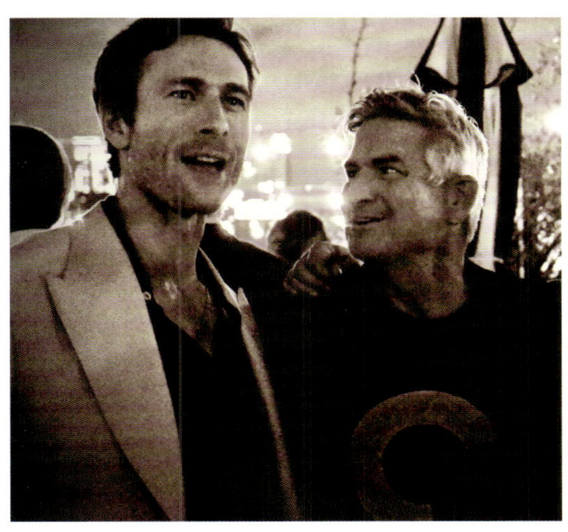

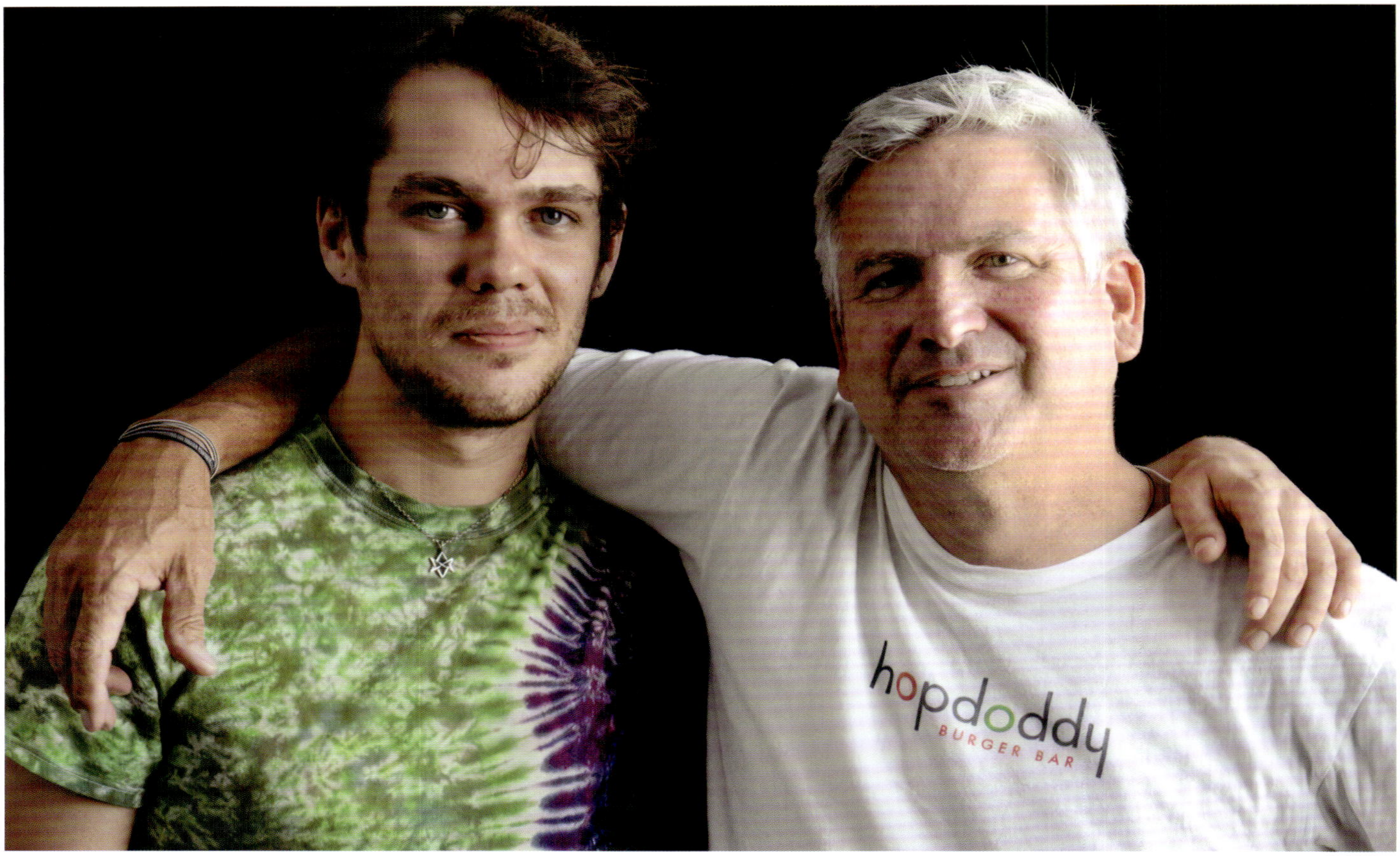

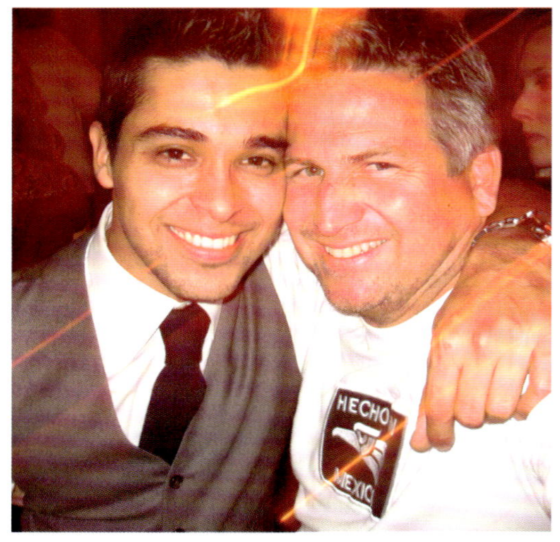

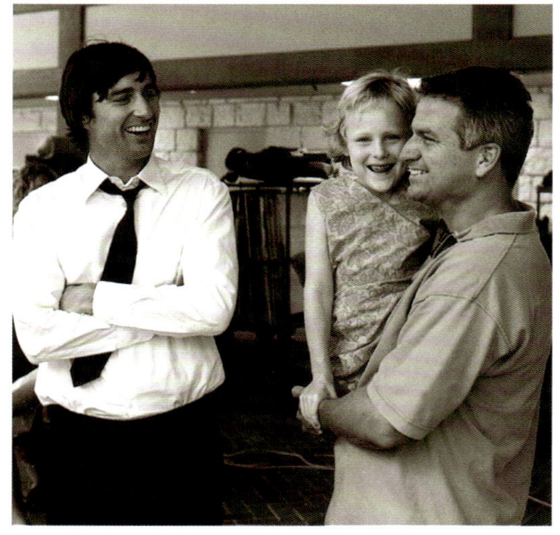

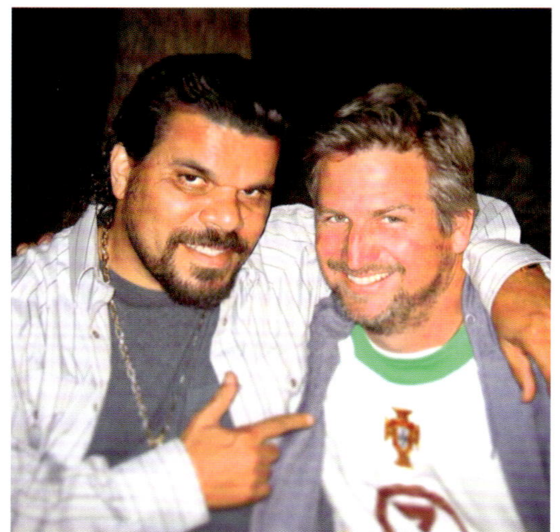

From top: ***Wilmer*** *Valderrama and* ***Matt****;* ***Luke*** *Wilson and* ***Matt****, with daughter* ***Sinéad****;* ***Luis*** *Guzmán and* ***Matt****. Opposite:* ***Matt*** *shooting* ***Ethan*** *Hawke on South Congress Avenue.*

Beyond his official role, Matt began a side project using a 4 x 5 camera and Polaroid Type 55 film, producing a remarkable portrait series that documented the cast's evolution. The results were collected in a stunning book published by University of Texas Press—a visual chronicle of a cinematic journey.

In the early 2000s, Matt met Jamie Nicholson while playing in a co-ed soccer league at Zilker Park. Smitten, he asked her out right there on the field.

Jamie, smart and beautiful, later became chair of the math department at Bowie High School. They married on December 20, 2008, and in 2012, their son, Nicholas, was born.

As he had done with *Boyhood*, Matt began a practice of photographing Nicholas. Each year, the images traced Nick's transformation—pale skin freckling under the Texas sun, steady blue eyes fixed on the lens. These portraits are among Matt's most personal and compelling work.

Matt remained eternally youthful—childlike in his fascination with people and the world around him. He was beloved; I can't think of anyone with more lifelong friends. That deep affection is woven into every photograph he took.

Look closely, and you'll see Matt in every frame.

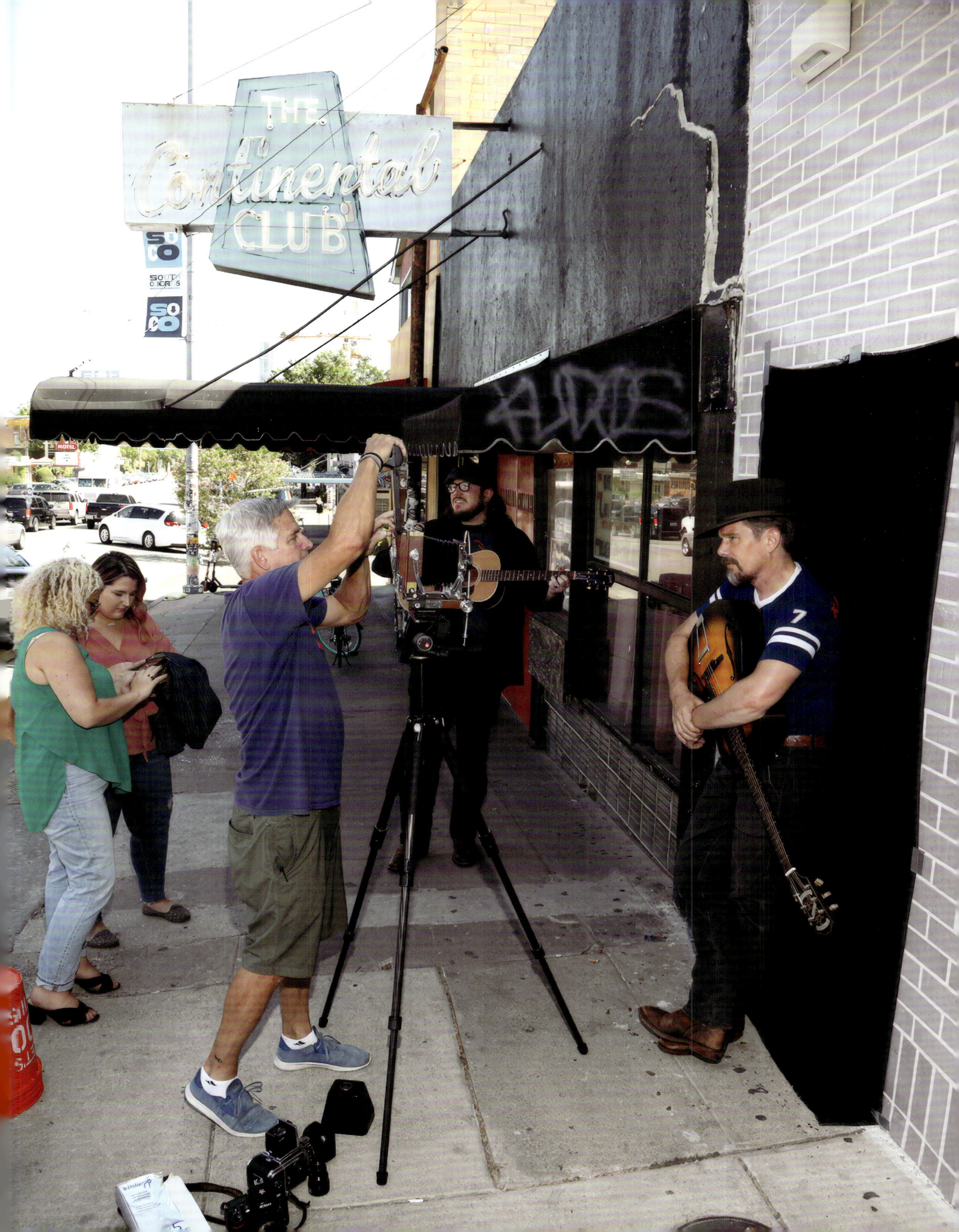
THE
Continental
CLUB

Film

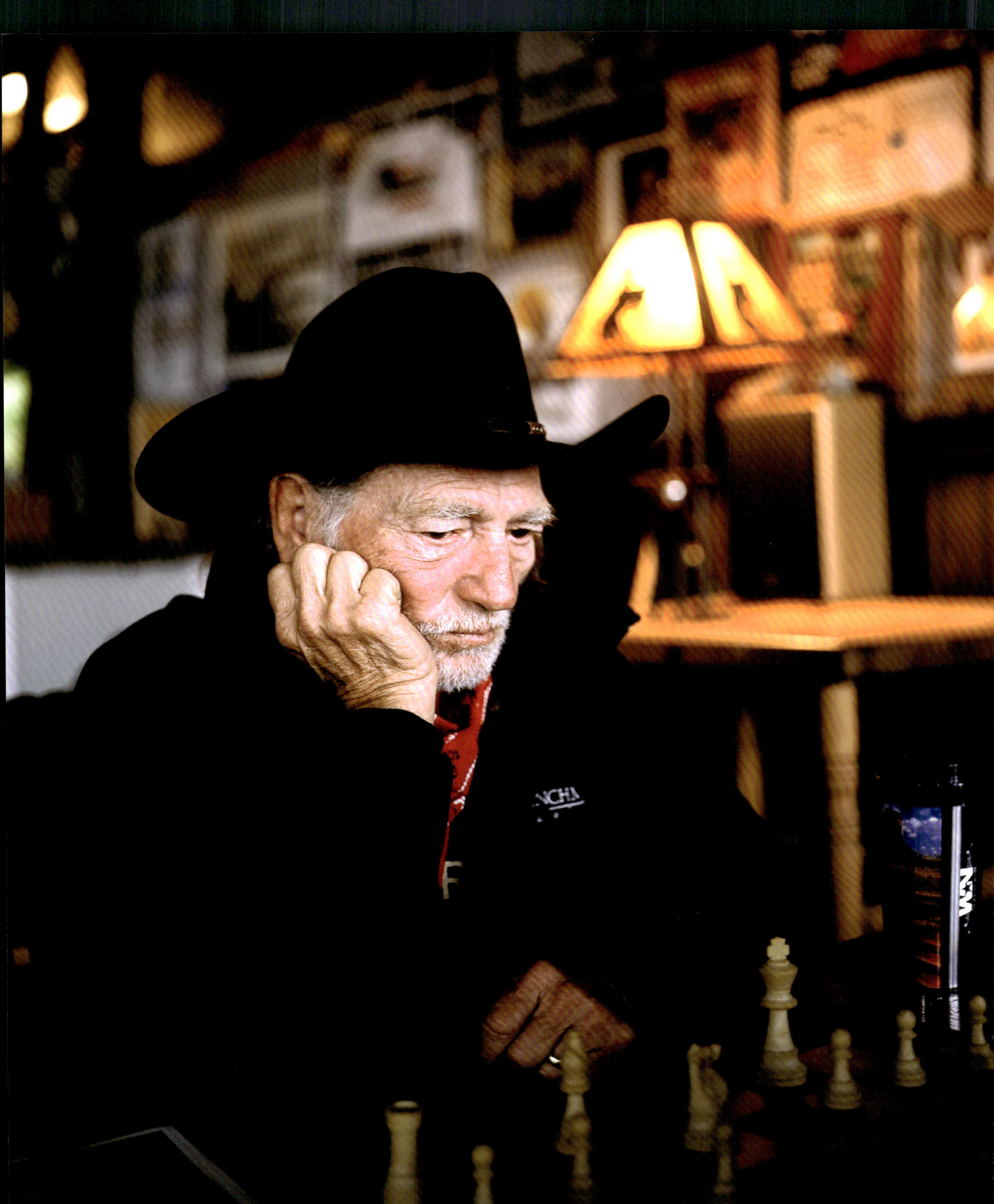
NCHA

Willie Nelson

Tommy Lee Jones

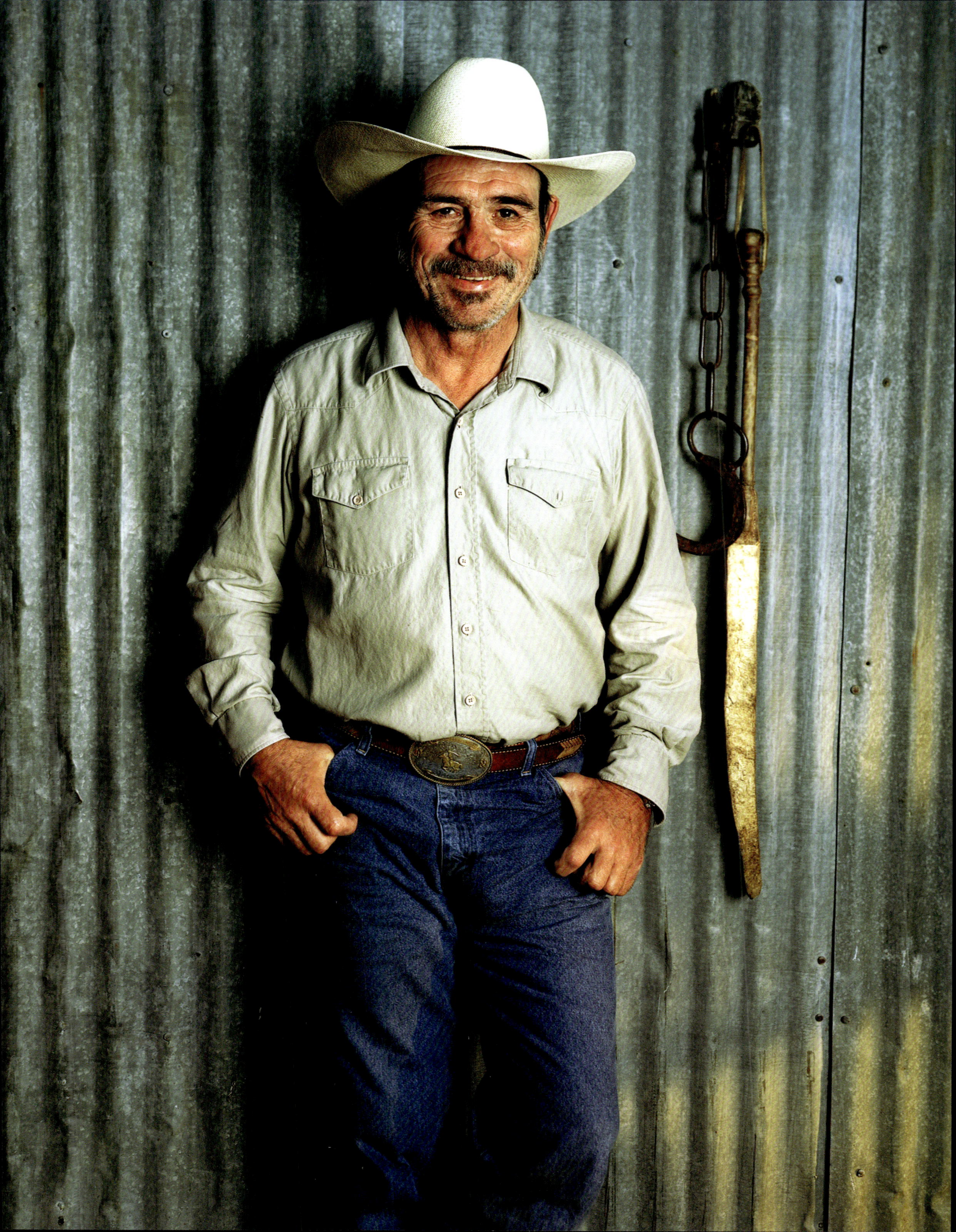

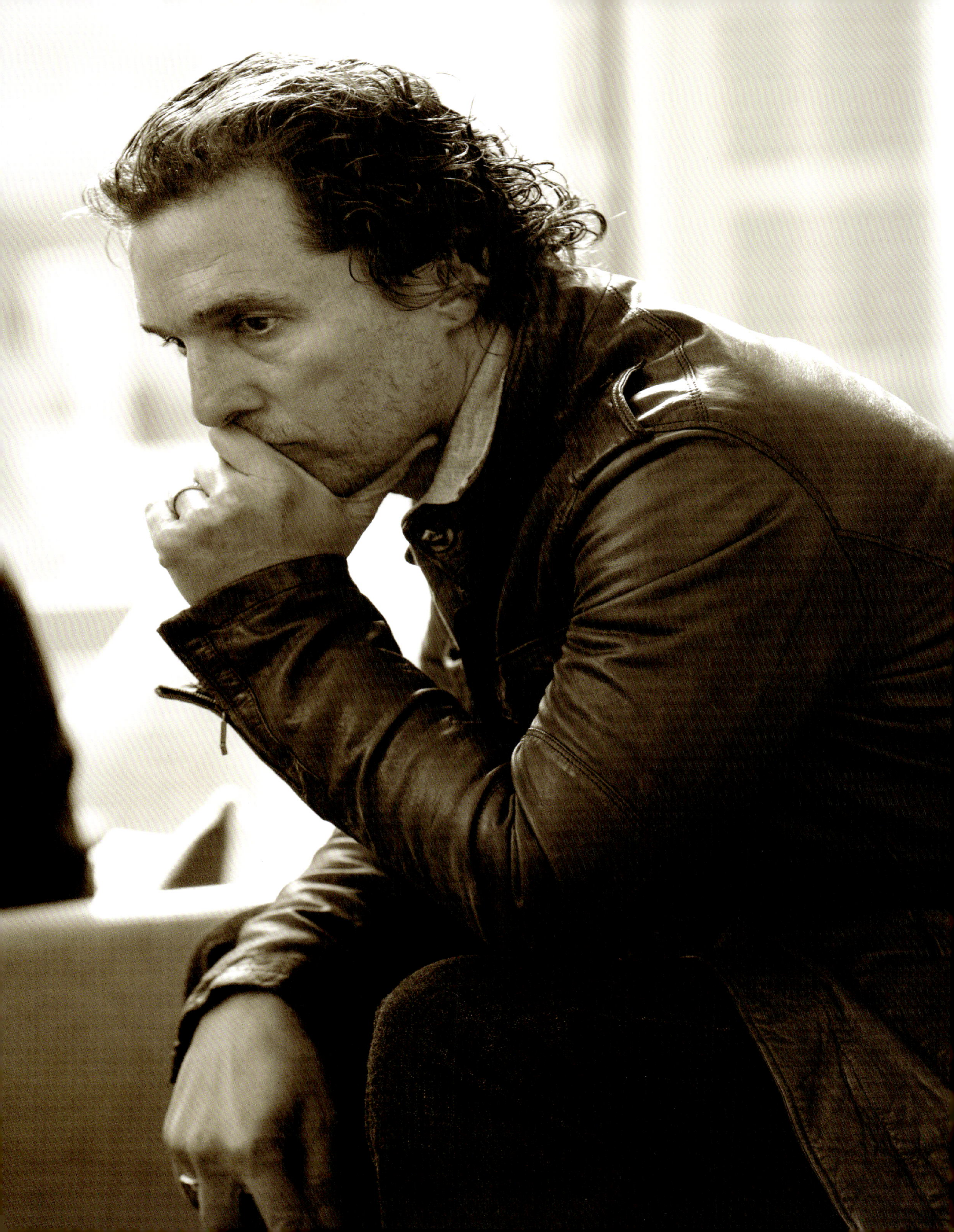

Matthew **McConaughey**

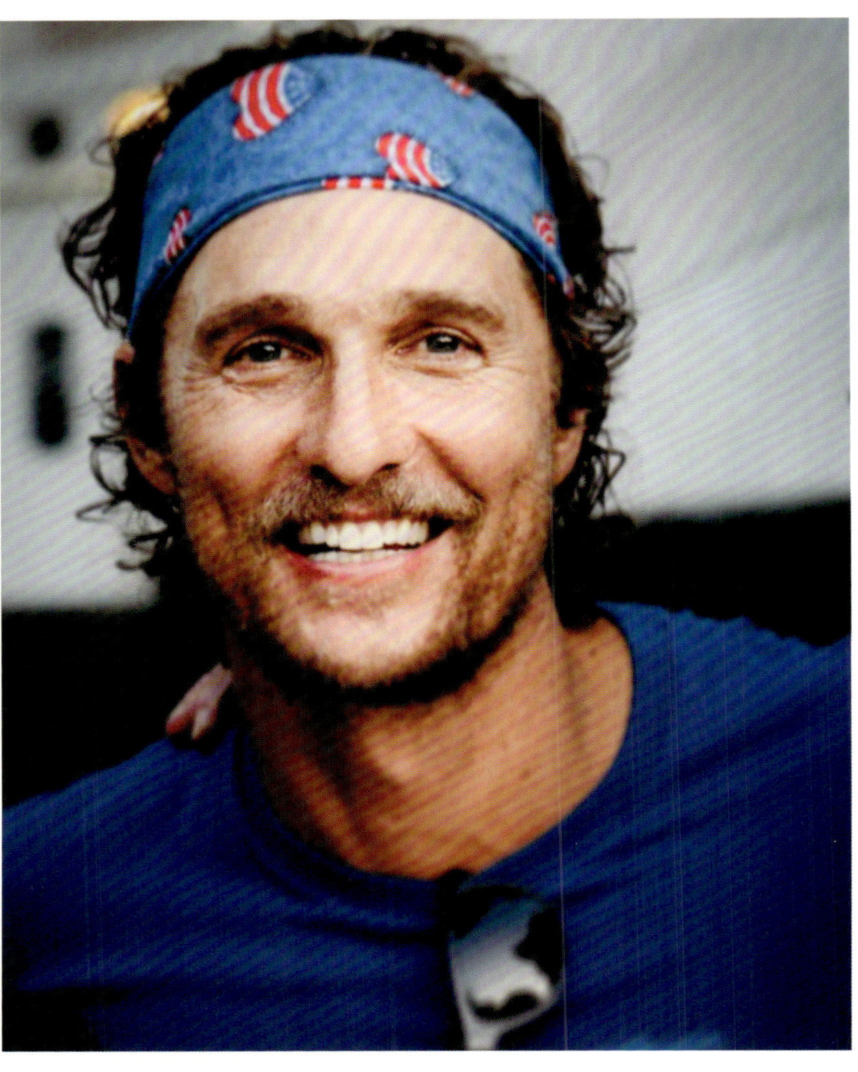

Luke Wilson

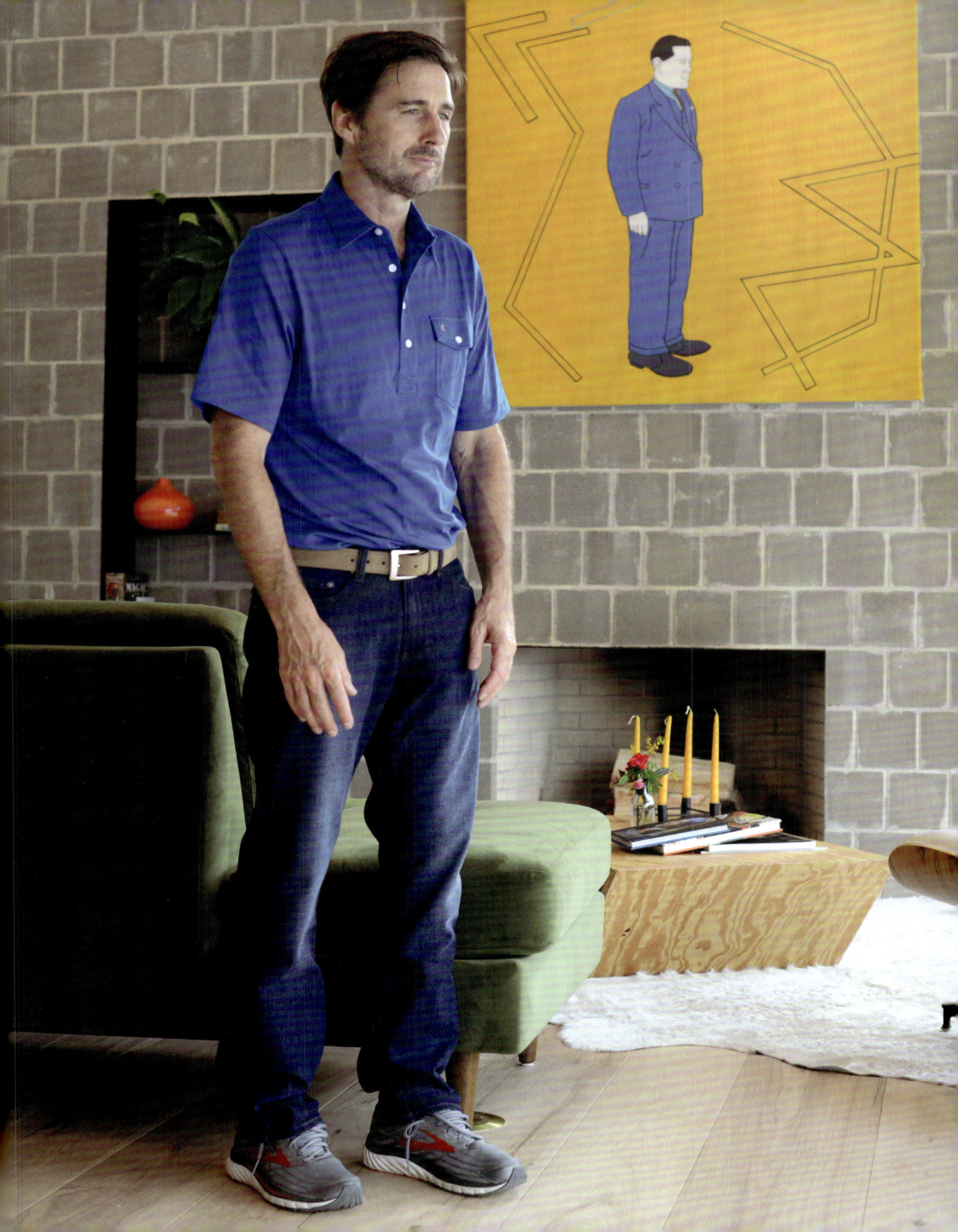

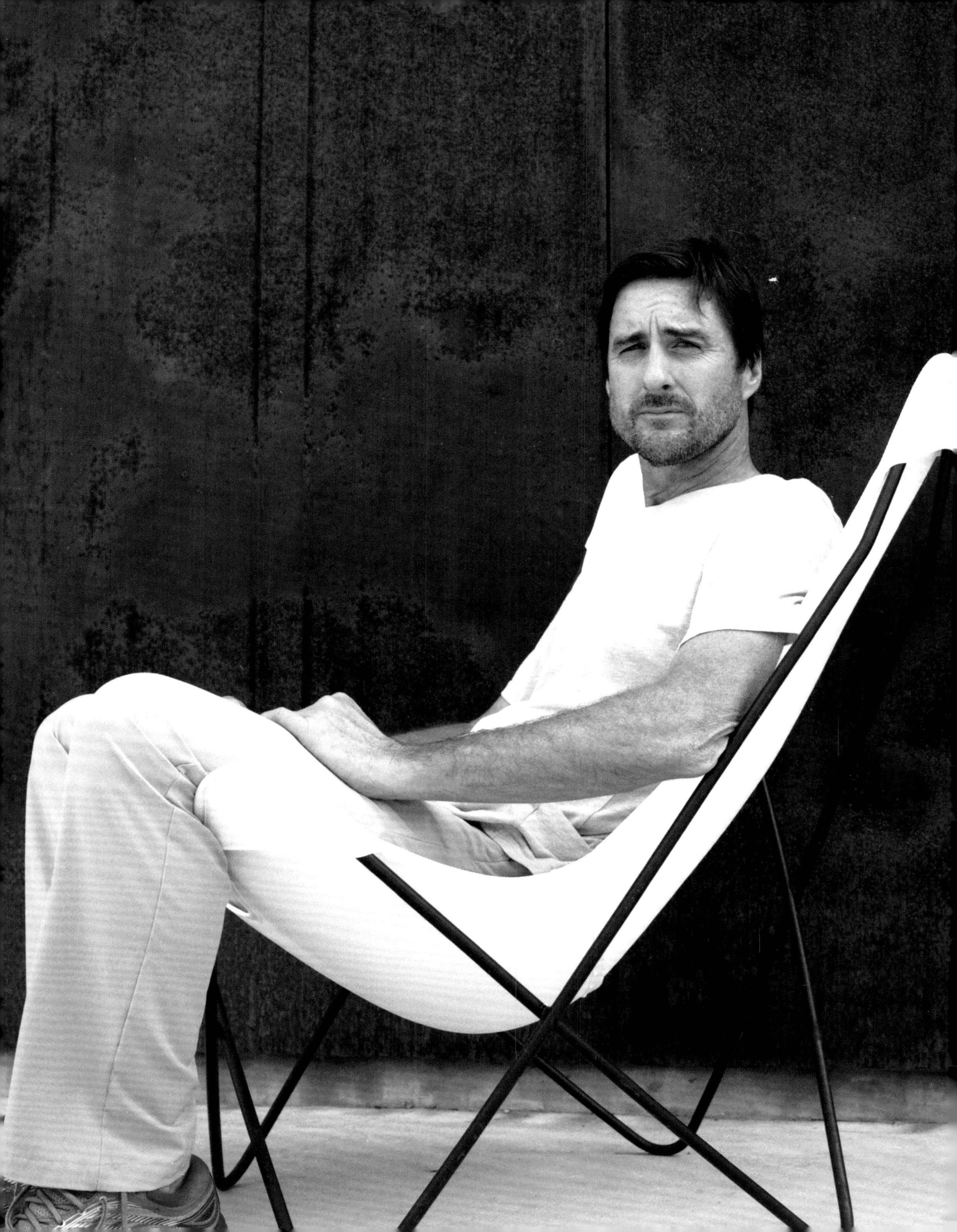

Luke Wilson

Ellar Coltrane

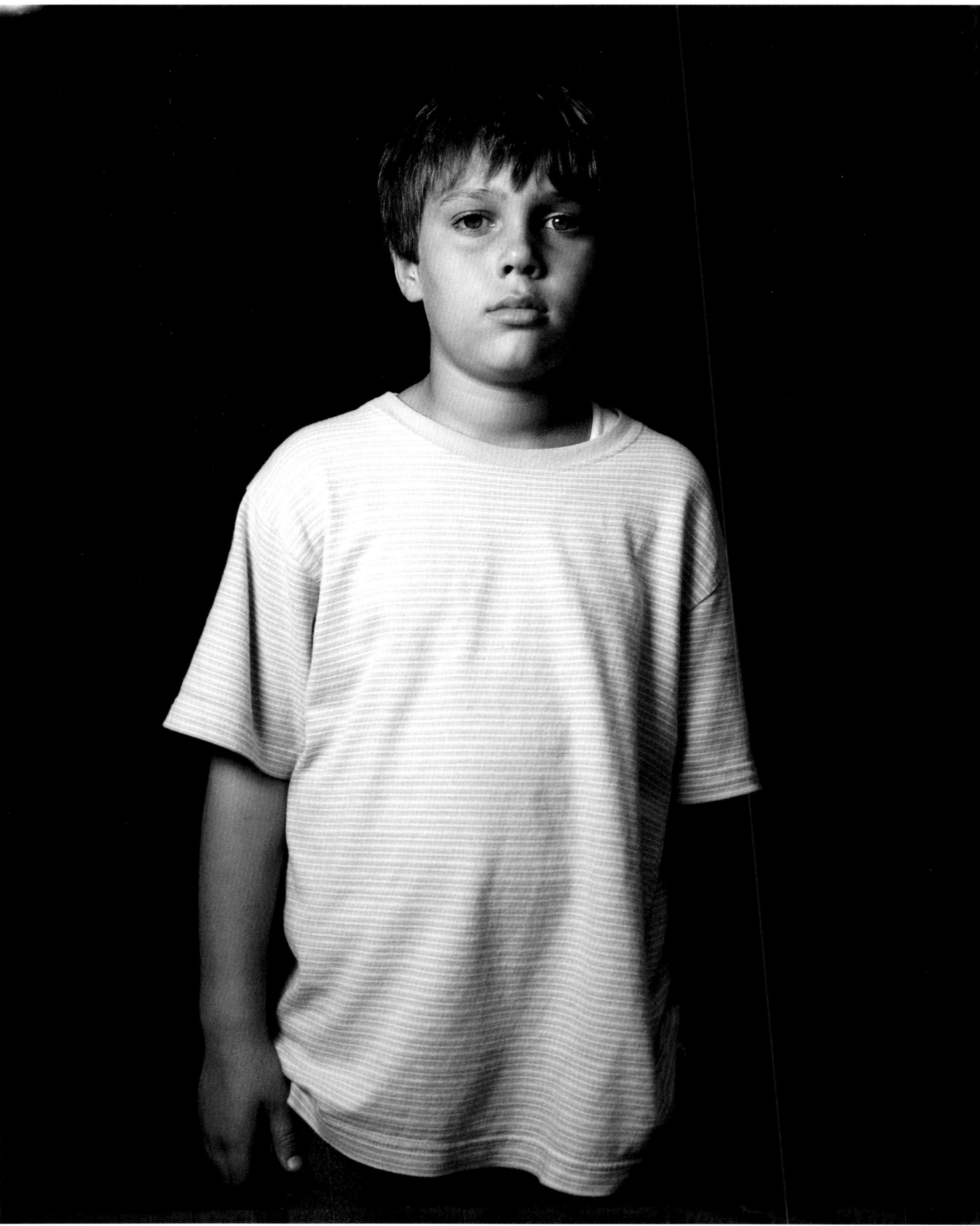

__Ellar__ Coltrane was "invited to simply exist," he says, by __Matt__, in front of the camera during their "annual return to the black velvet sheet." While filming Boyhood, *__Matt__ captured the first 6 years, this page, and years 7 to 12, opposite.*

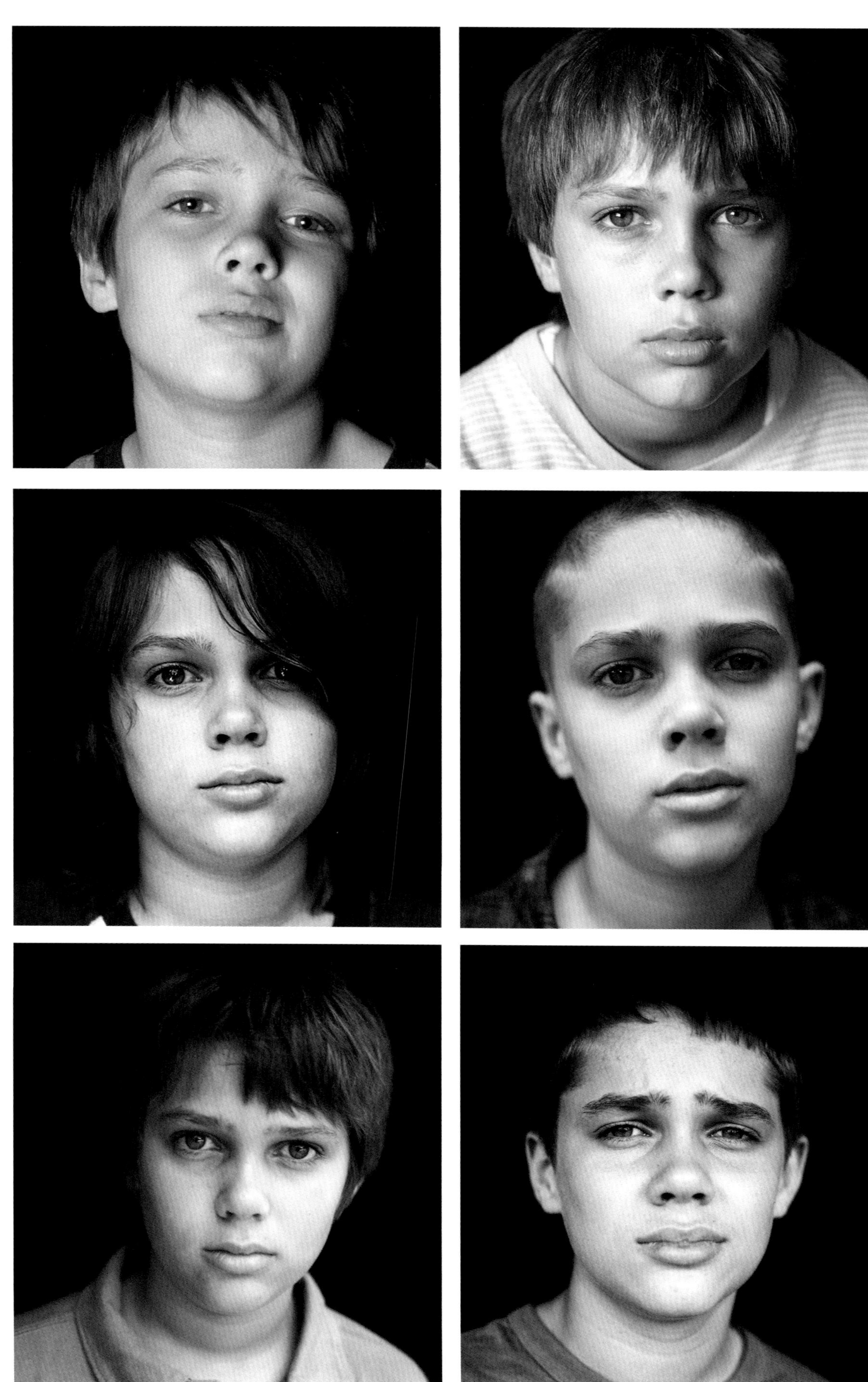

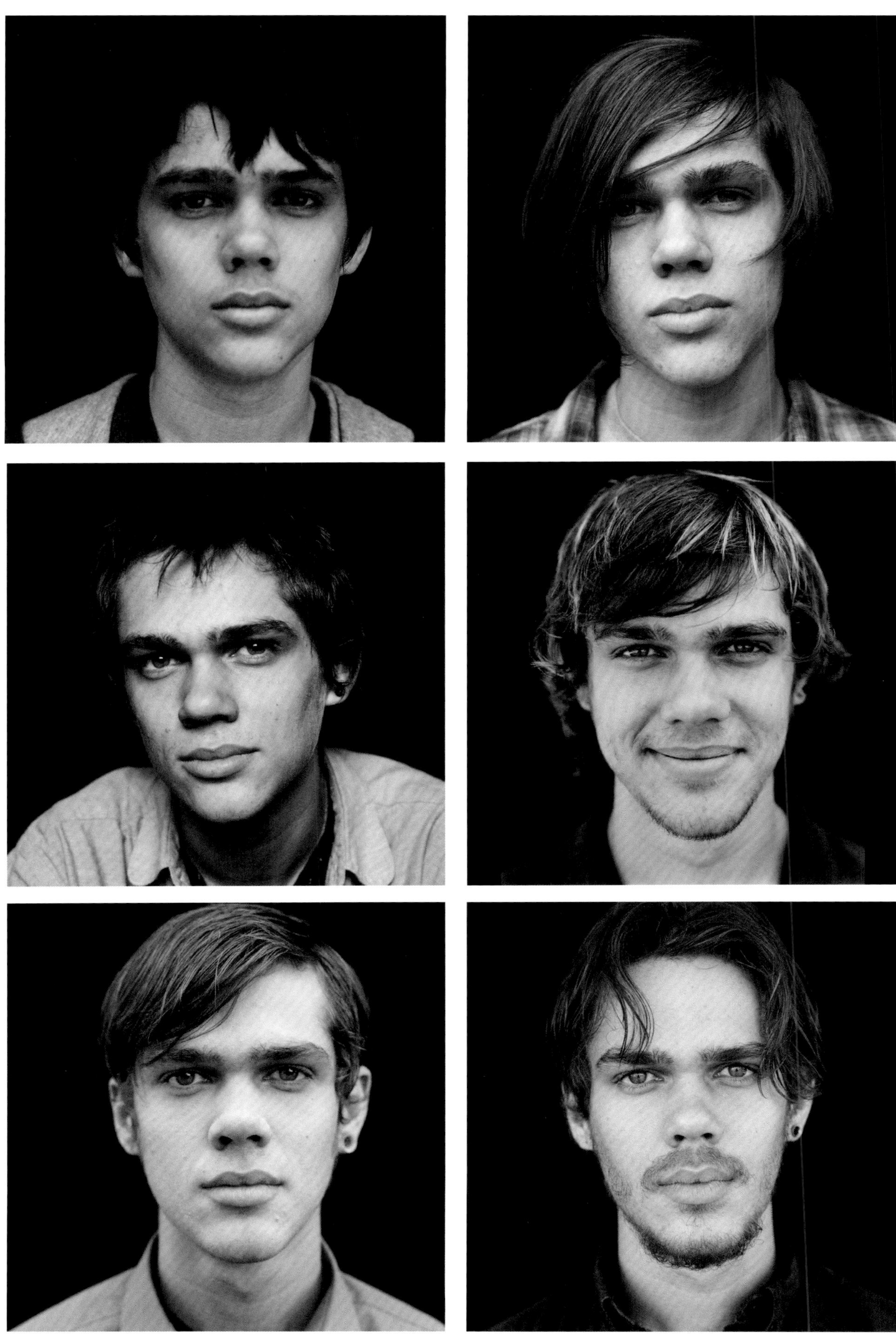

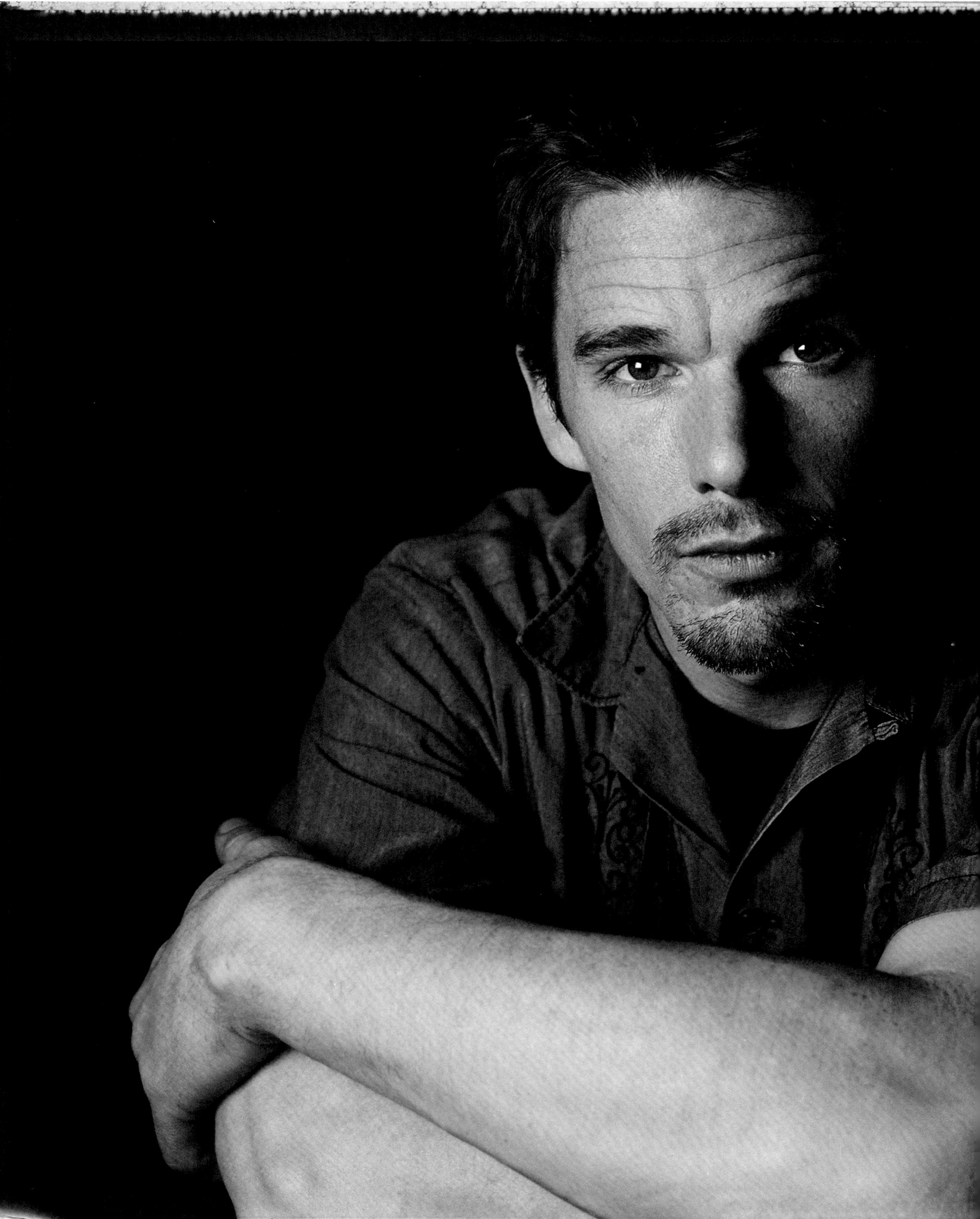

Ethan Hawke

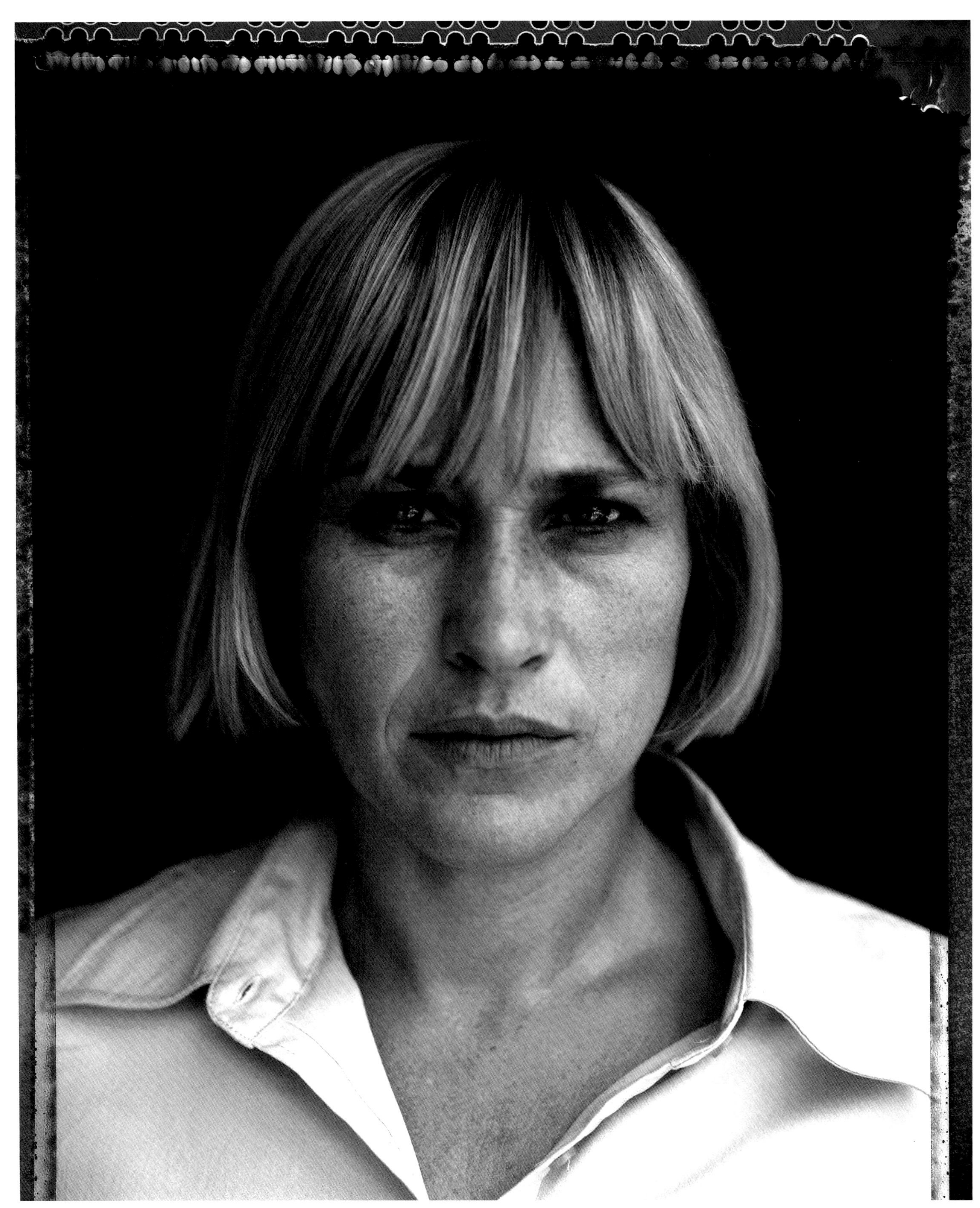

Patricia Arquette

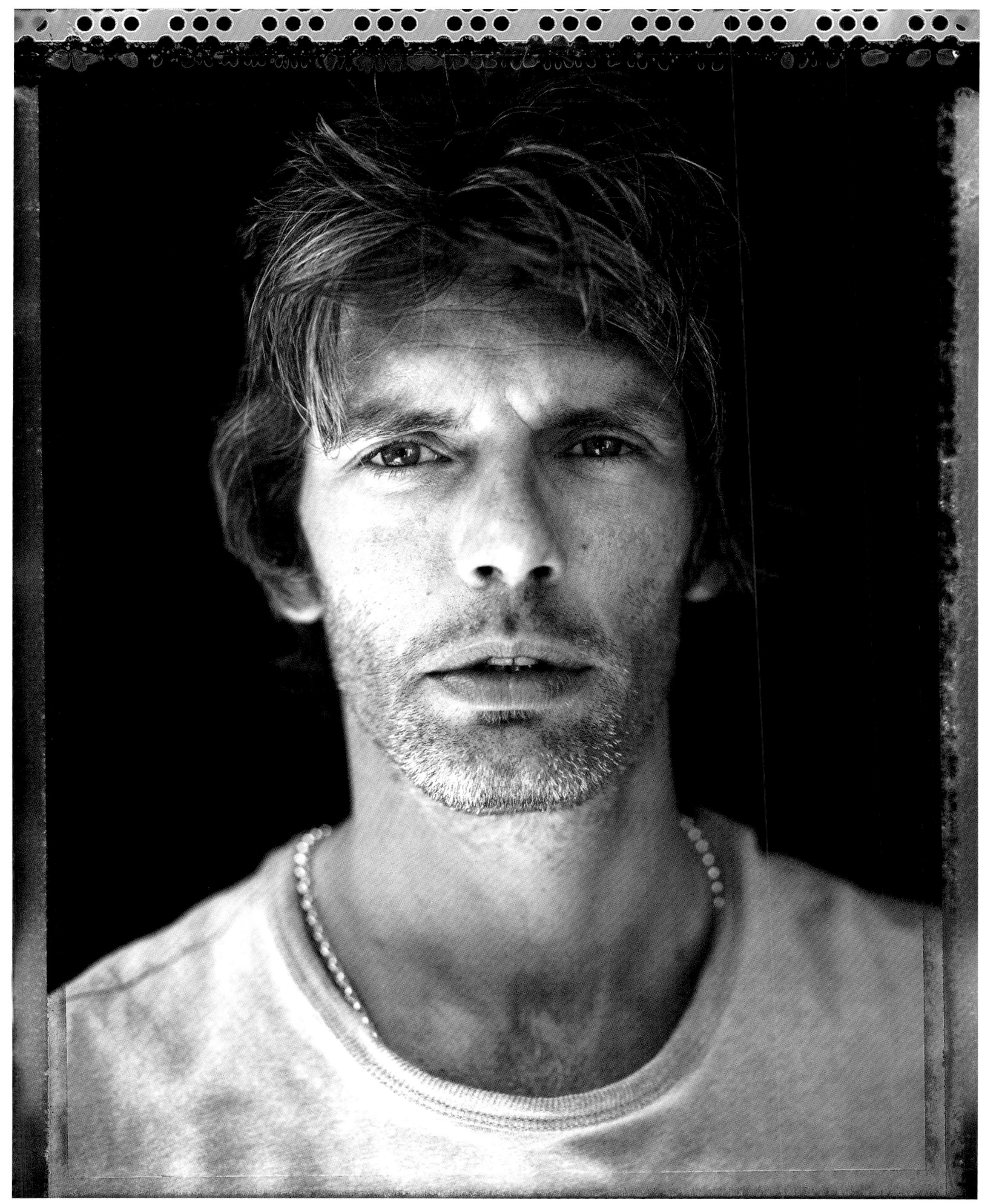

Charlie Sexton

Savannah Welch

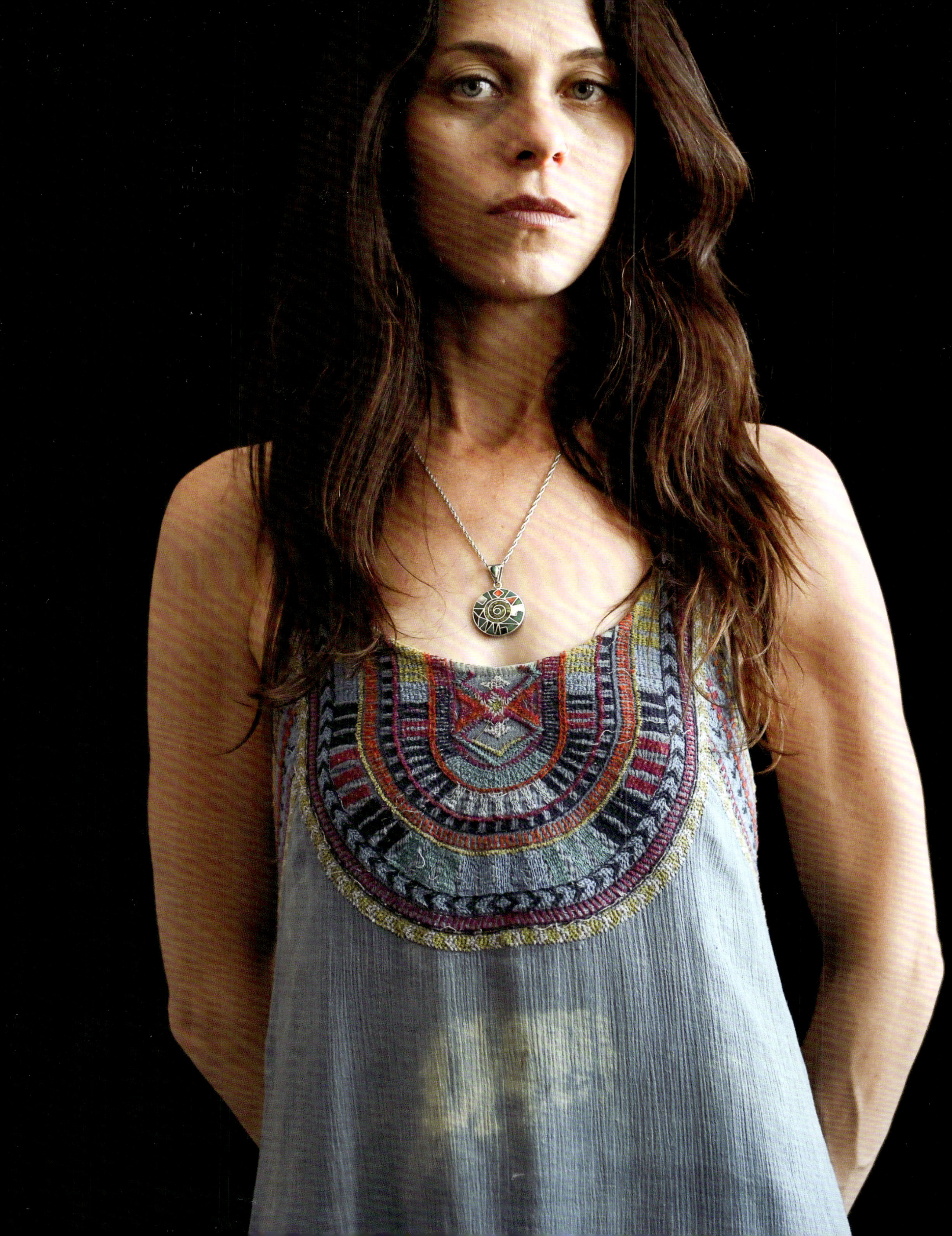

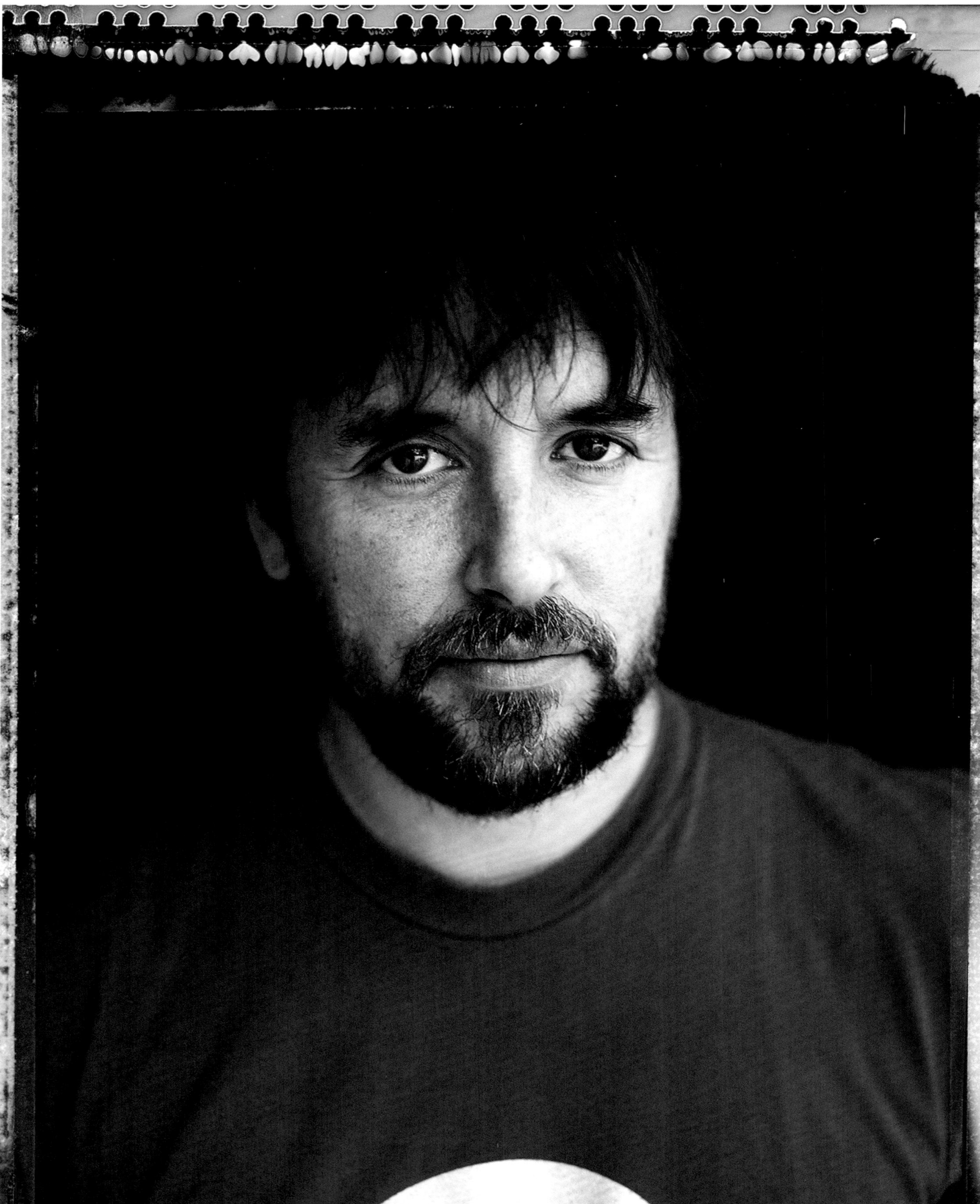

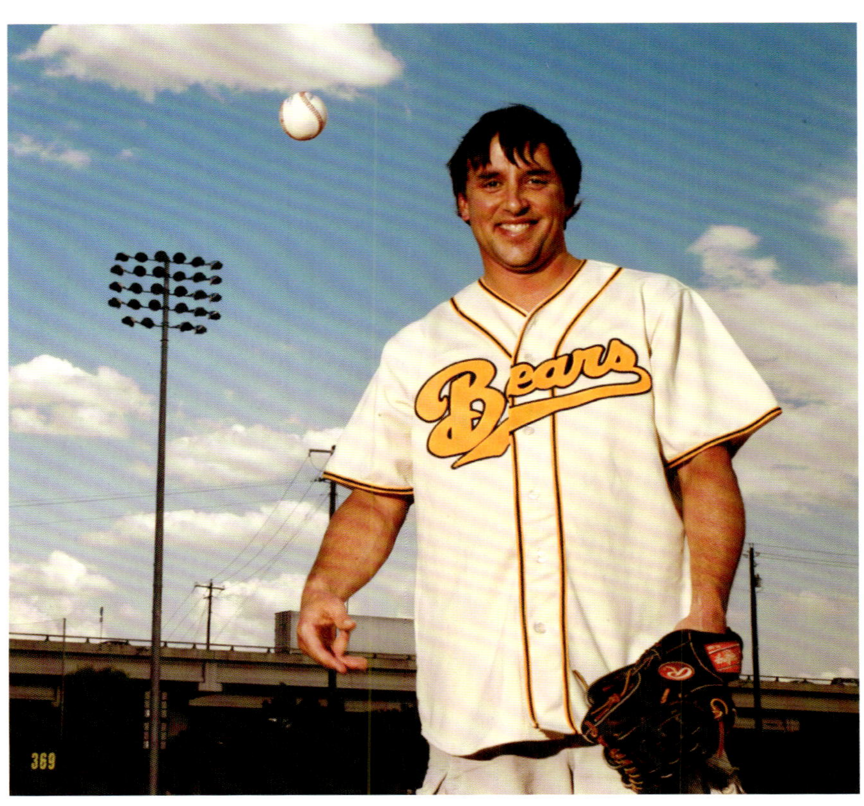

Richard **Linklater**

Keanu Reeves

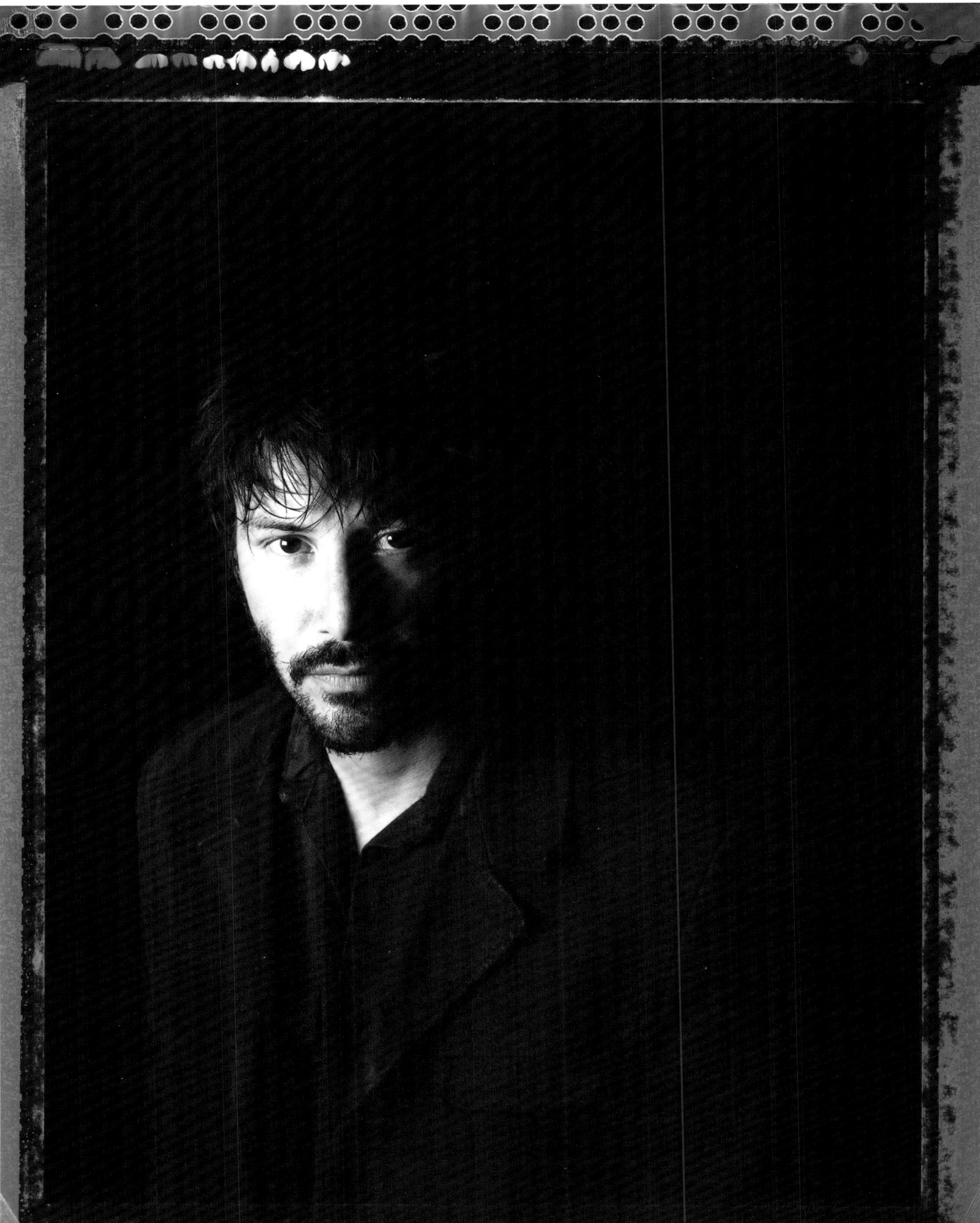

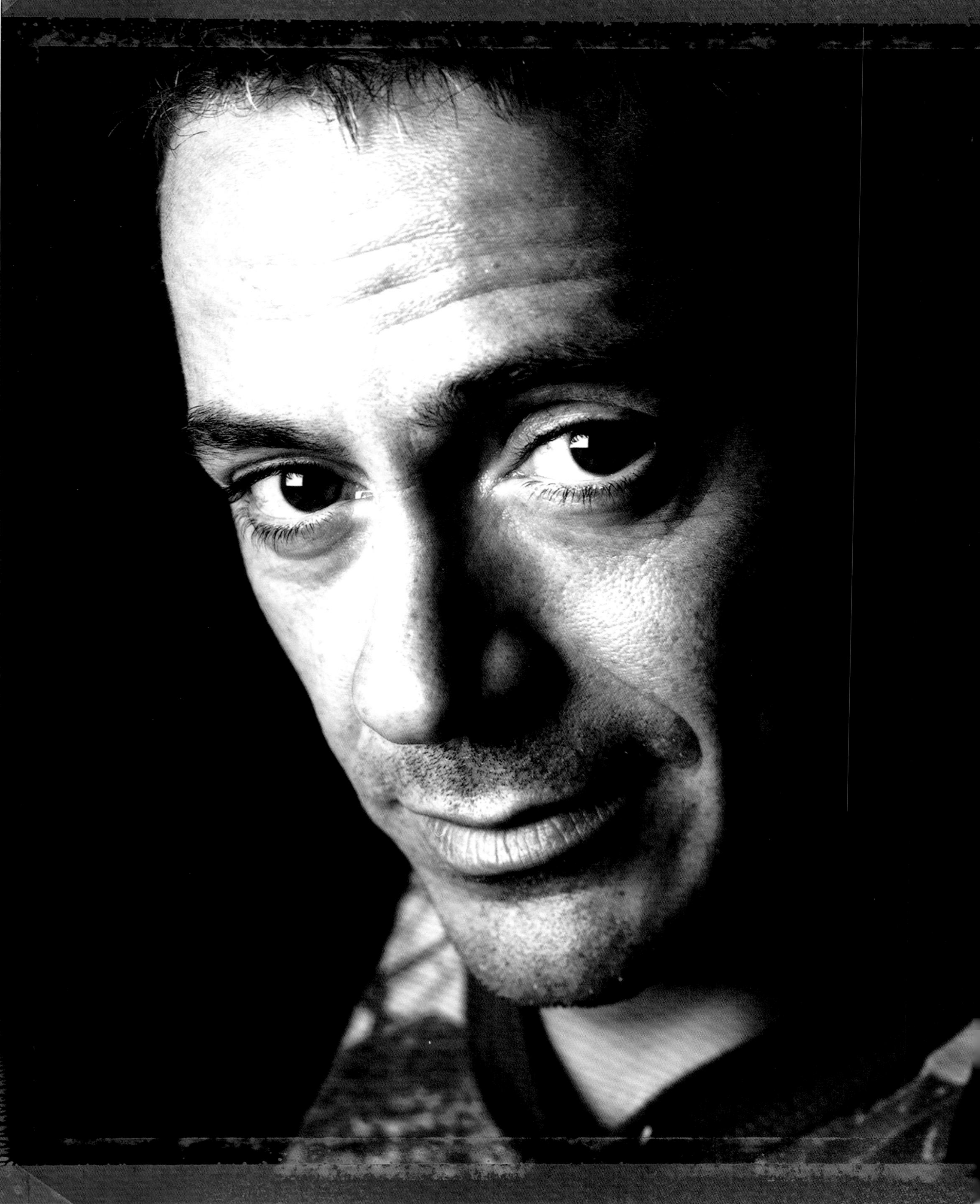

Robert Downey Jr.

Winona Ryder

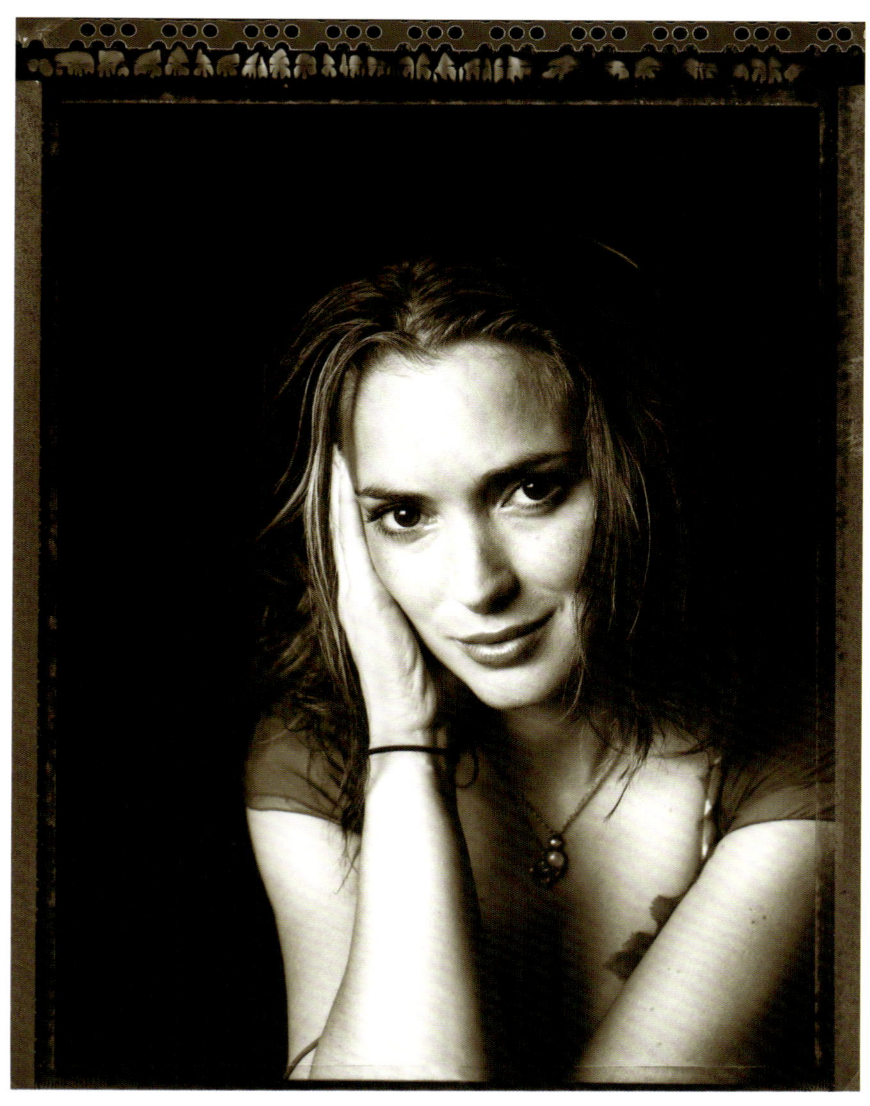

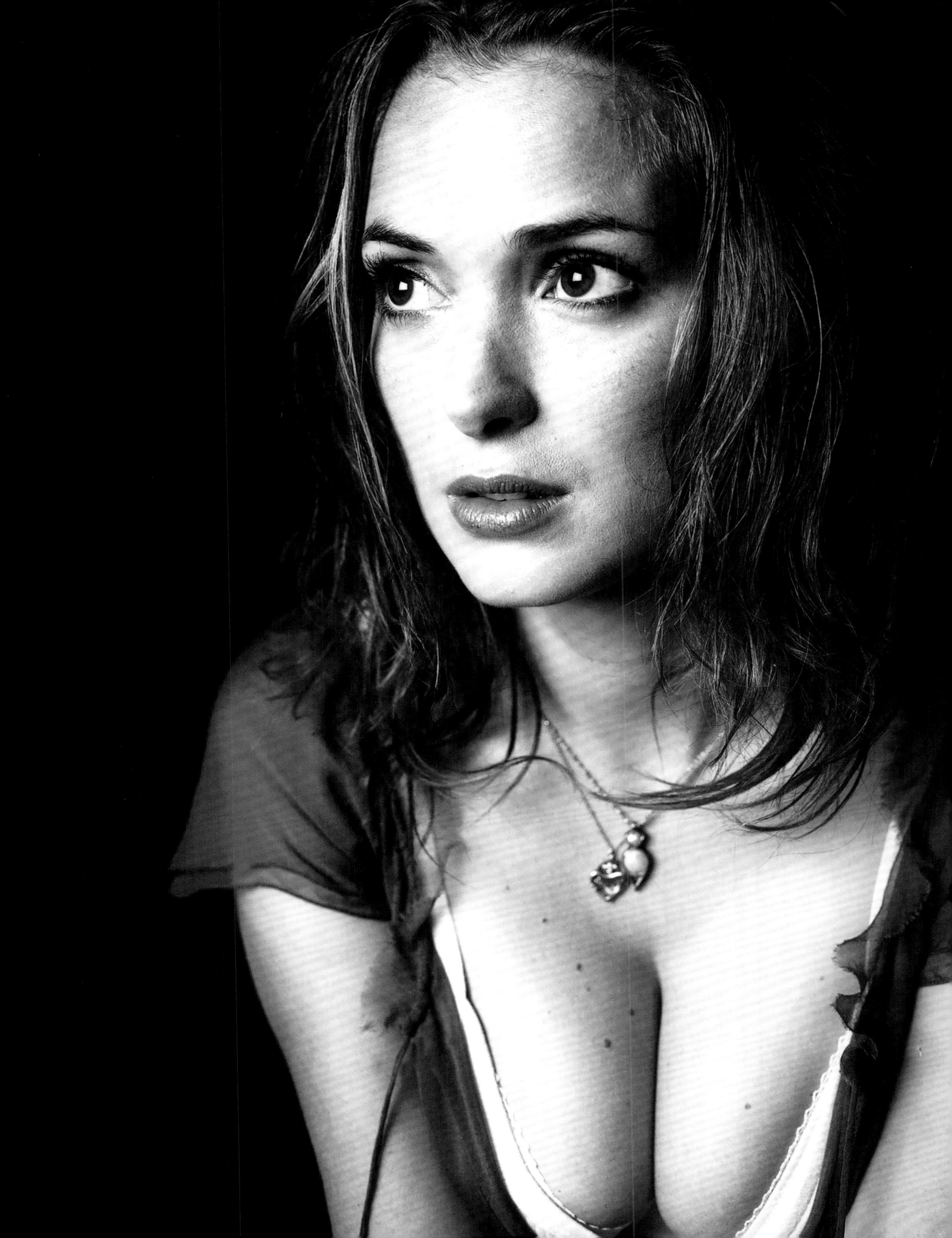

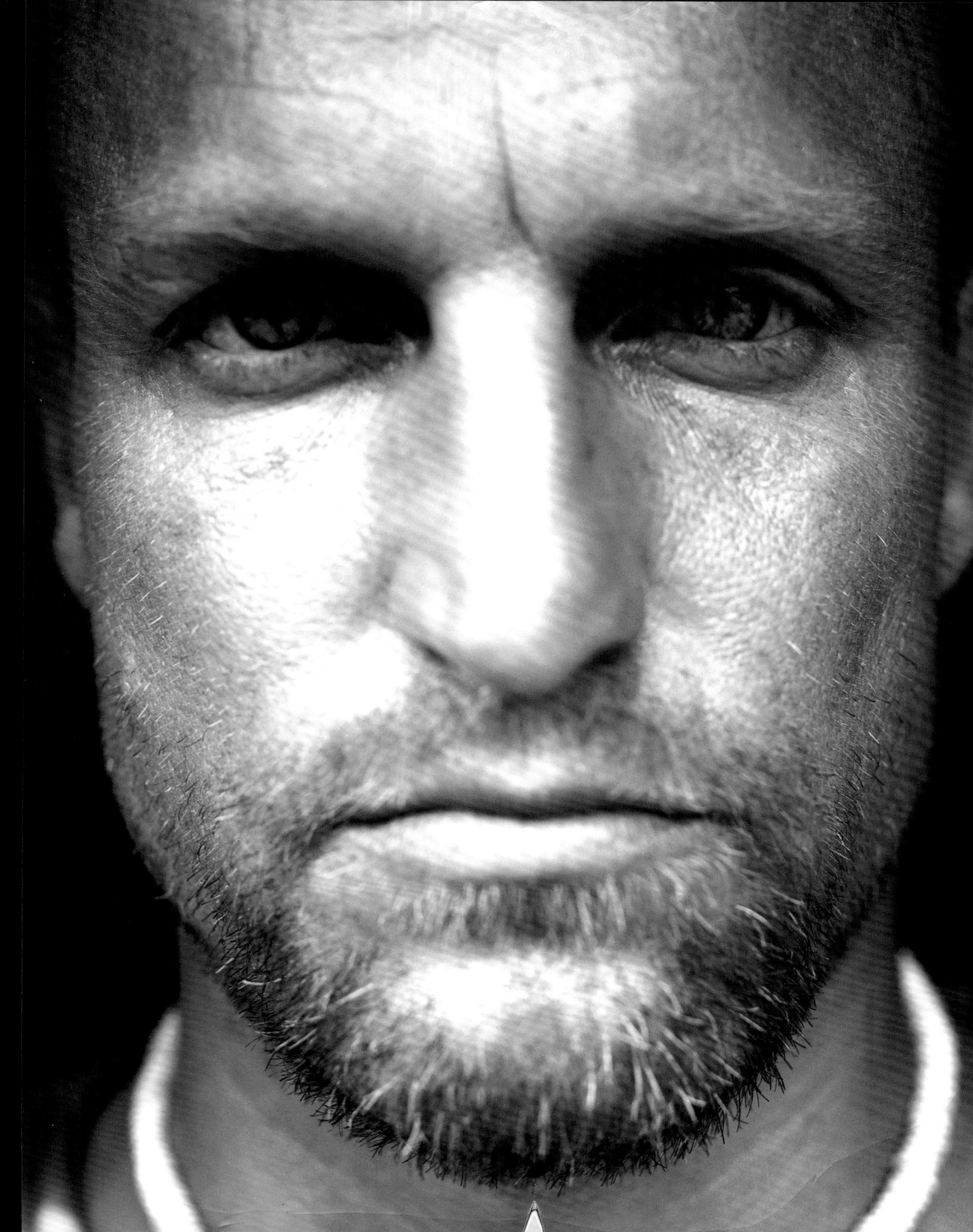

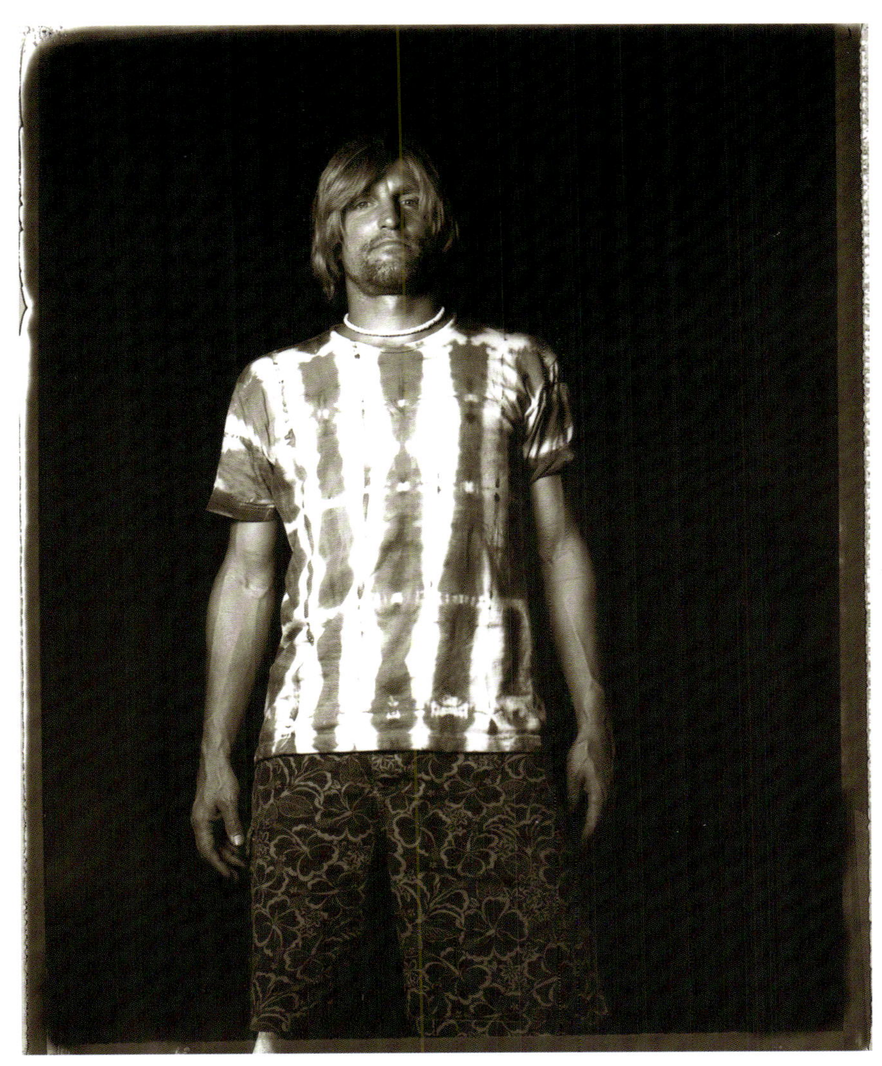

Woody Harrelson

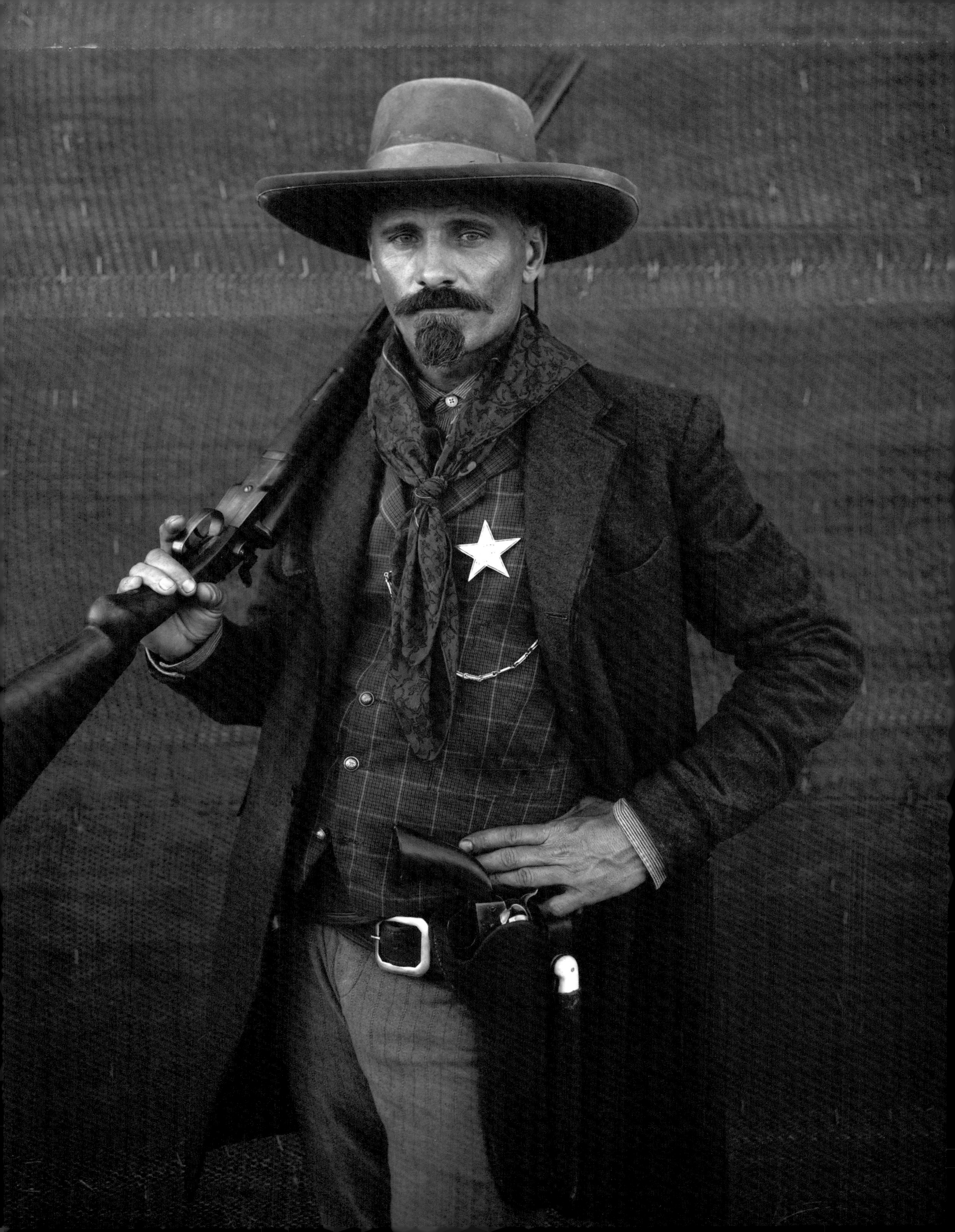

Viggo Mortensen

Lance Henriksen

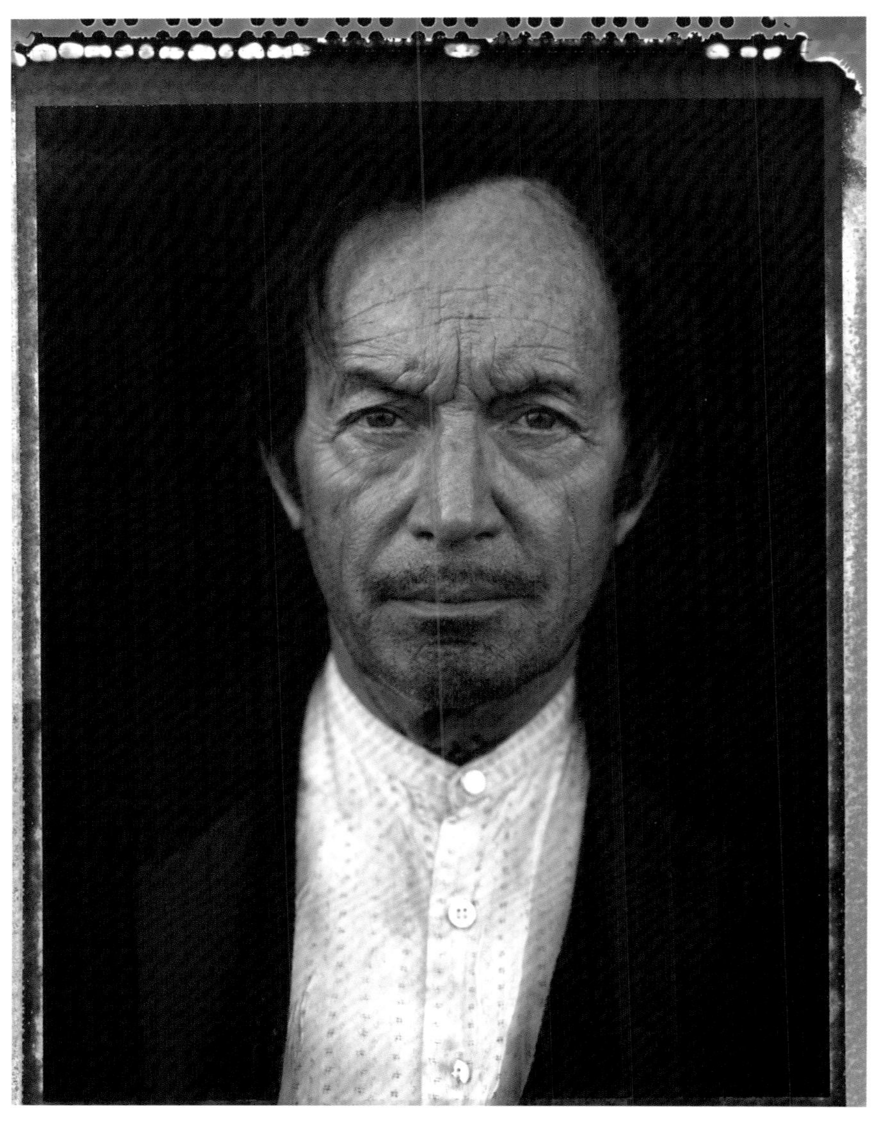

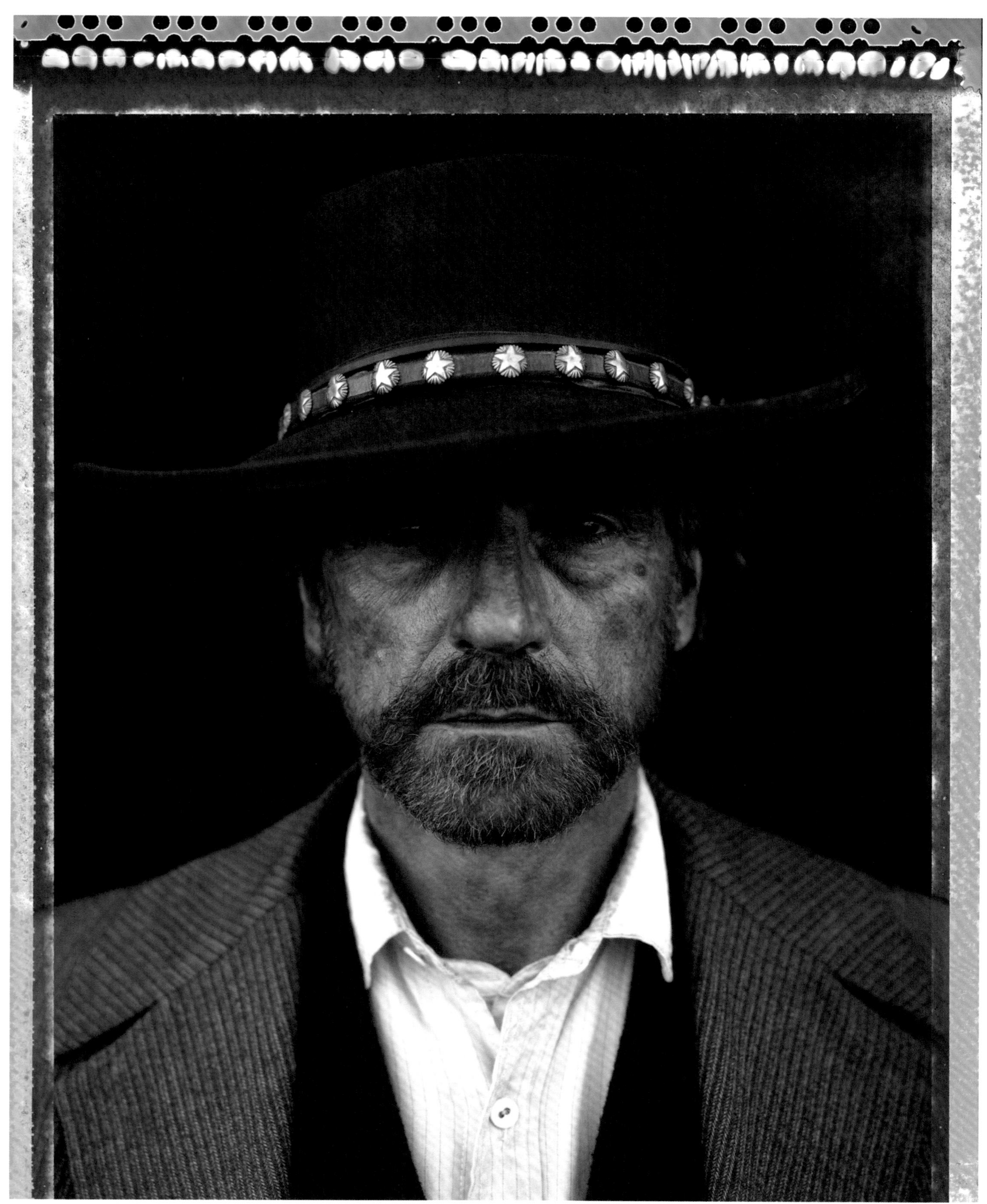

Jeremy Irons

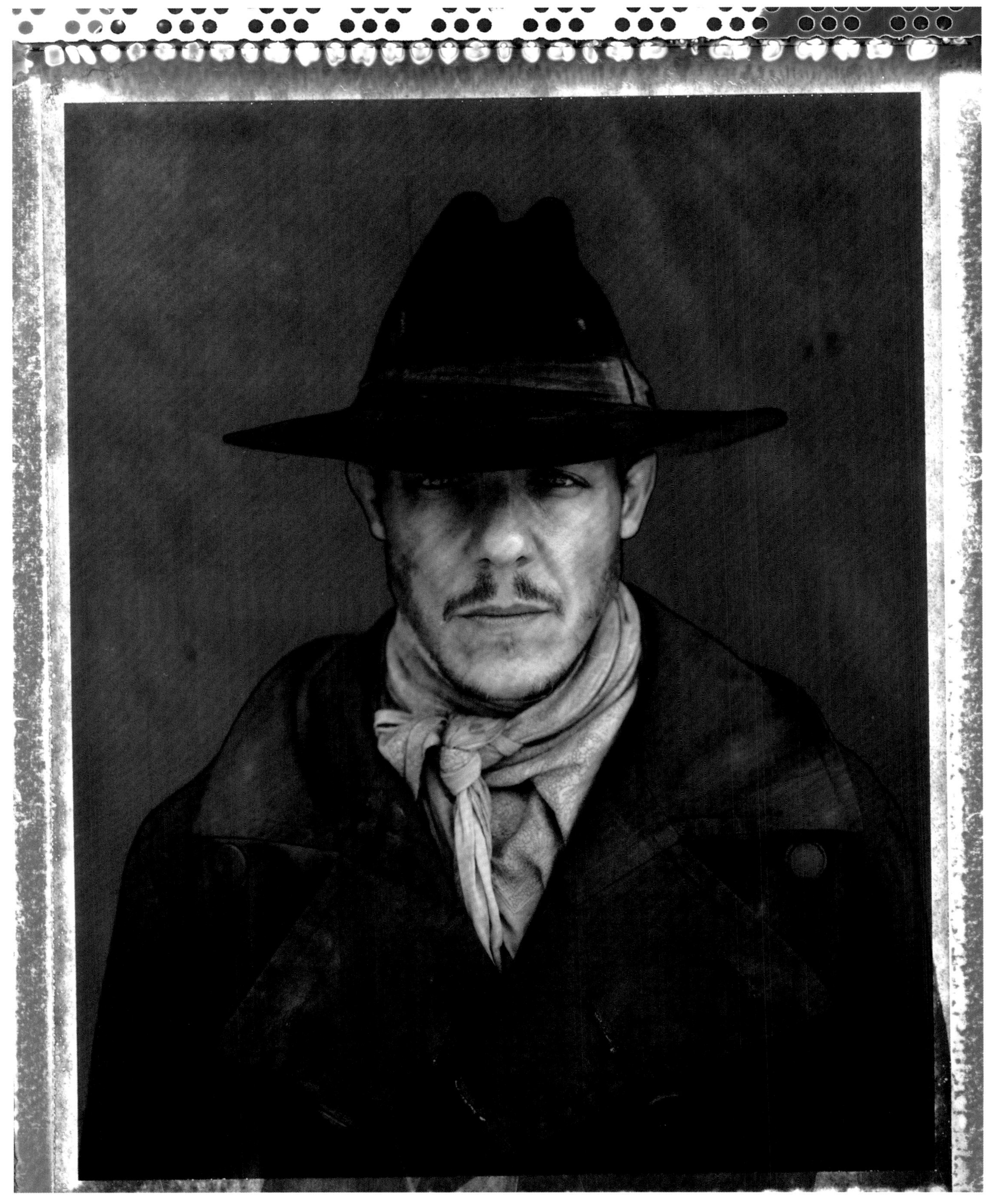

Theo Rossi

Argos MacCallum

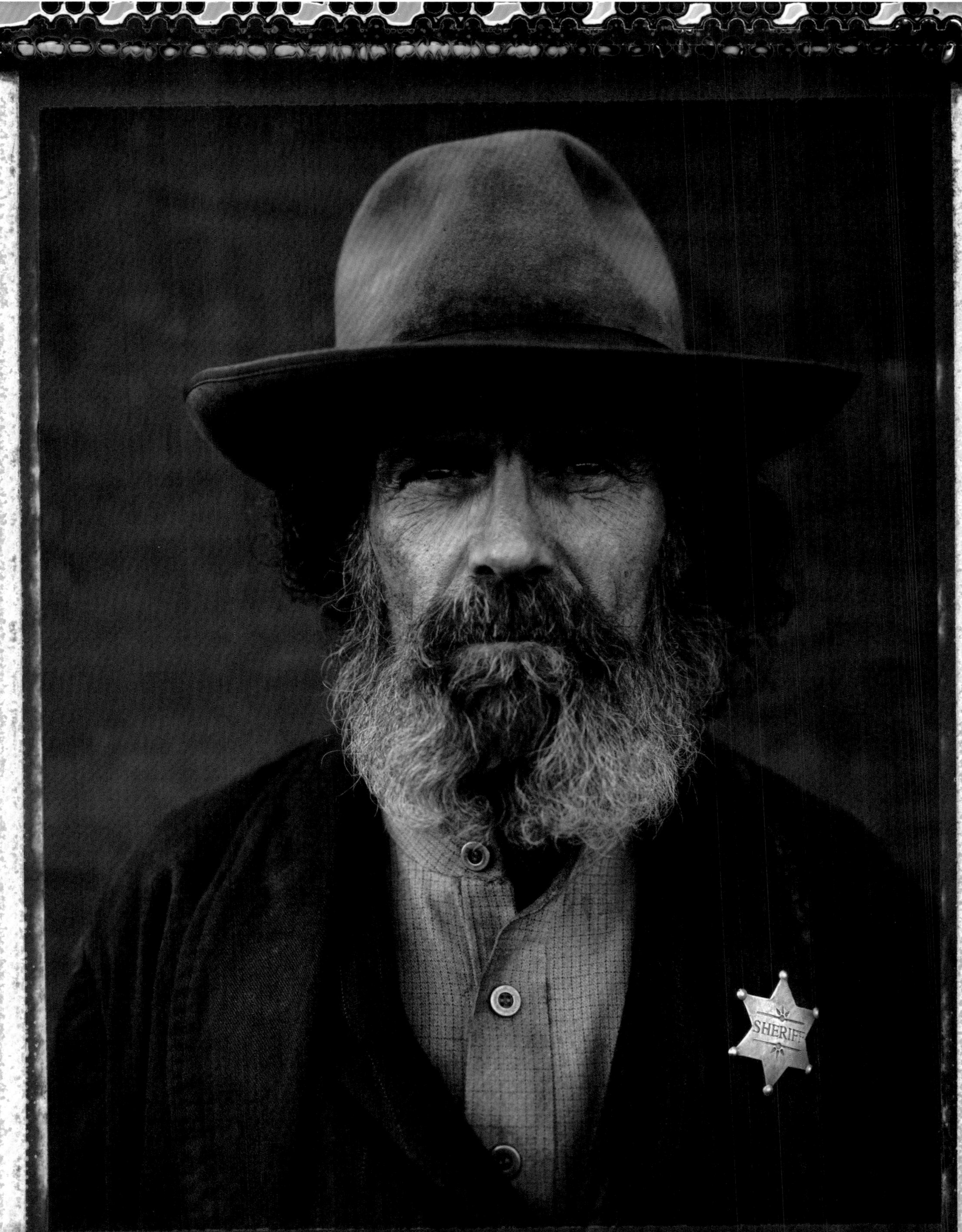
SHERIFF

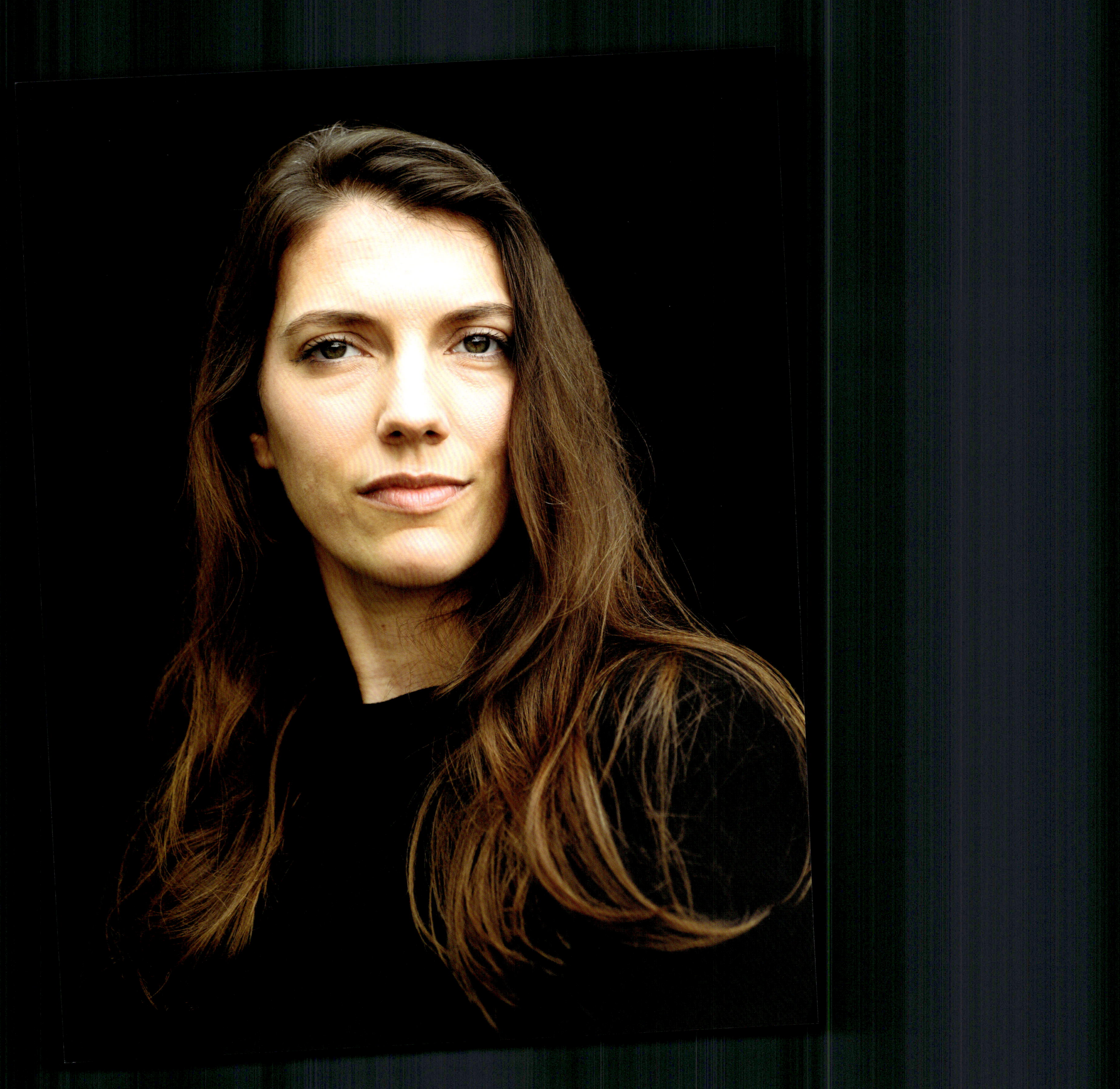

Teresa May Nichta

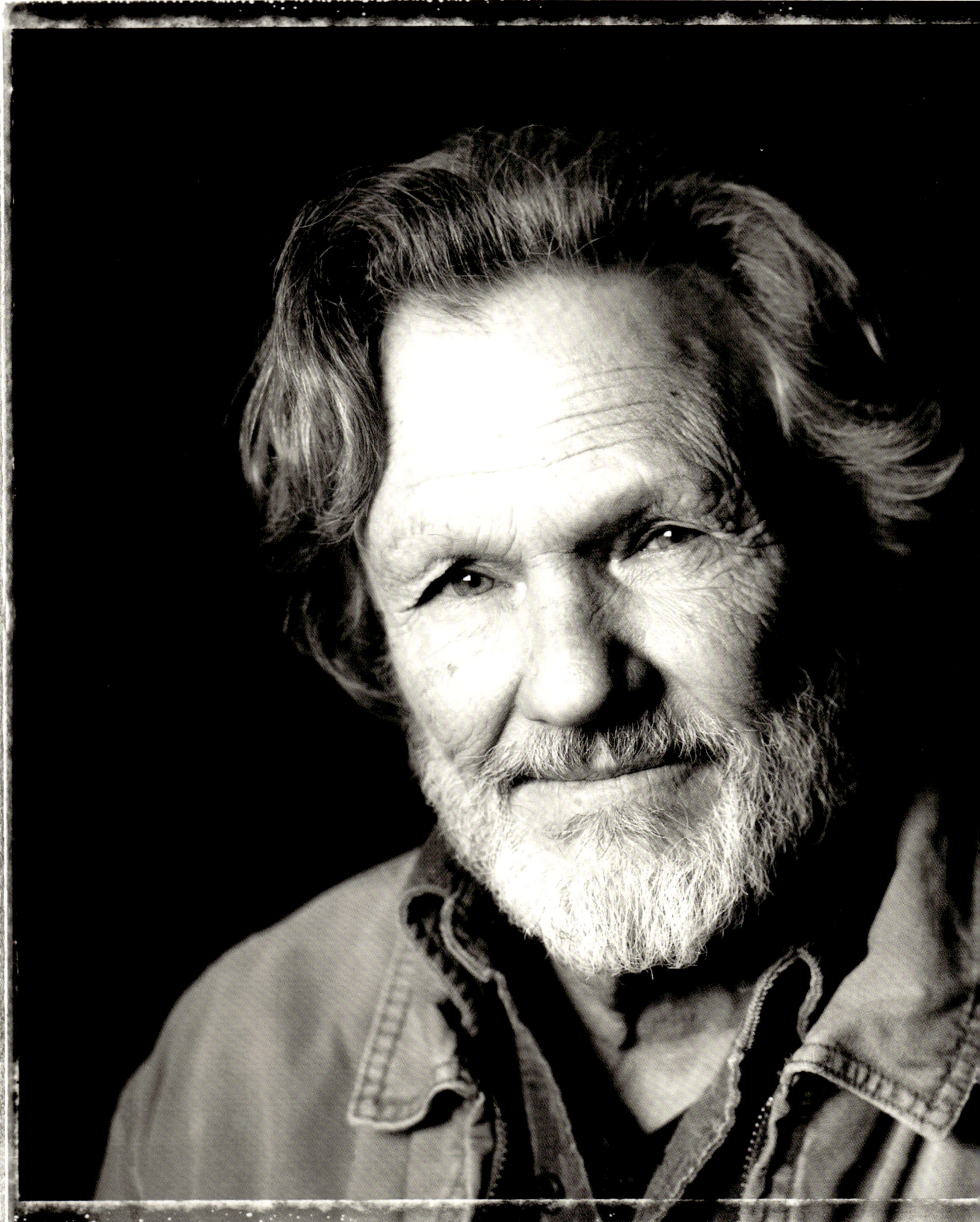

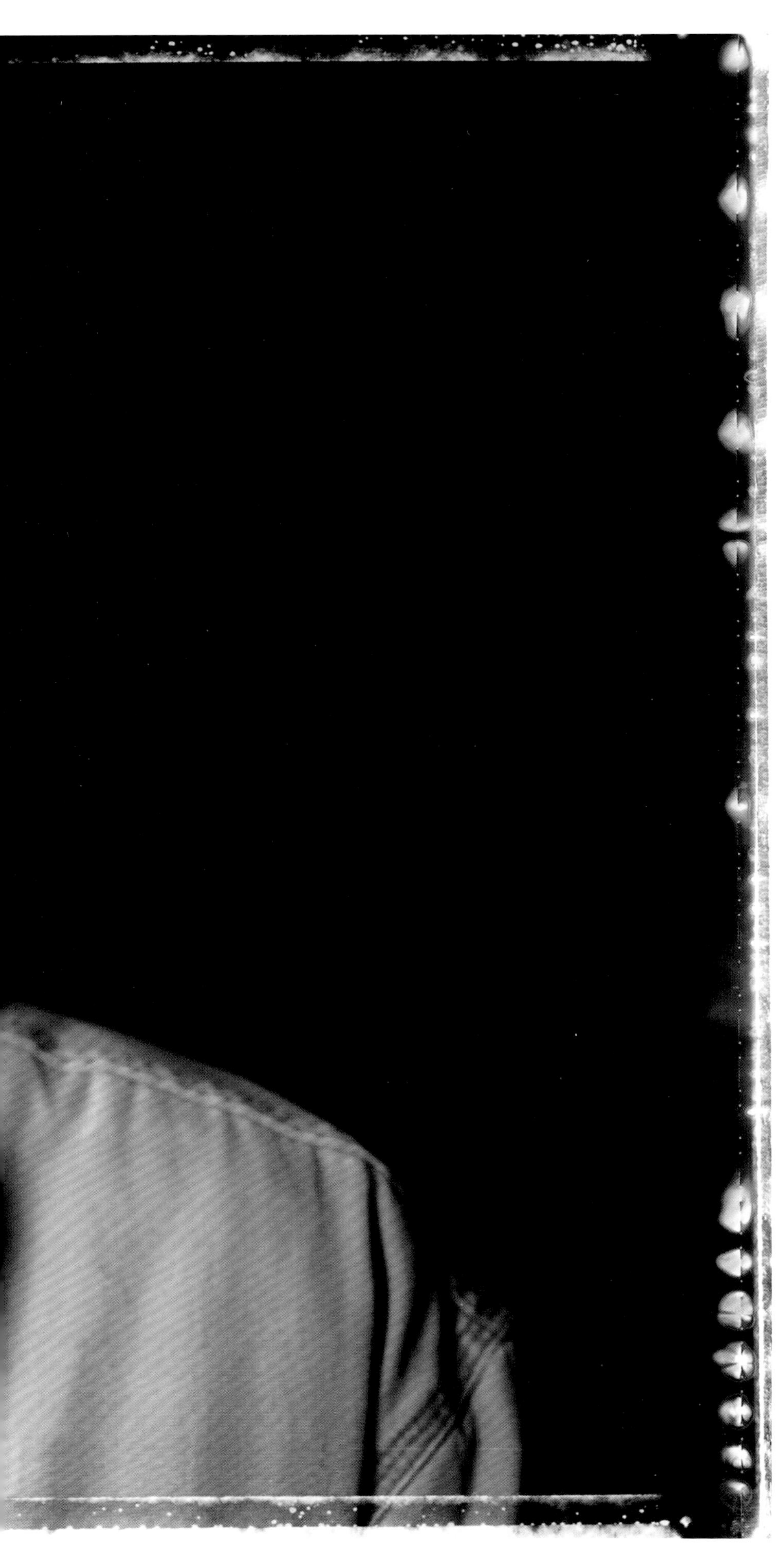

Kris Kristofferson

Kris Kristofferson

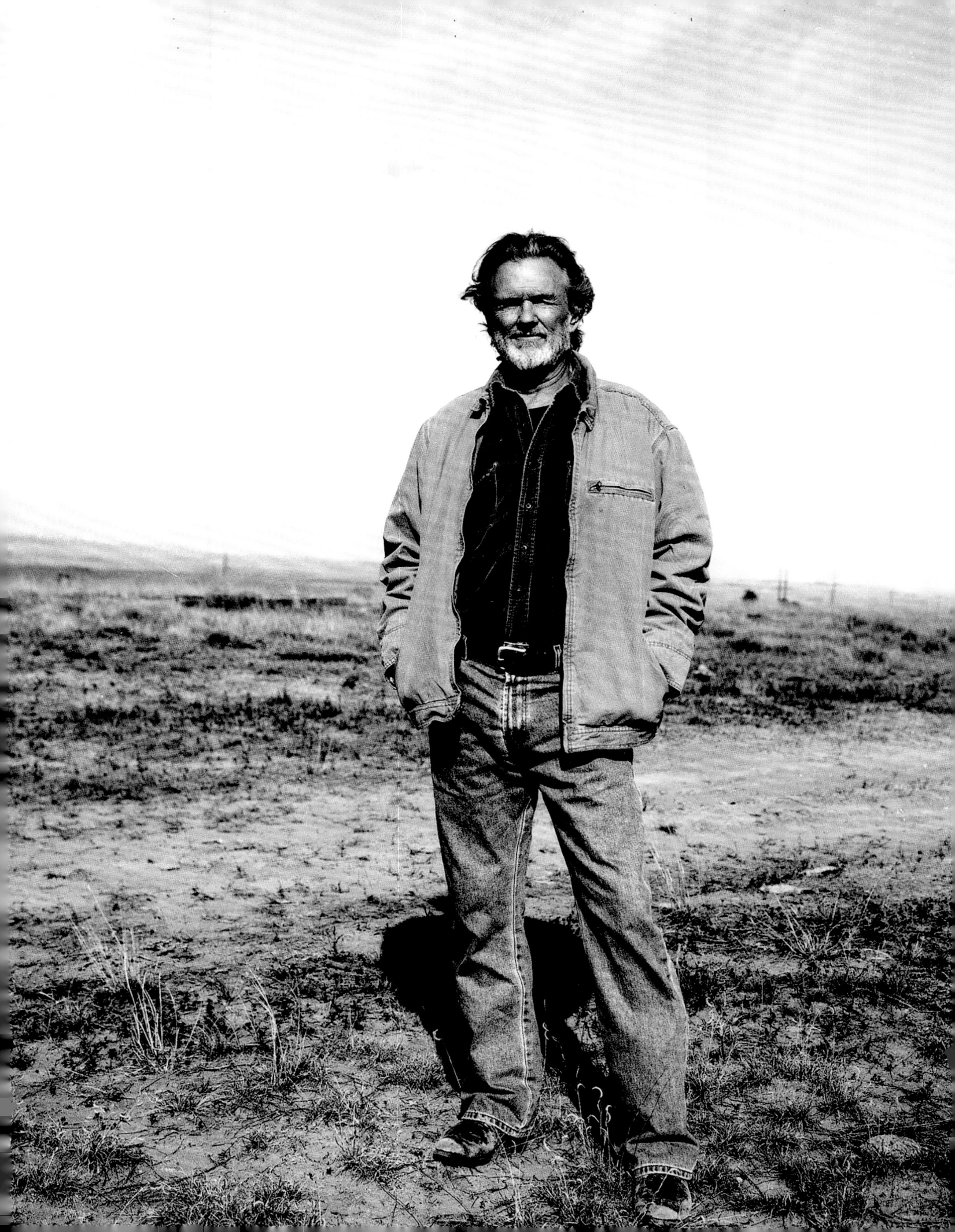

Catalina Sandino Moreno

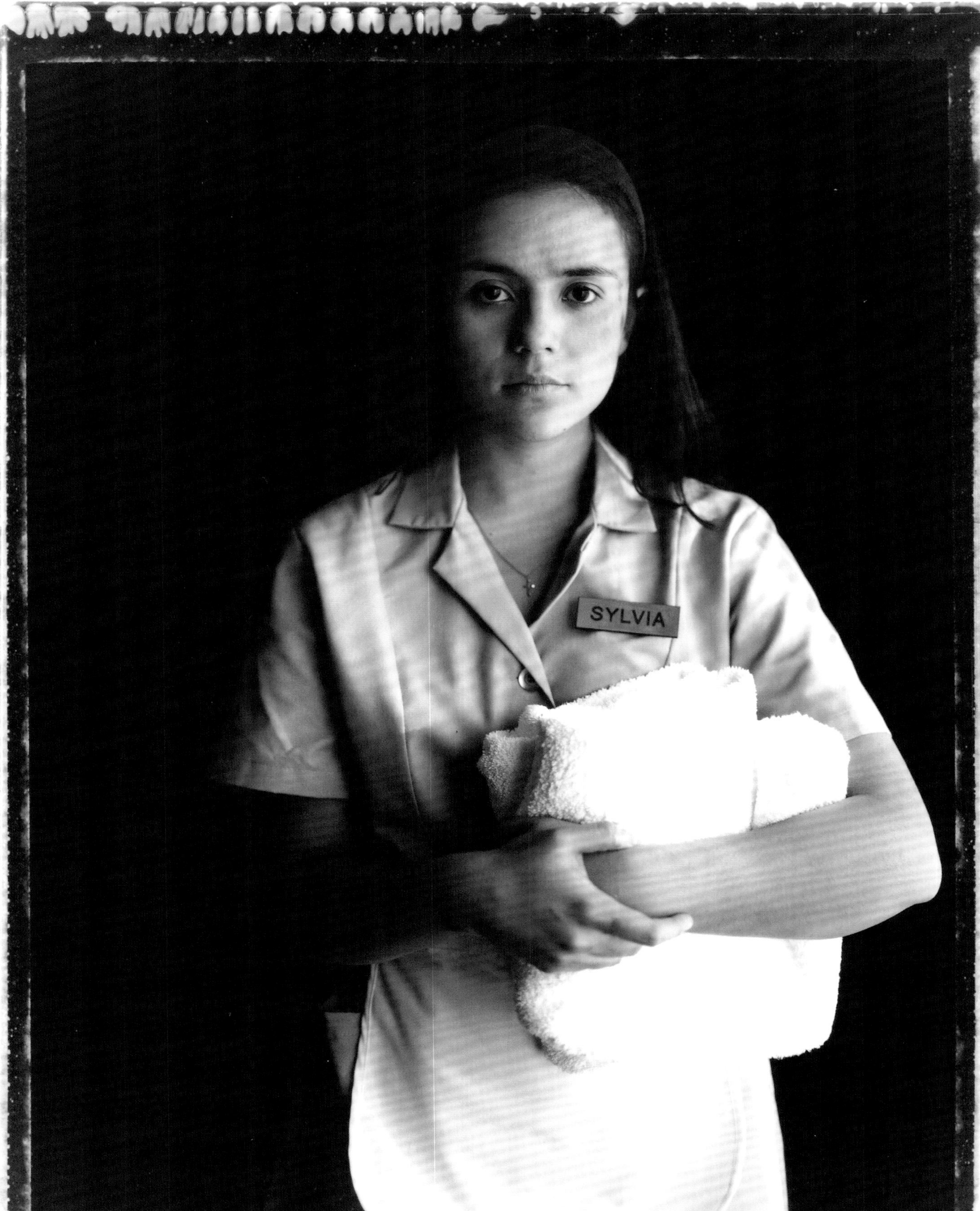
SYLVIA

Wilmer Valderrama

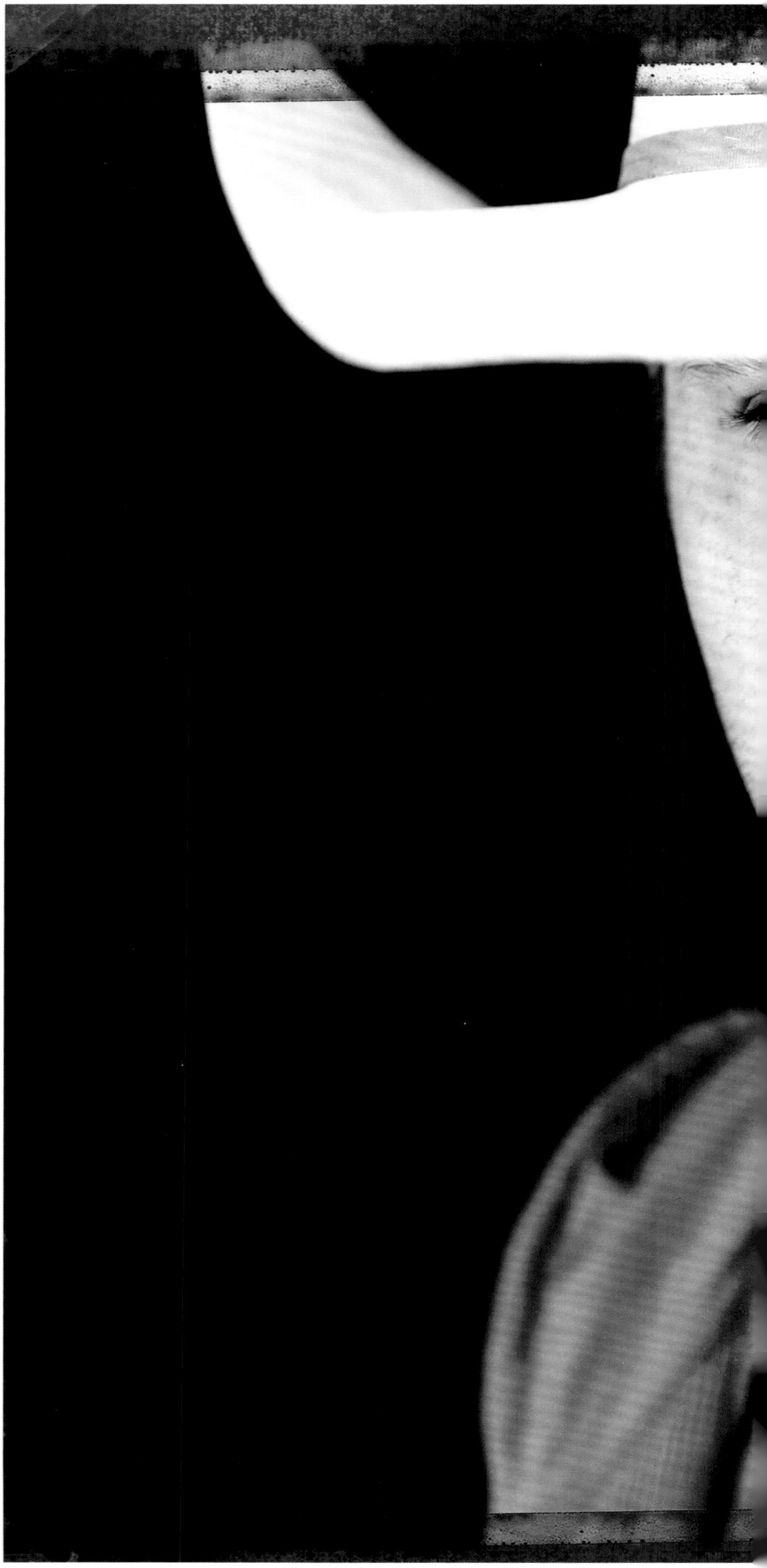

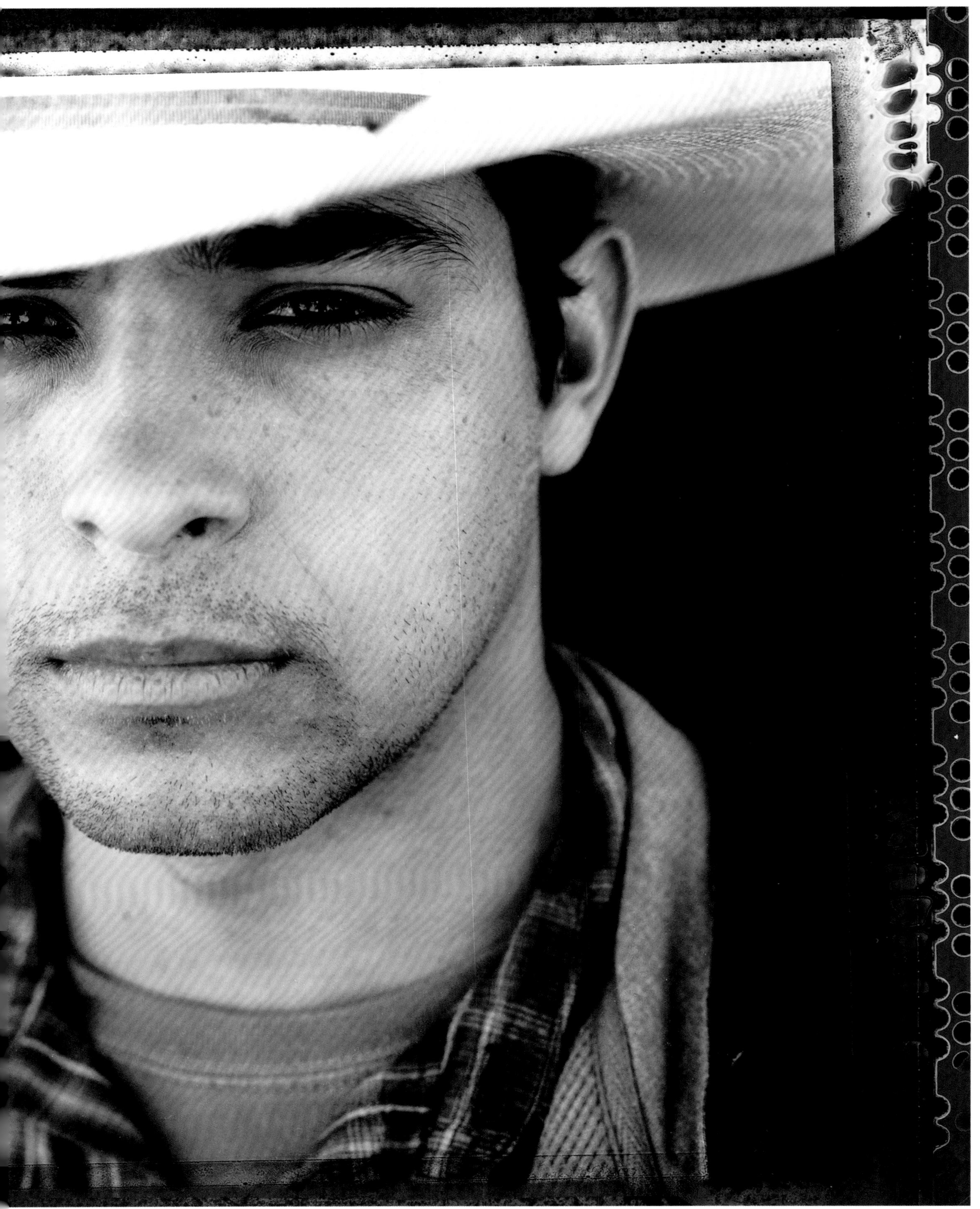

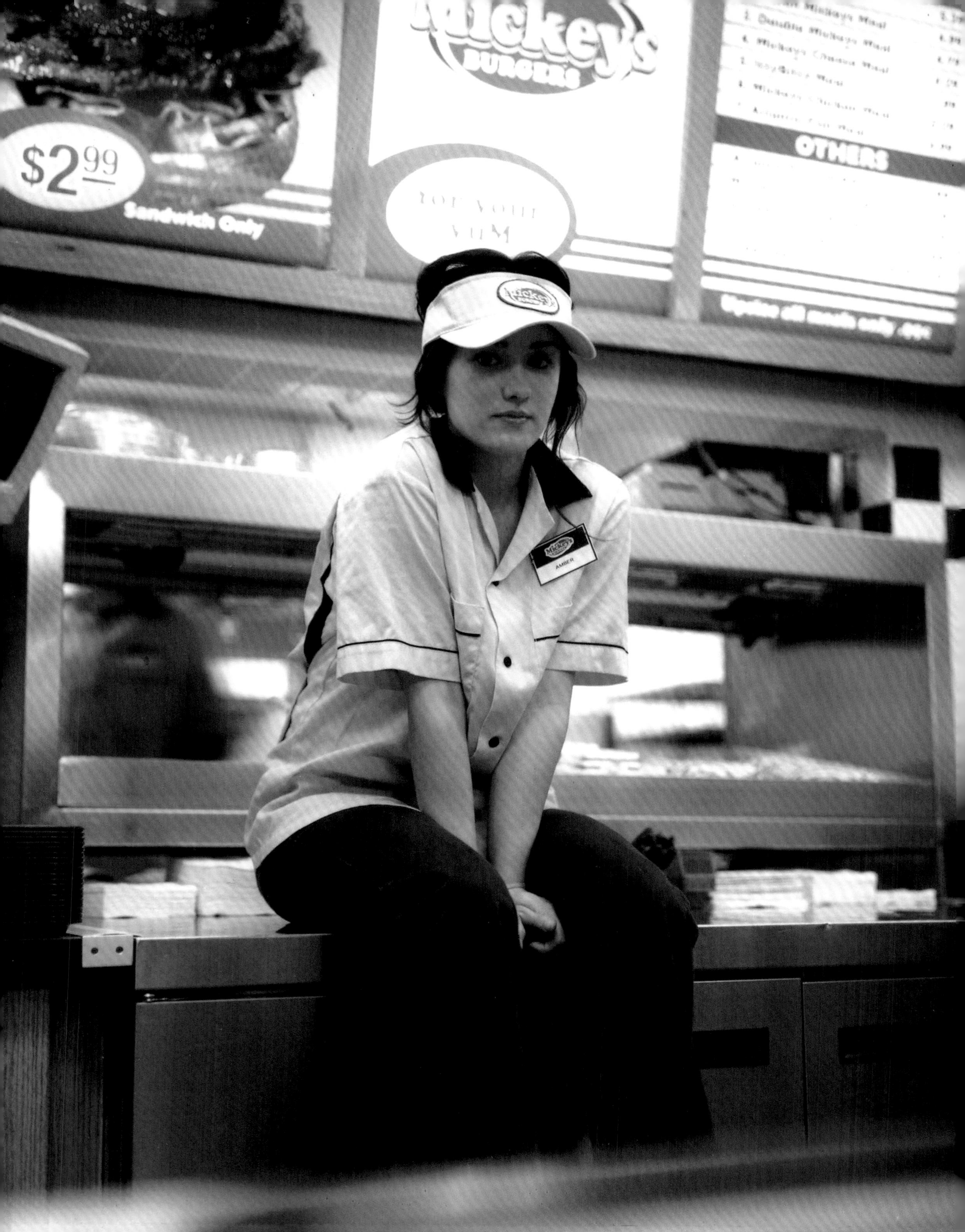
$2.99
Sandwich Only
Mickey's
BURGERS
OTHERS
AMBER

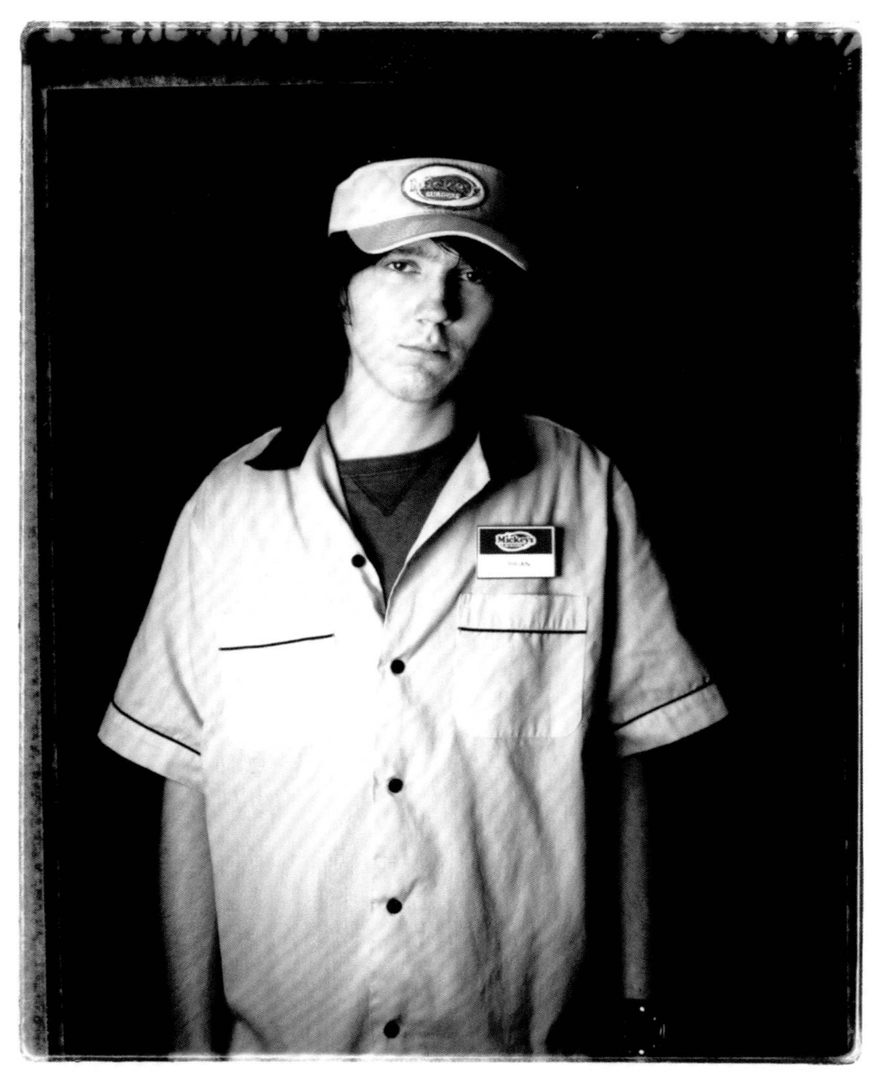

Paul Dano

Ashley Johnson

Greg Kinnear

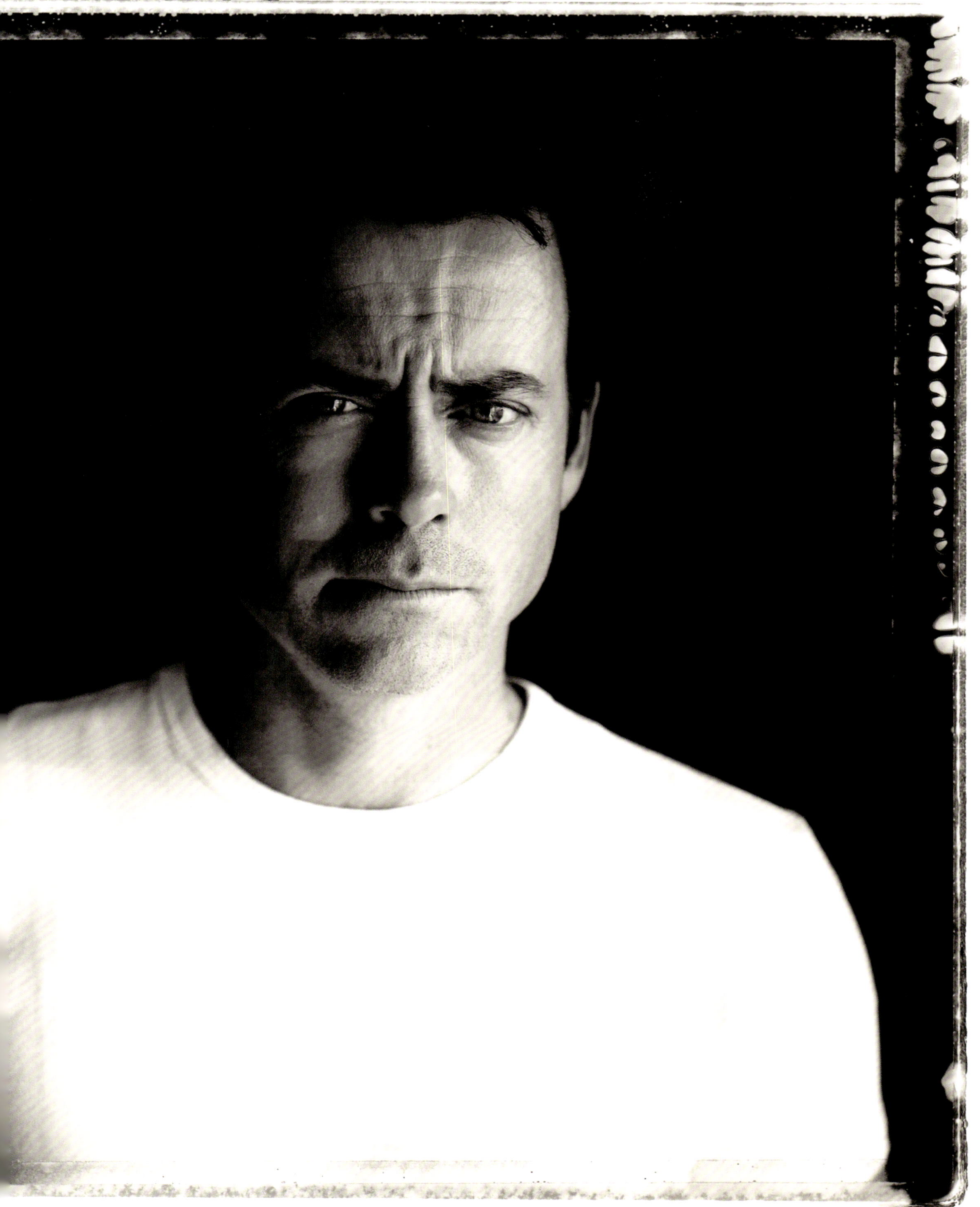

Luis Guzmán

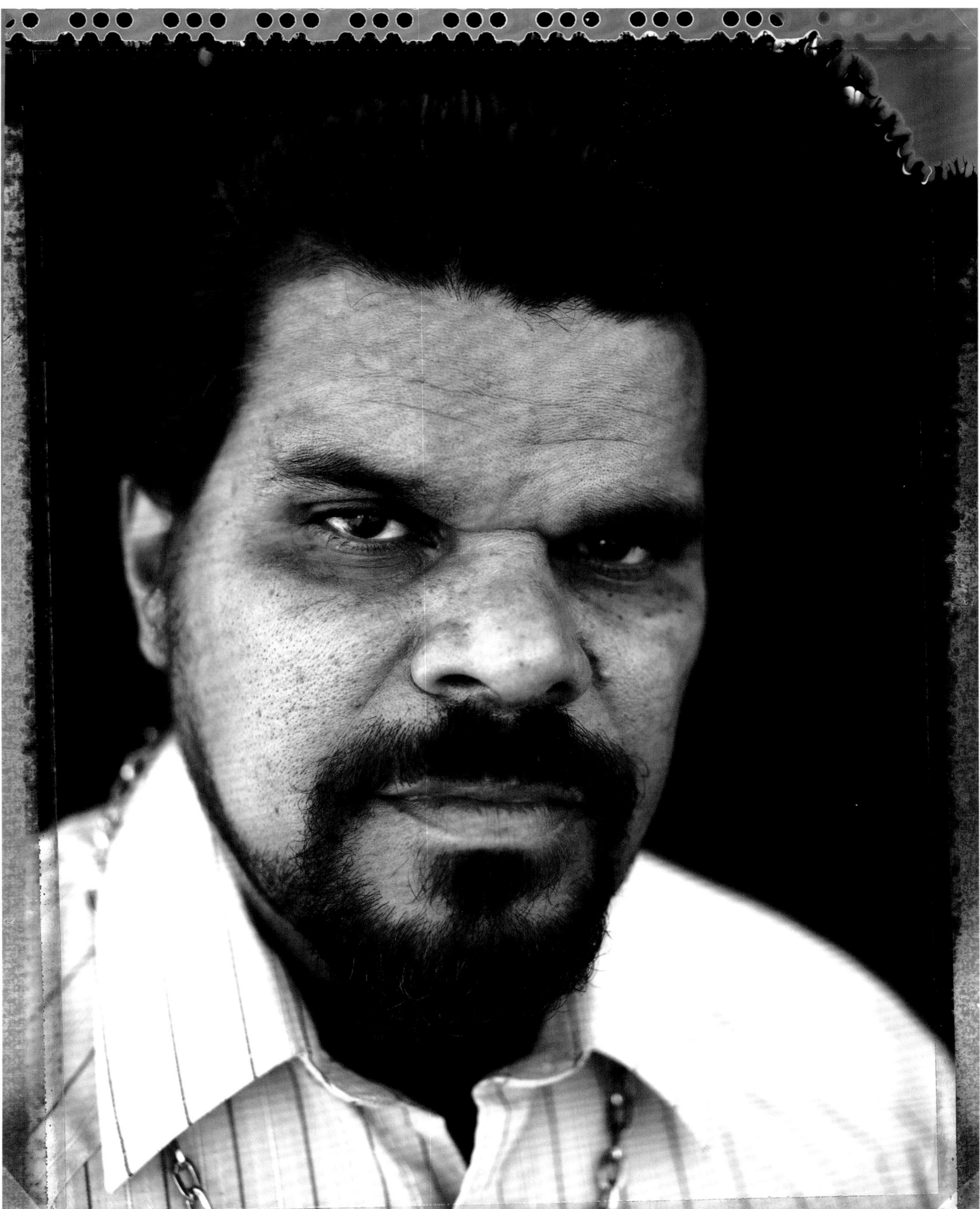

Juan Carlos Serrán

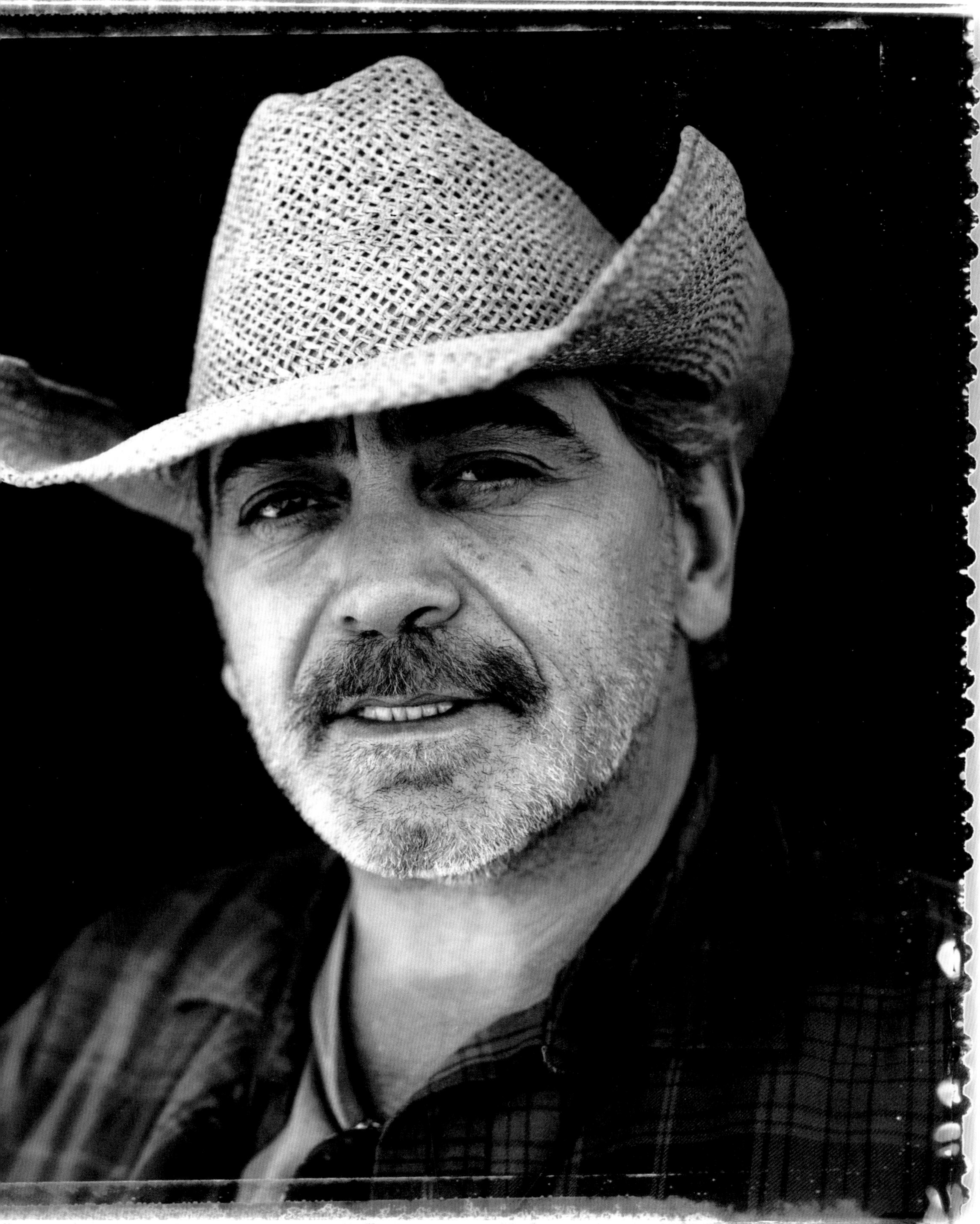

Glen Powell

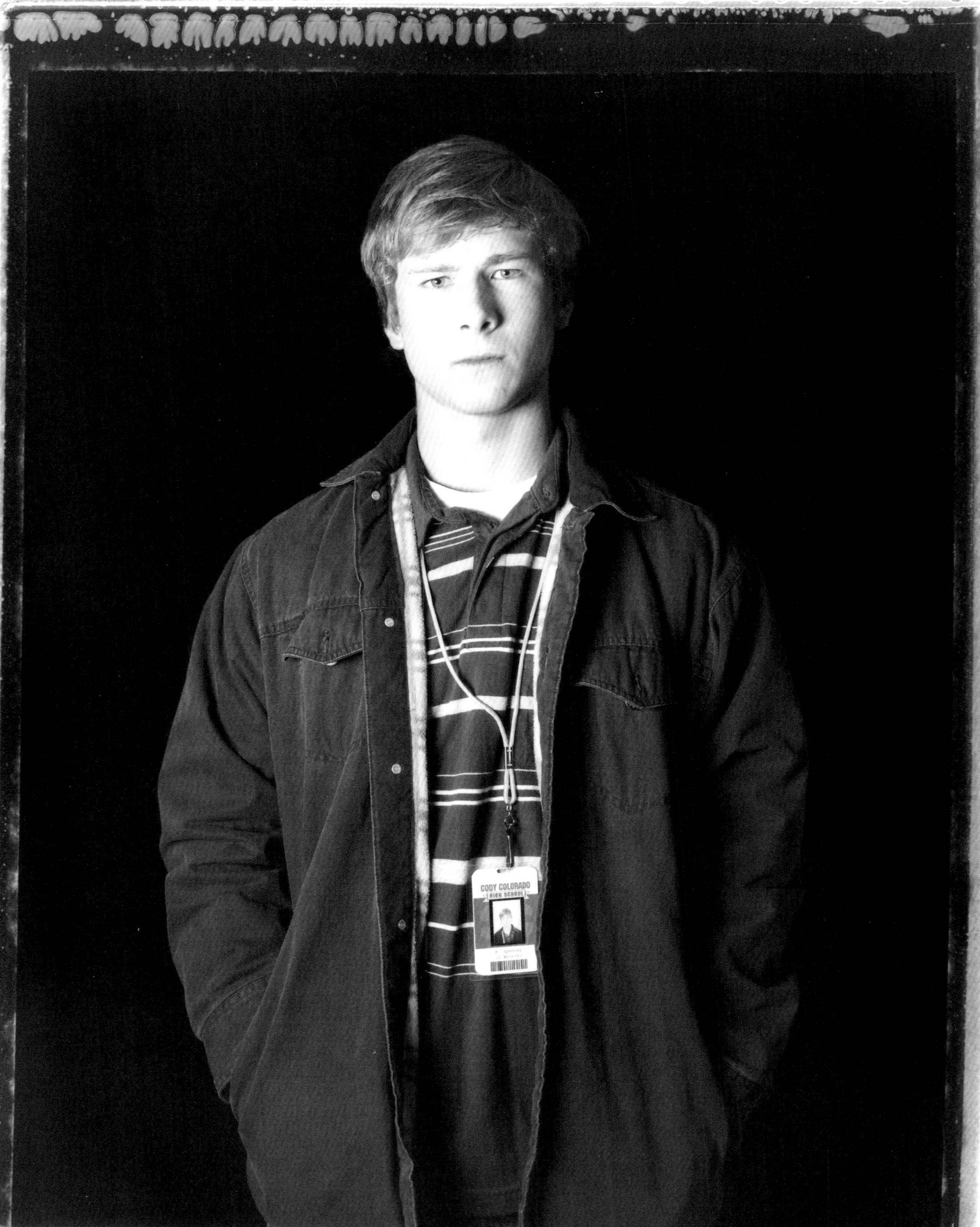
CODY COLORADO
HIGH SCHOOL

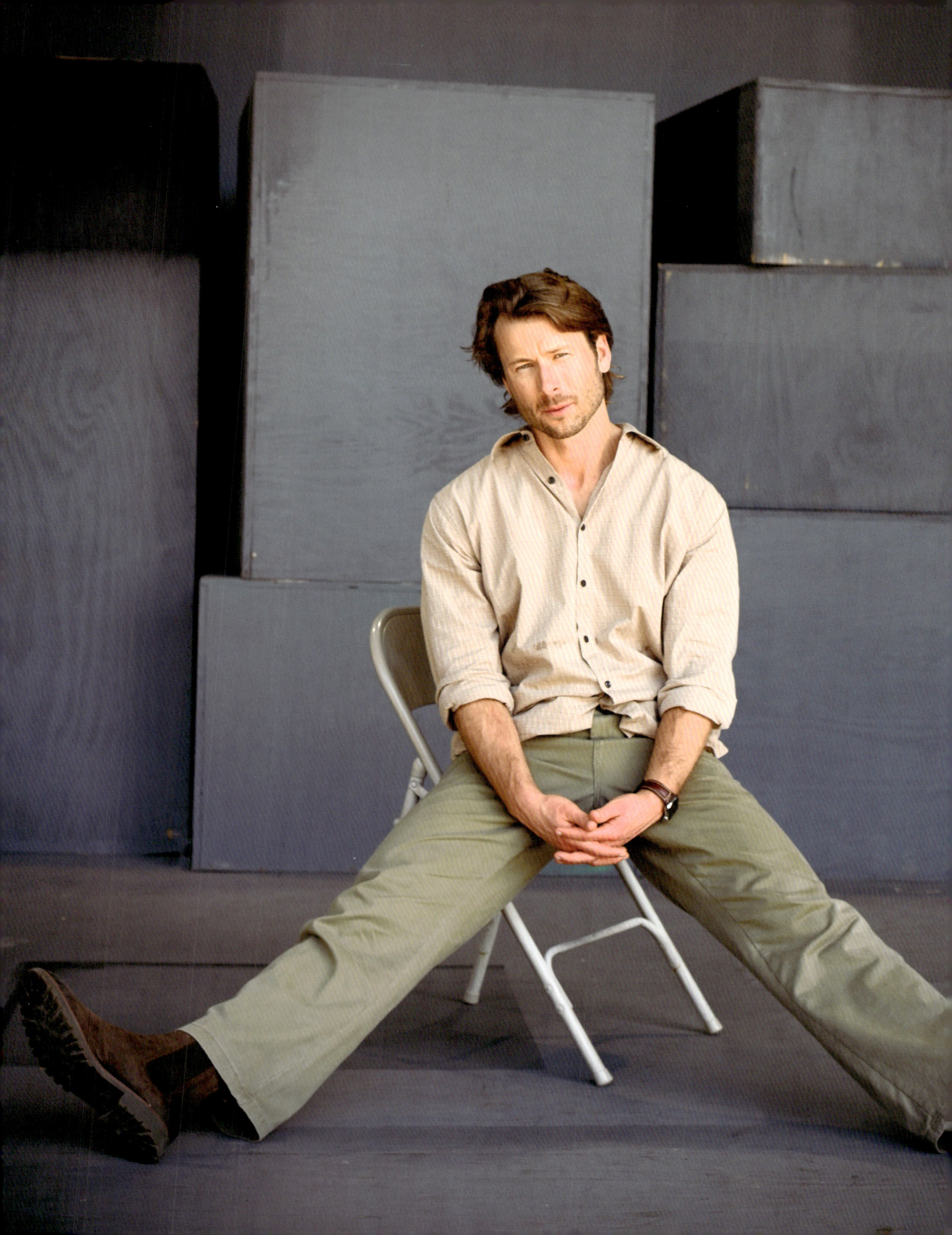

Glen Po

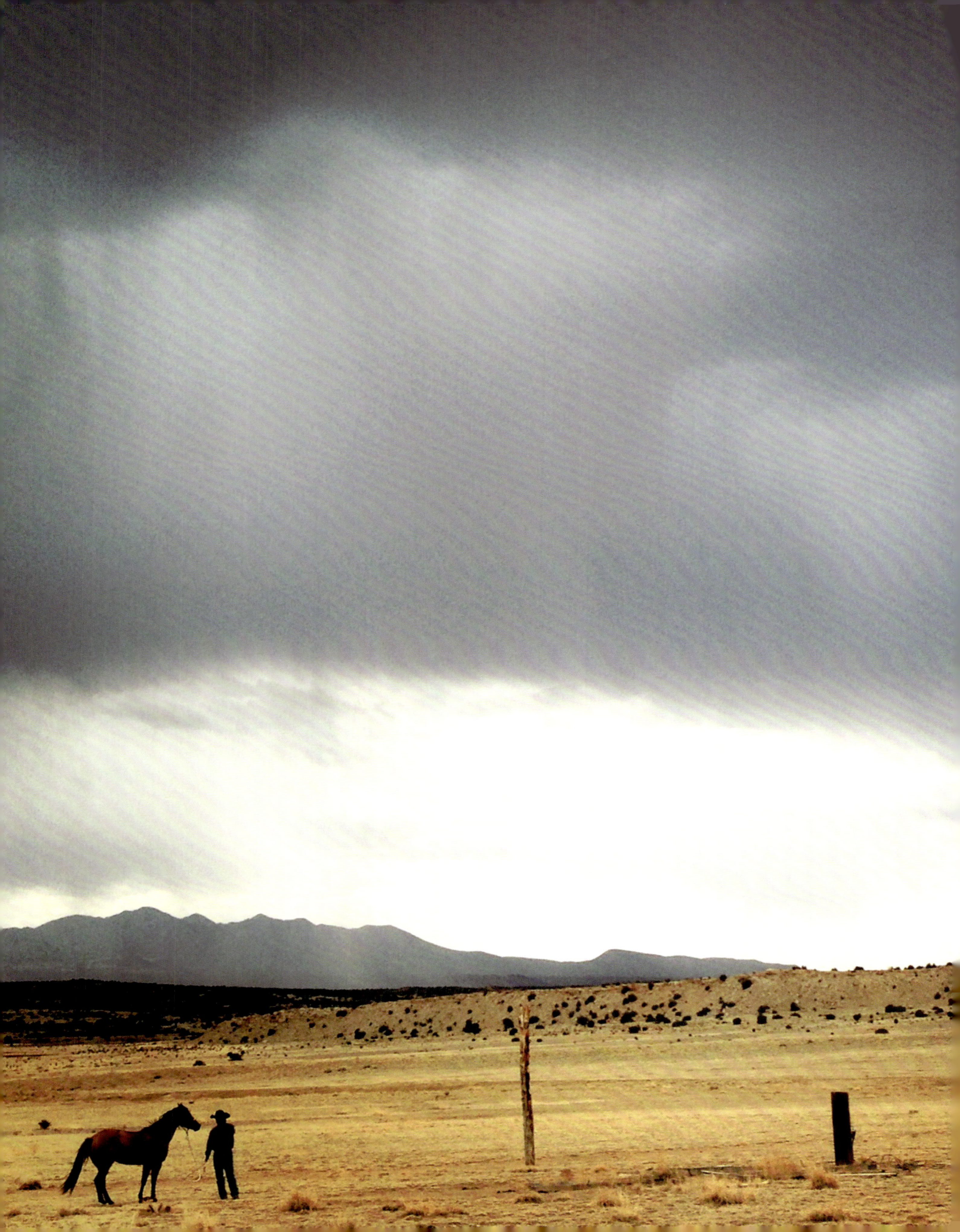

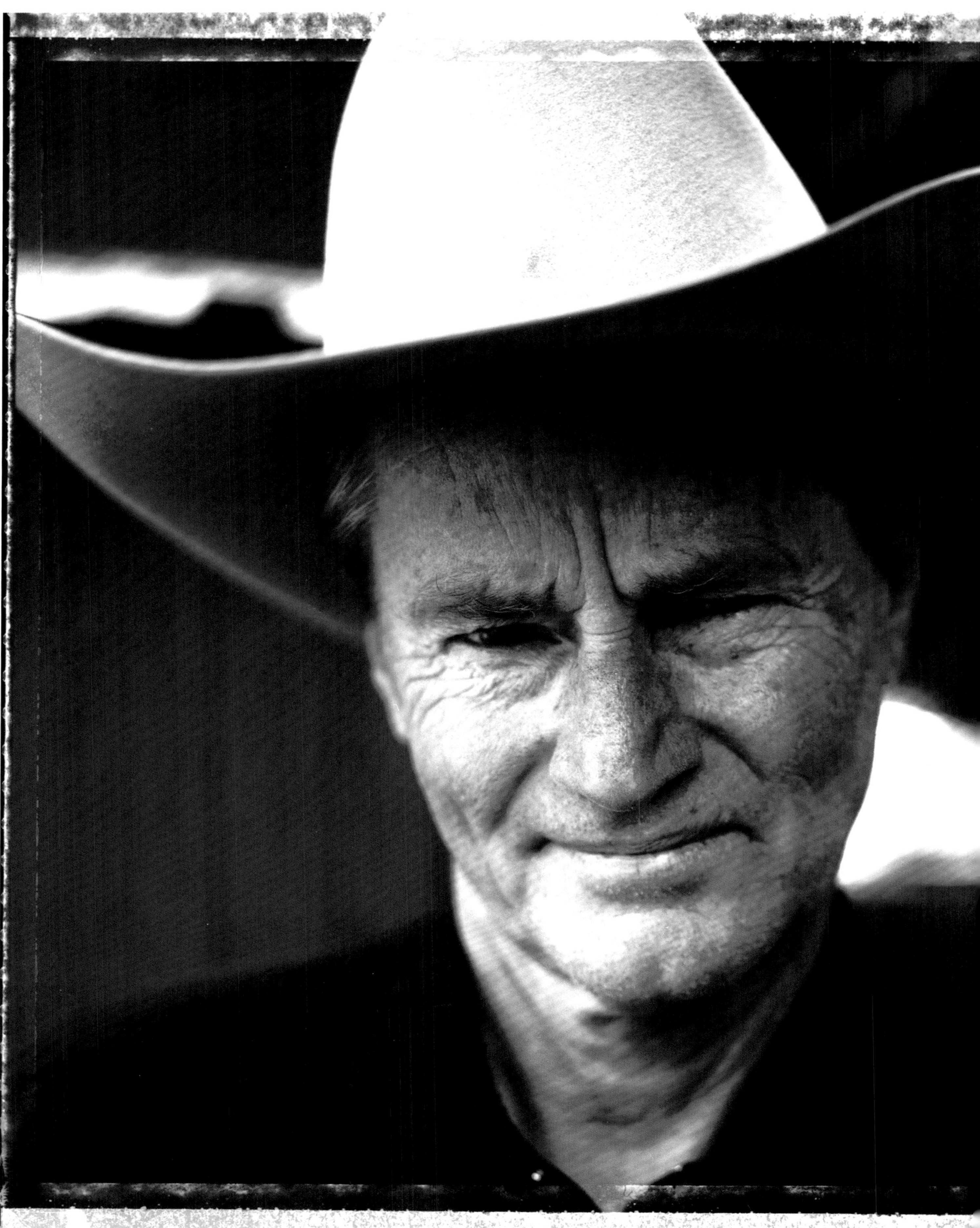

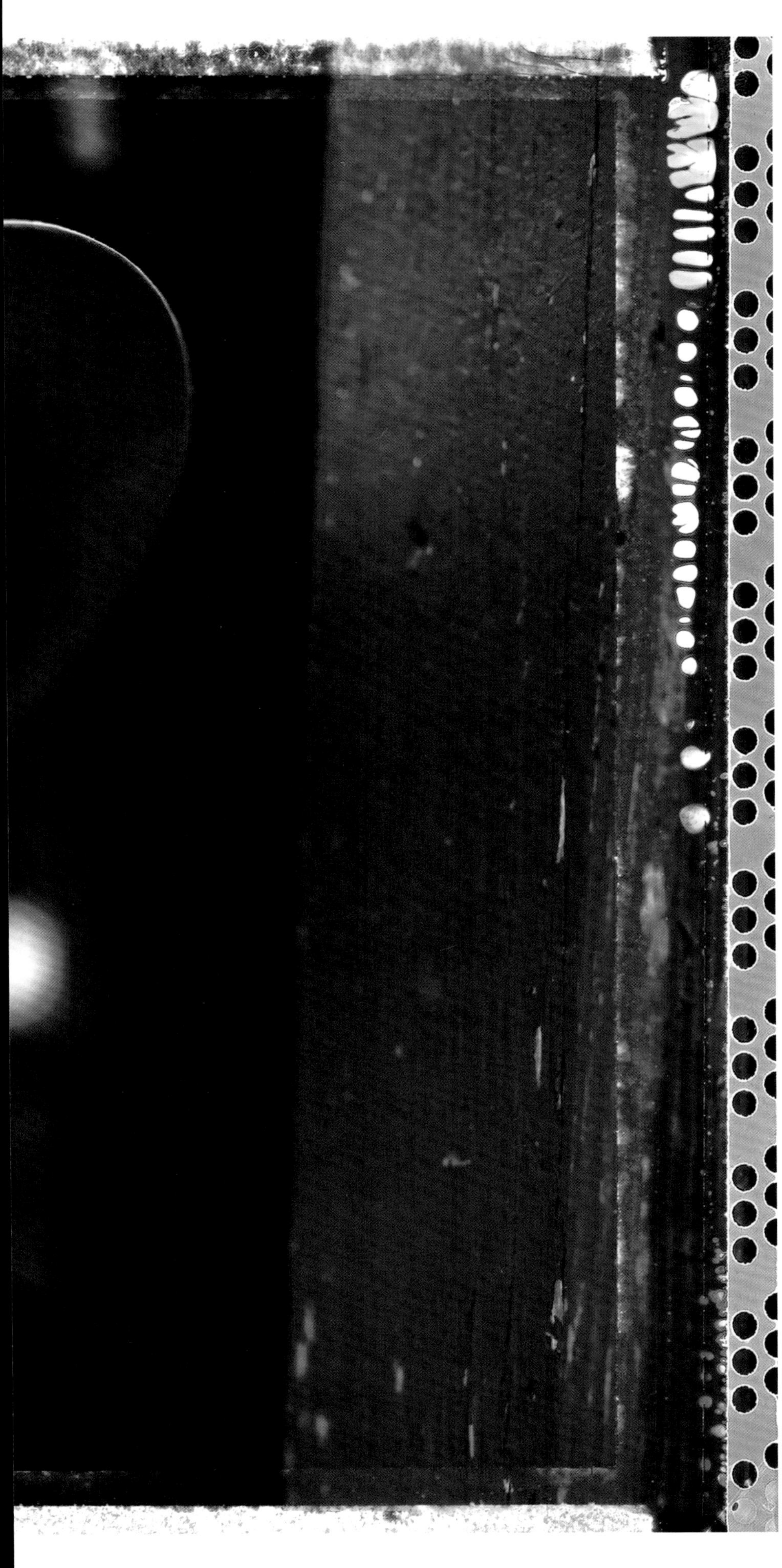

Sam Shepard

Harry Dean Stanton

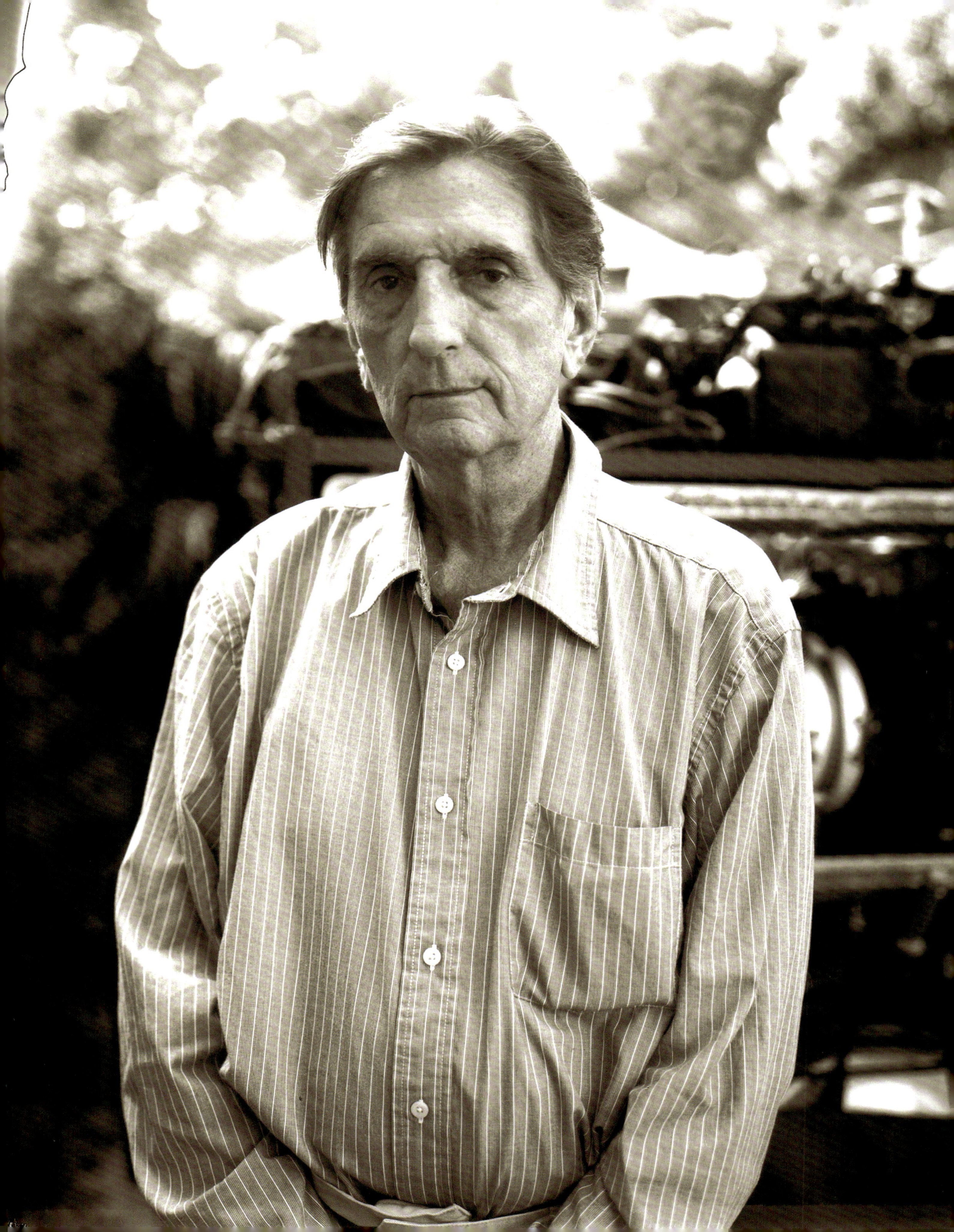

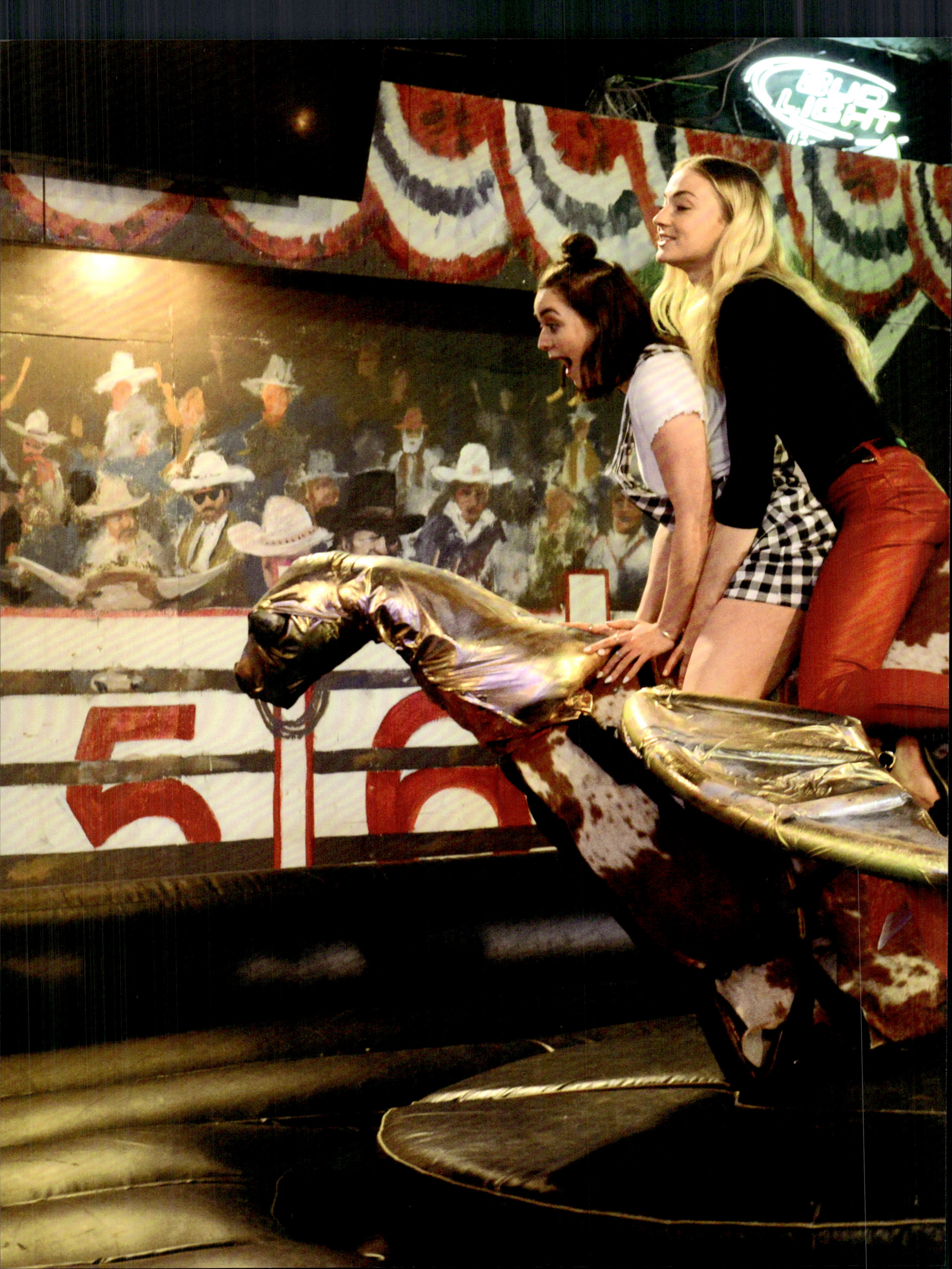
BUD LIGHT

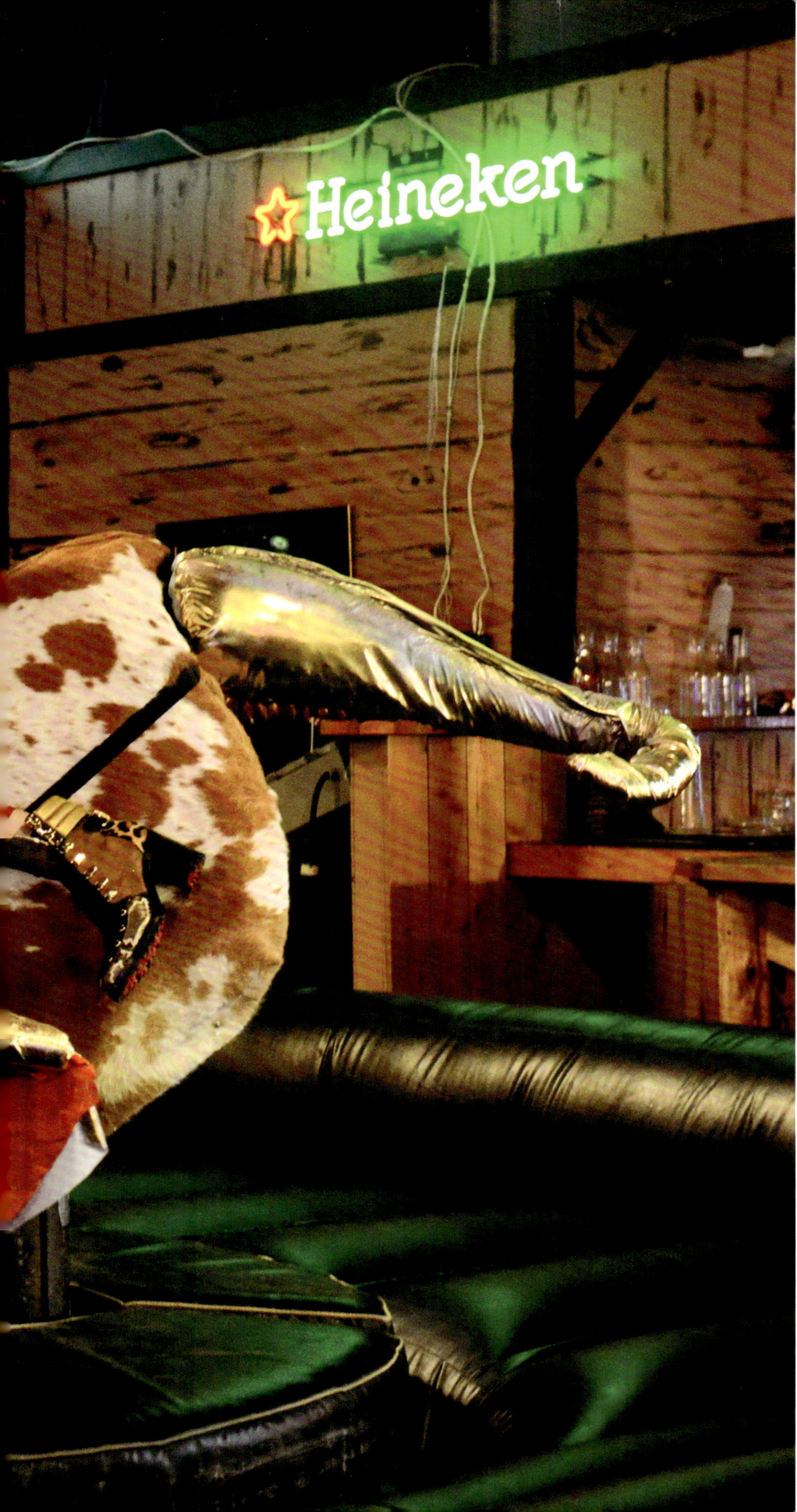

Maisie Williams and **Sophie** Turner

Sophie Turner

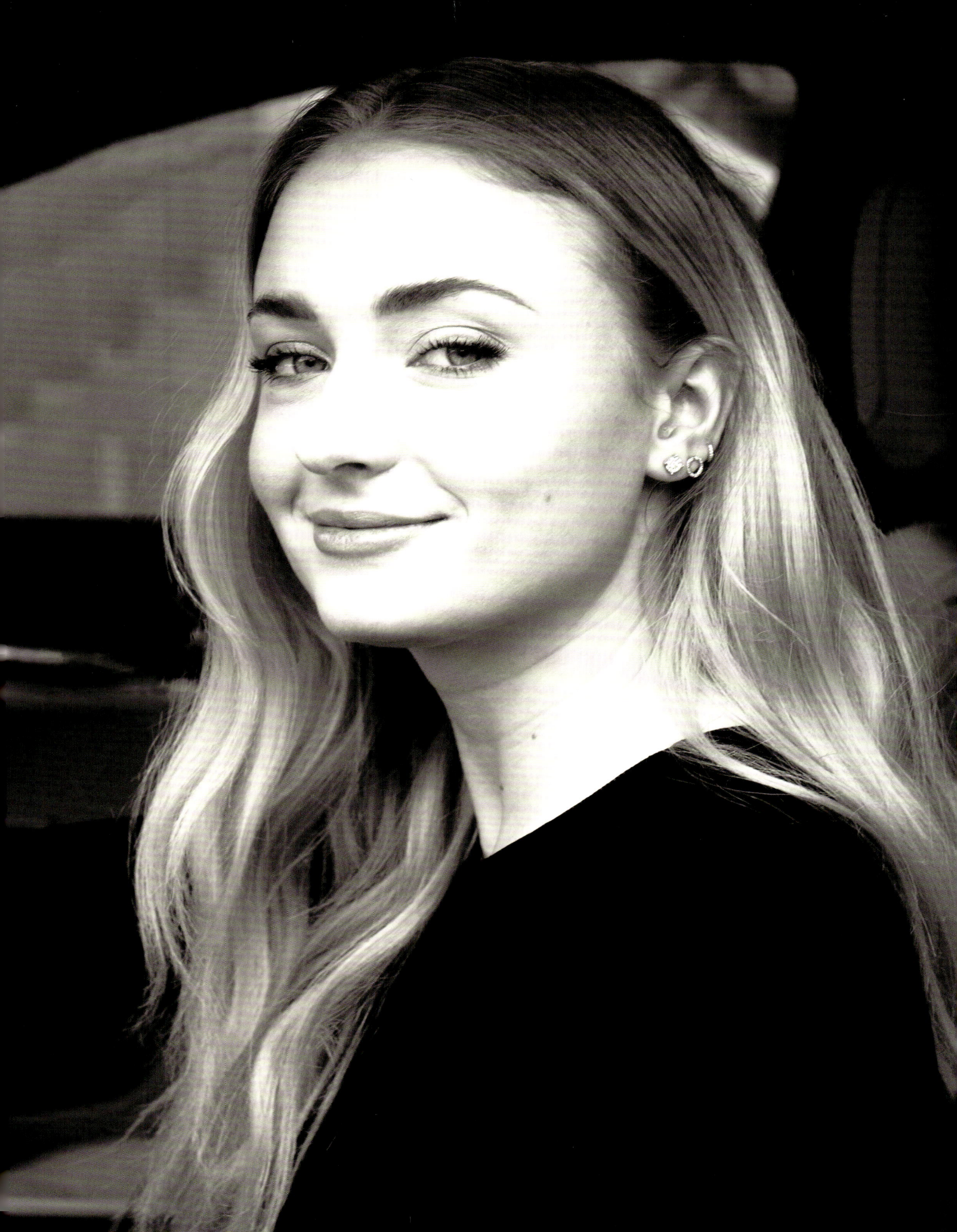

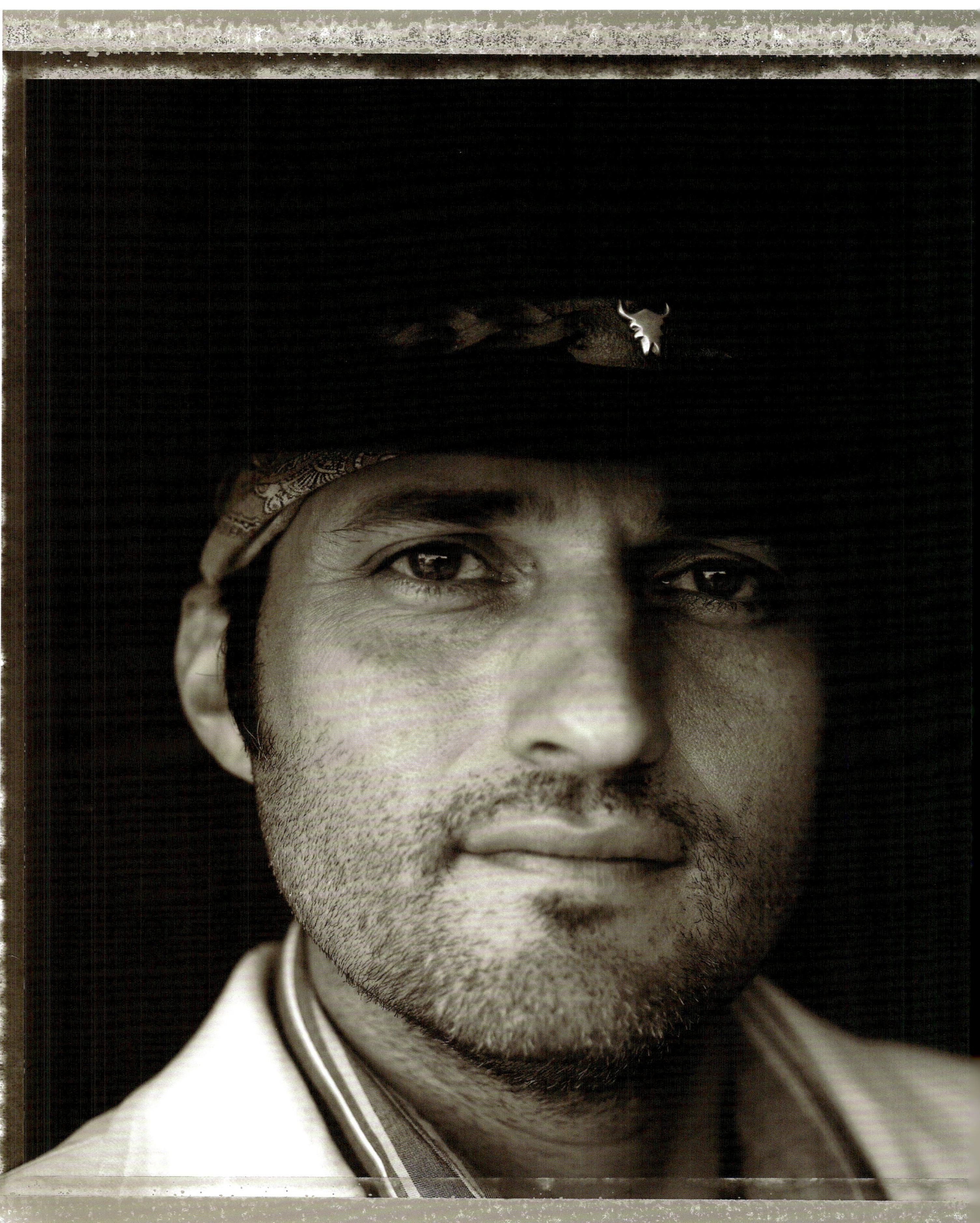

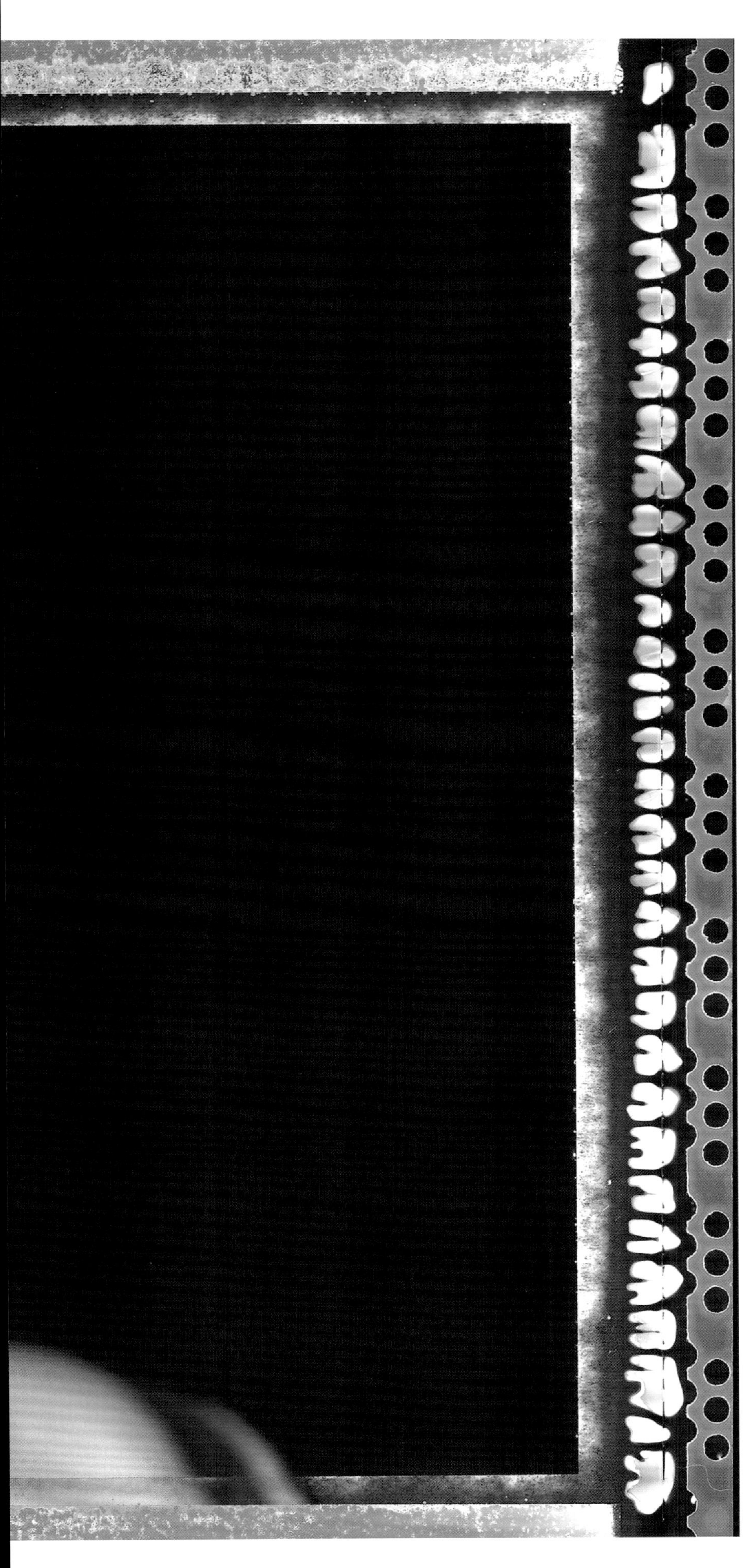

Robert Rodriguez

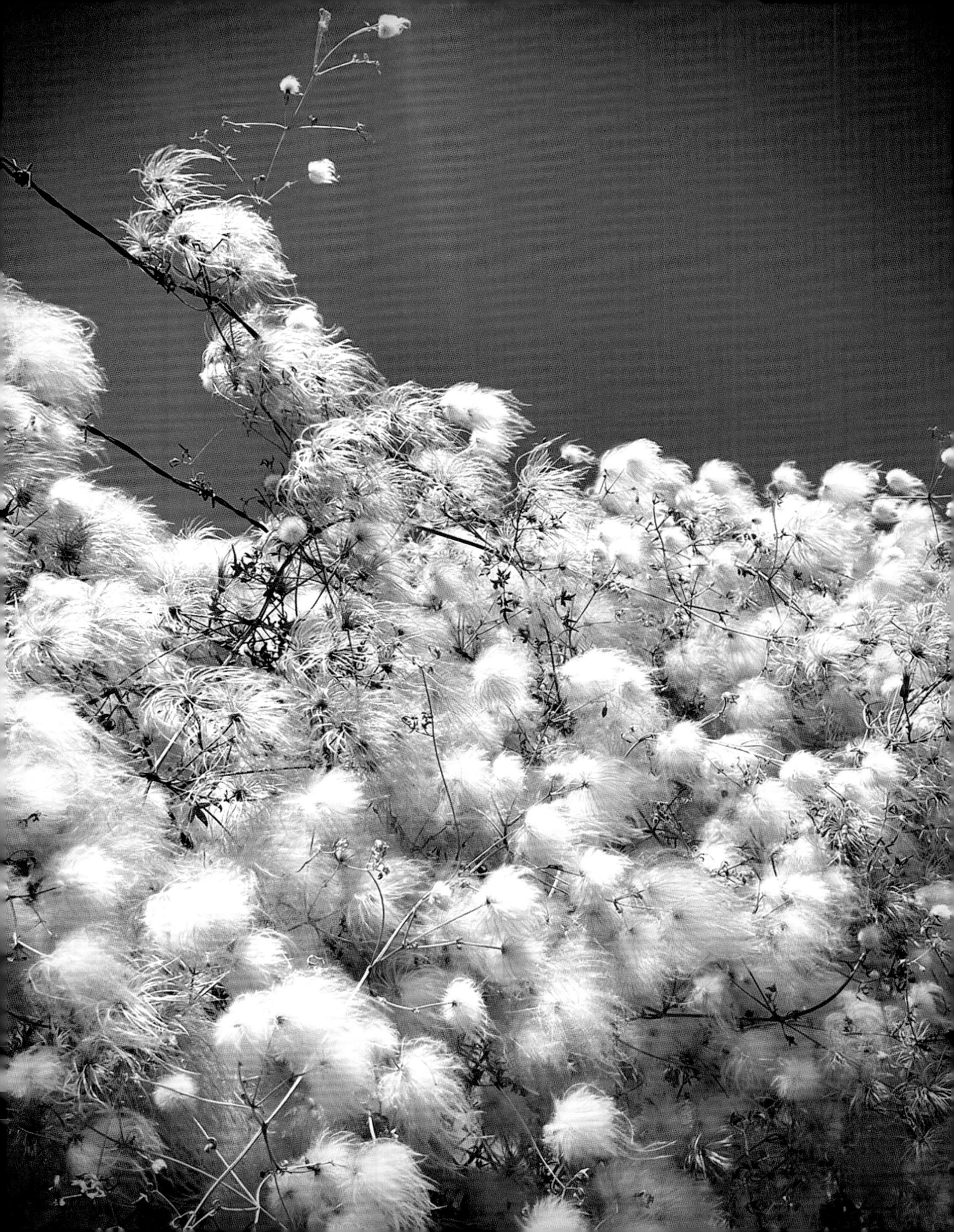

Music

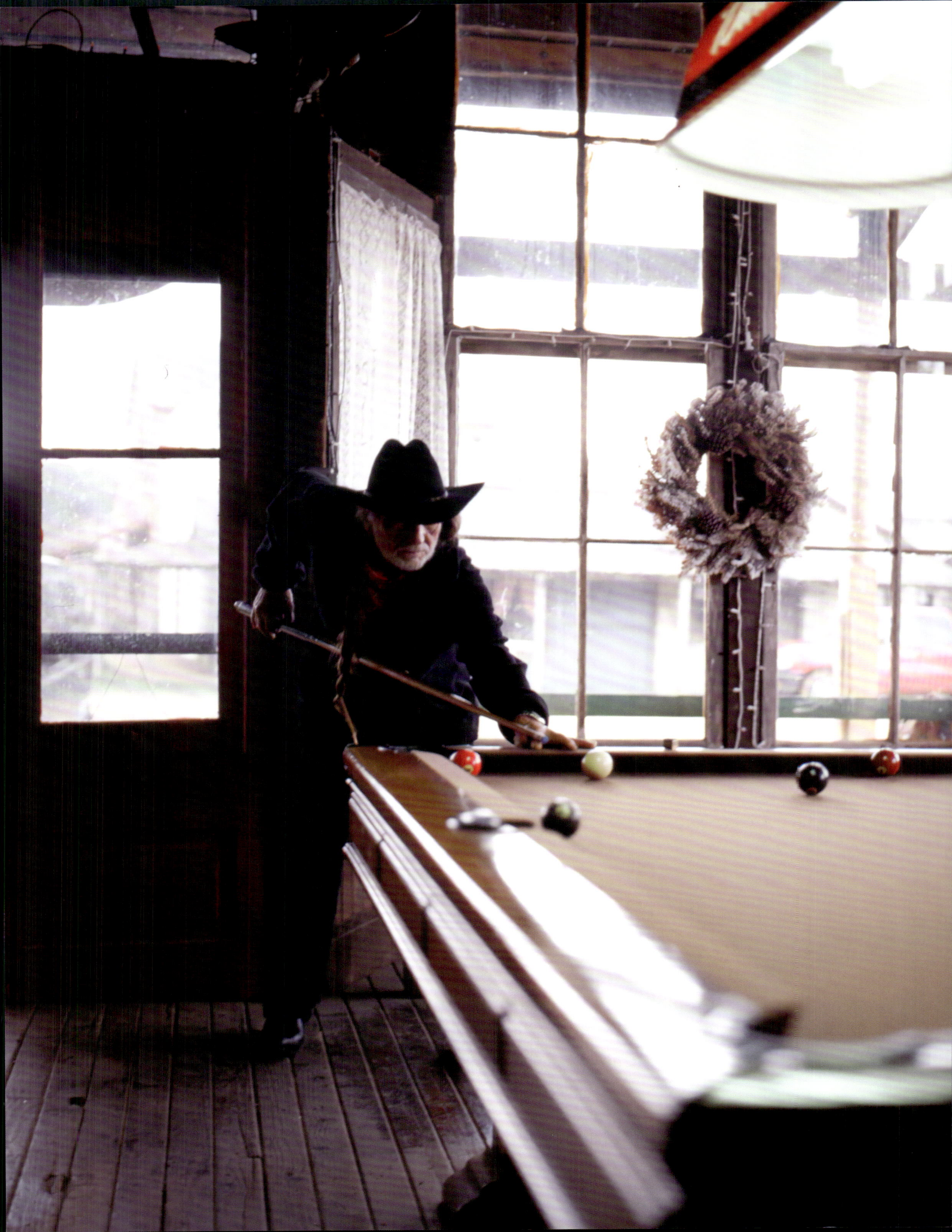

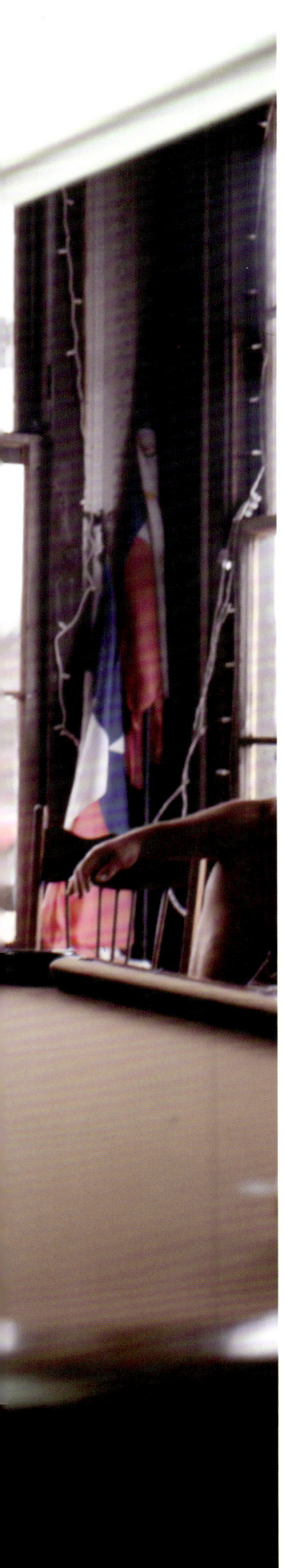

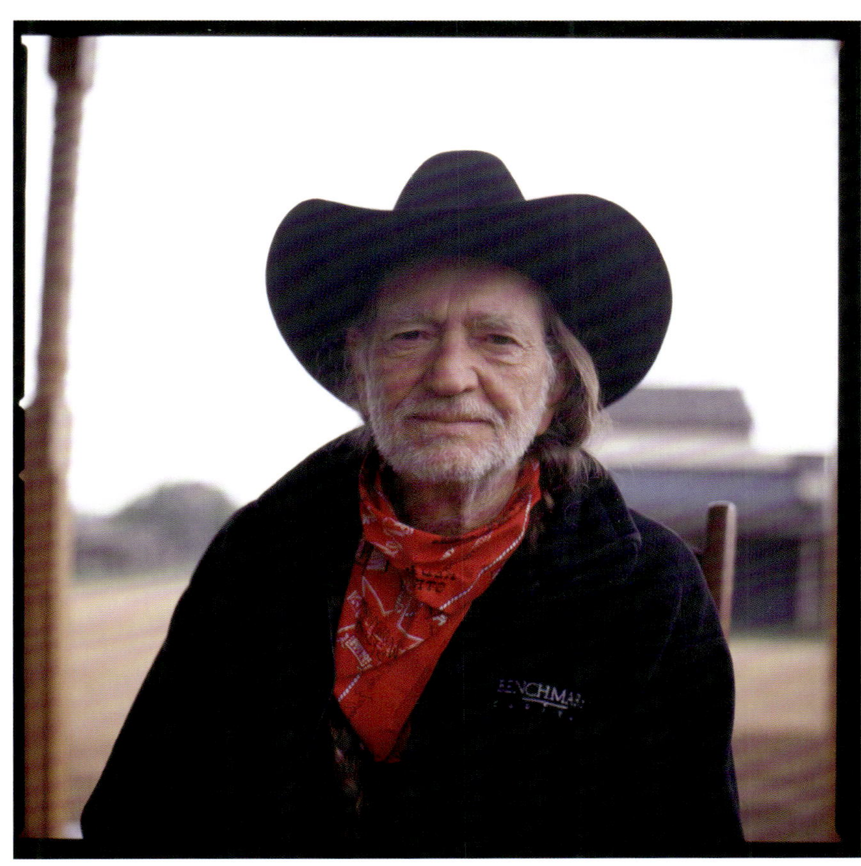

Willie Nelson

Willie Nelson

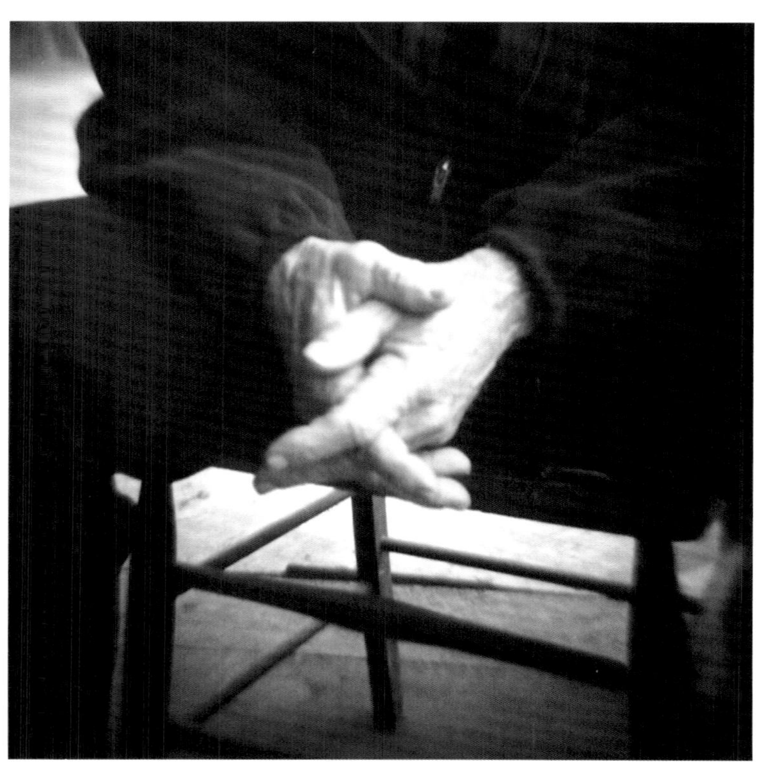

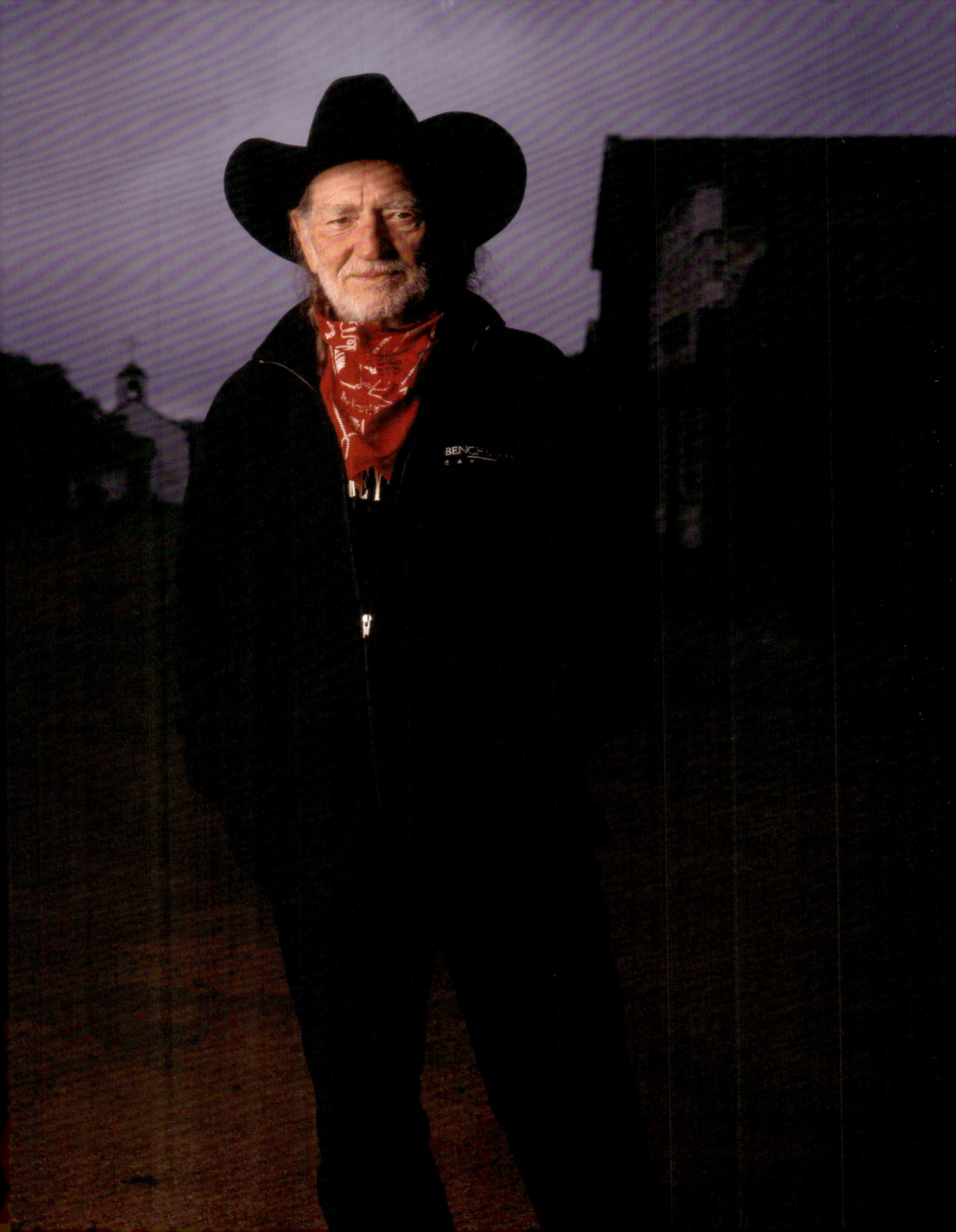

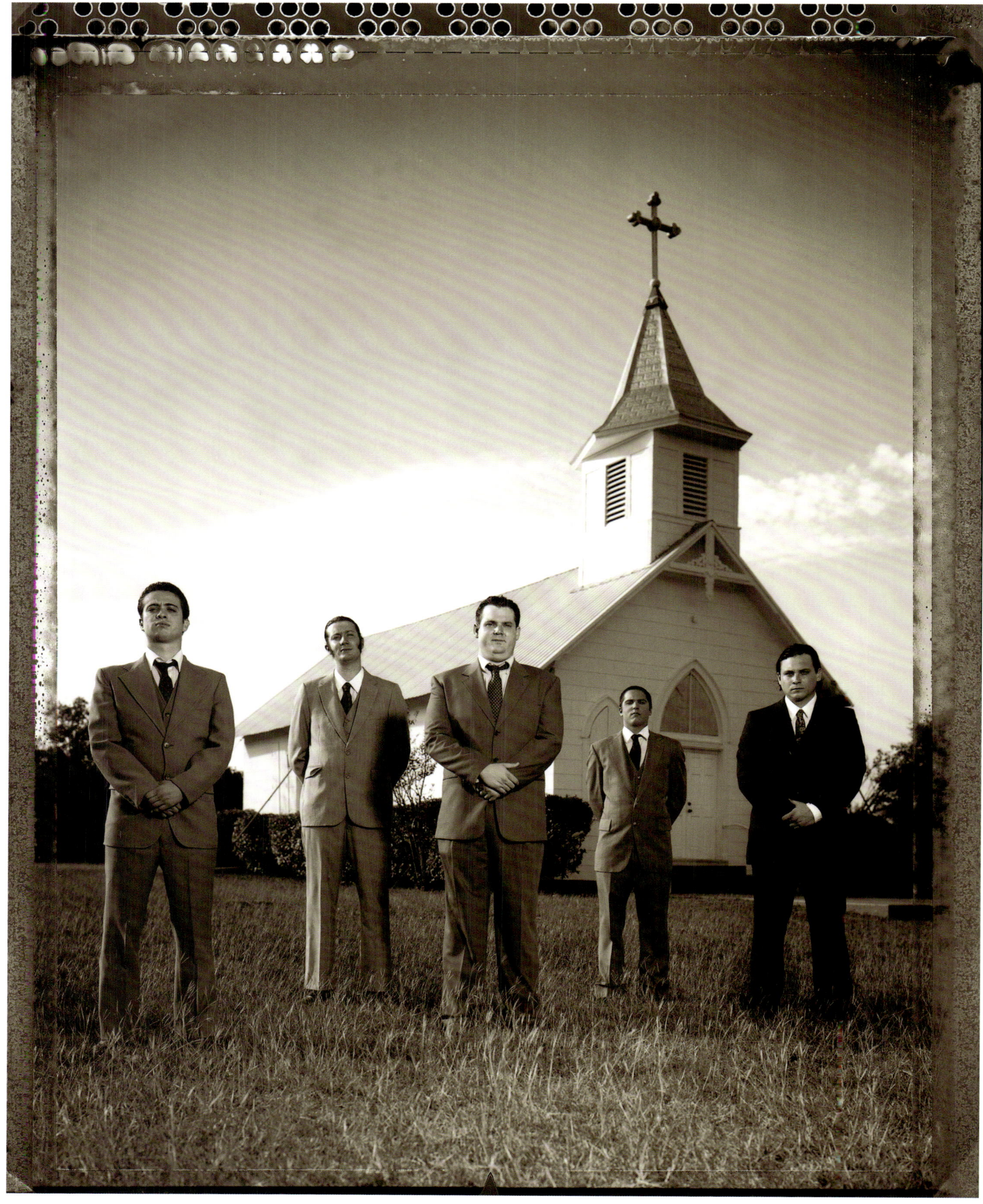

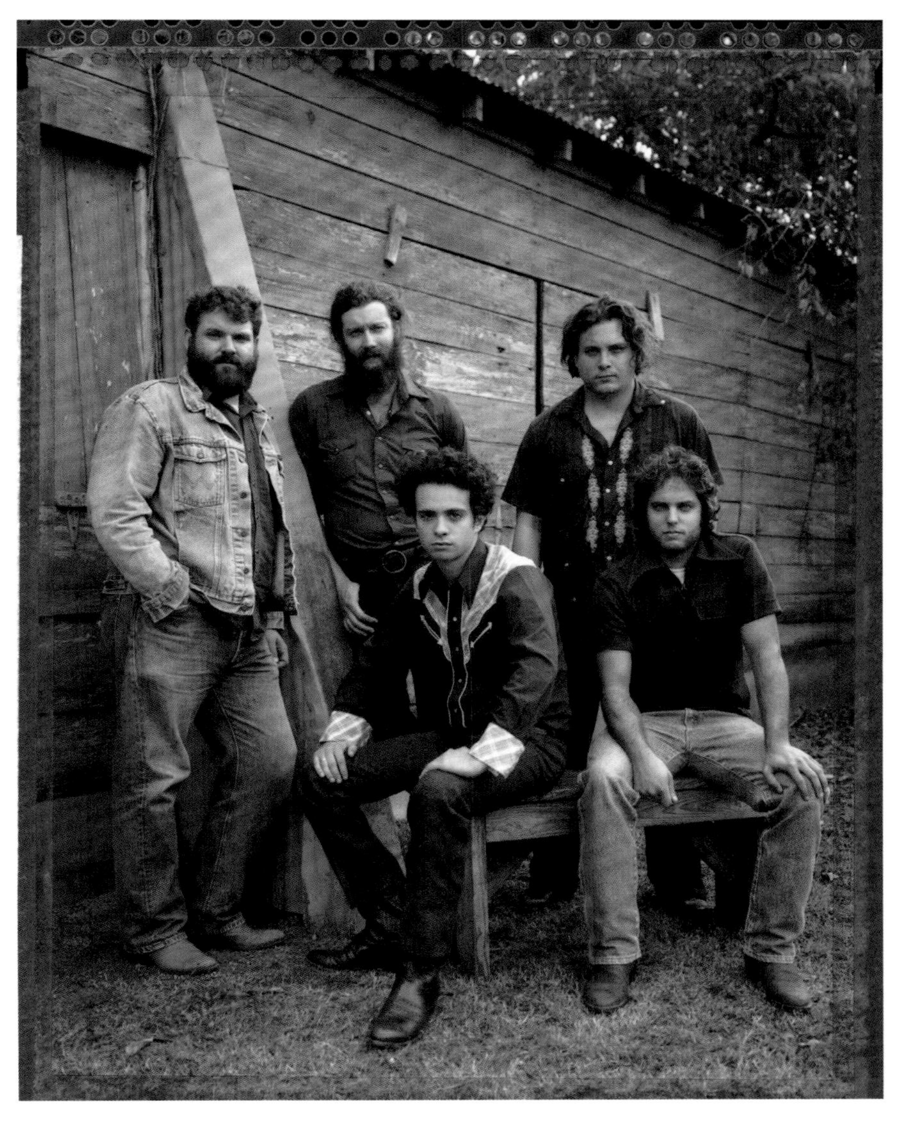

The **Weary Boys**

Jon Dee Graham

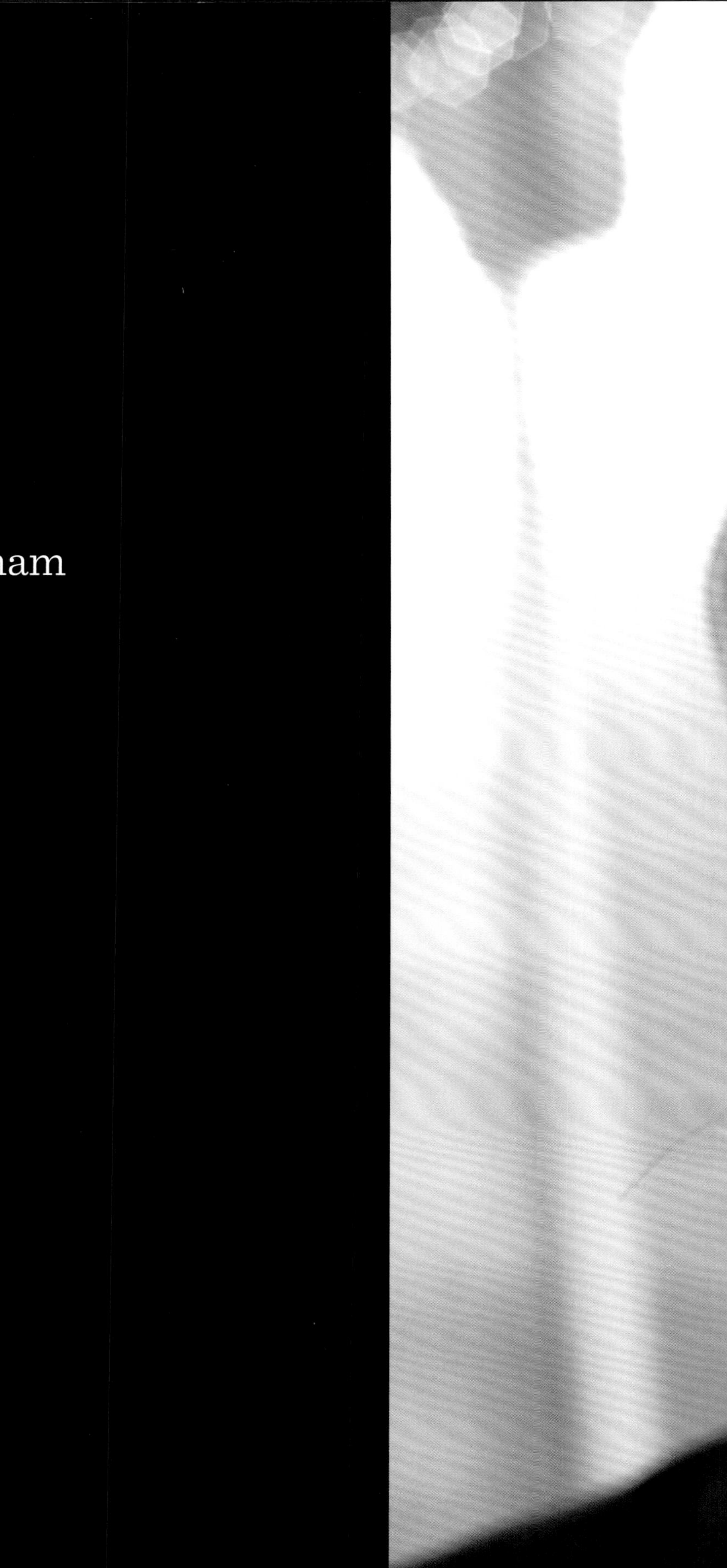

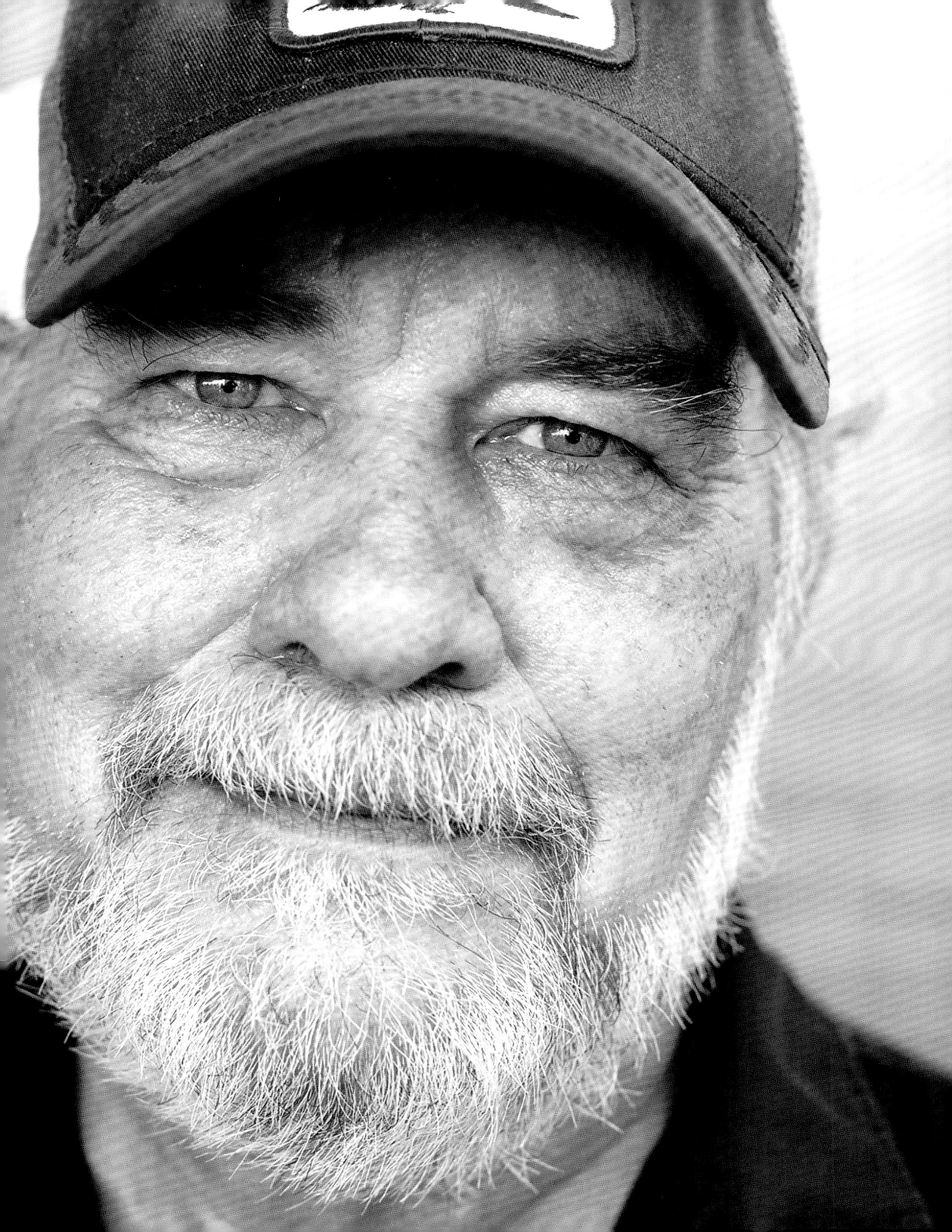

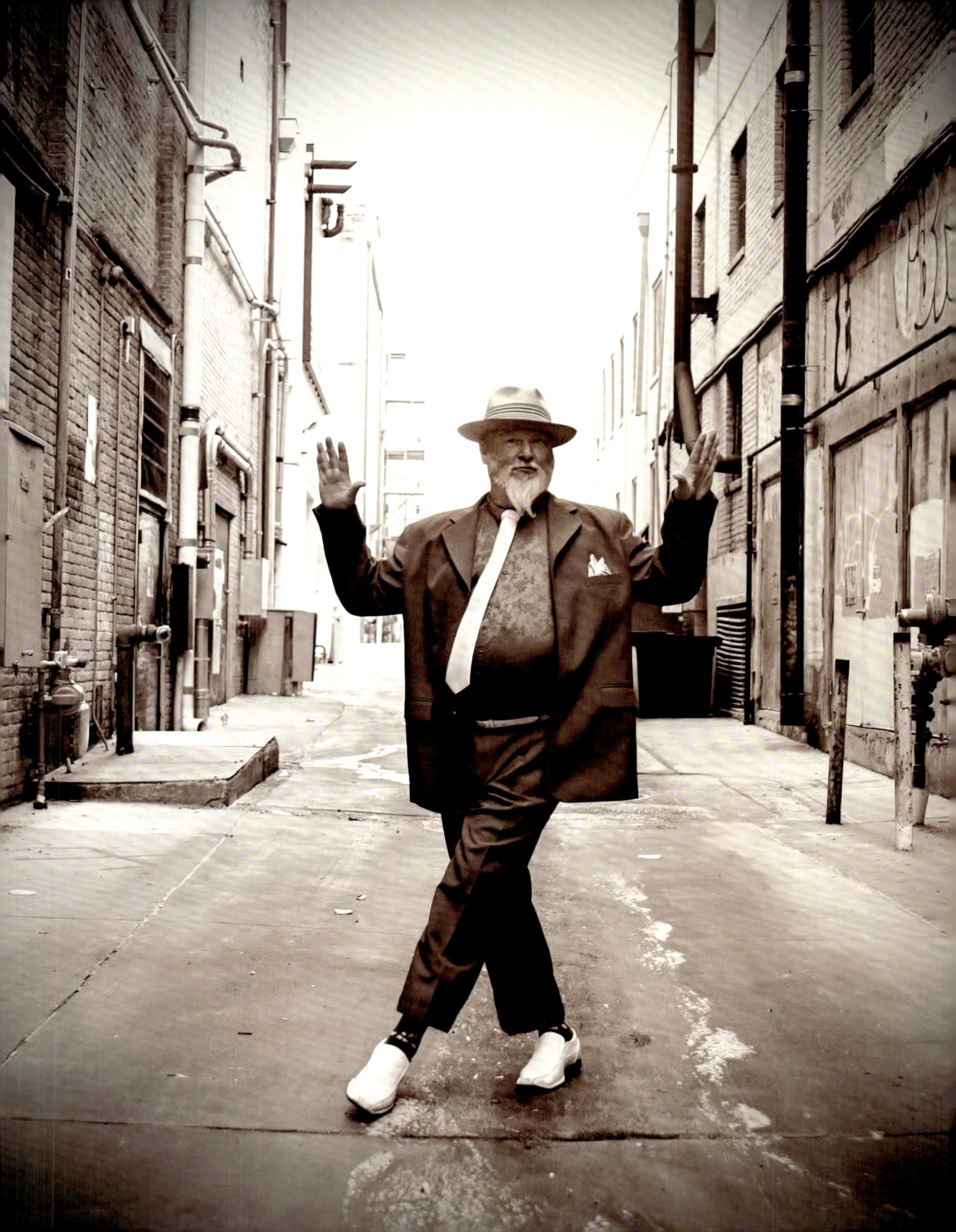

Kevin Russell

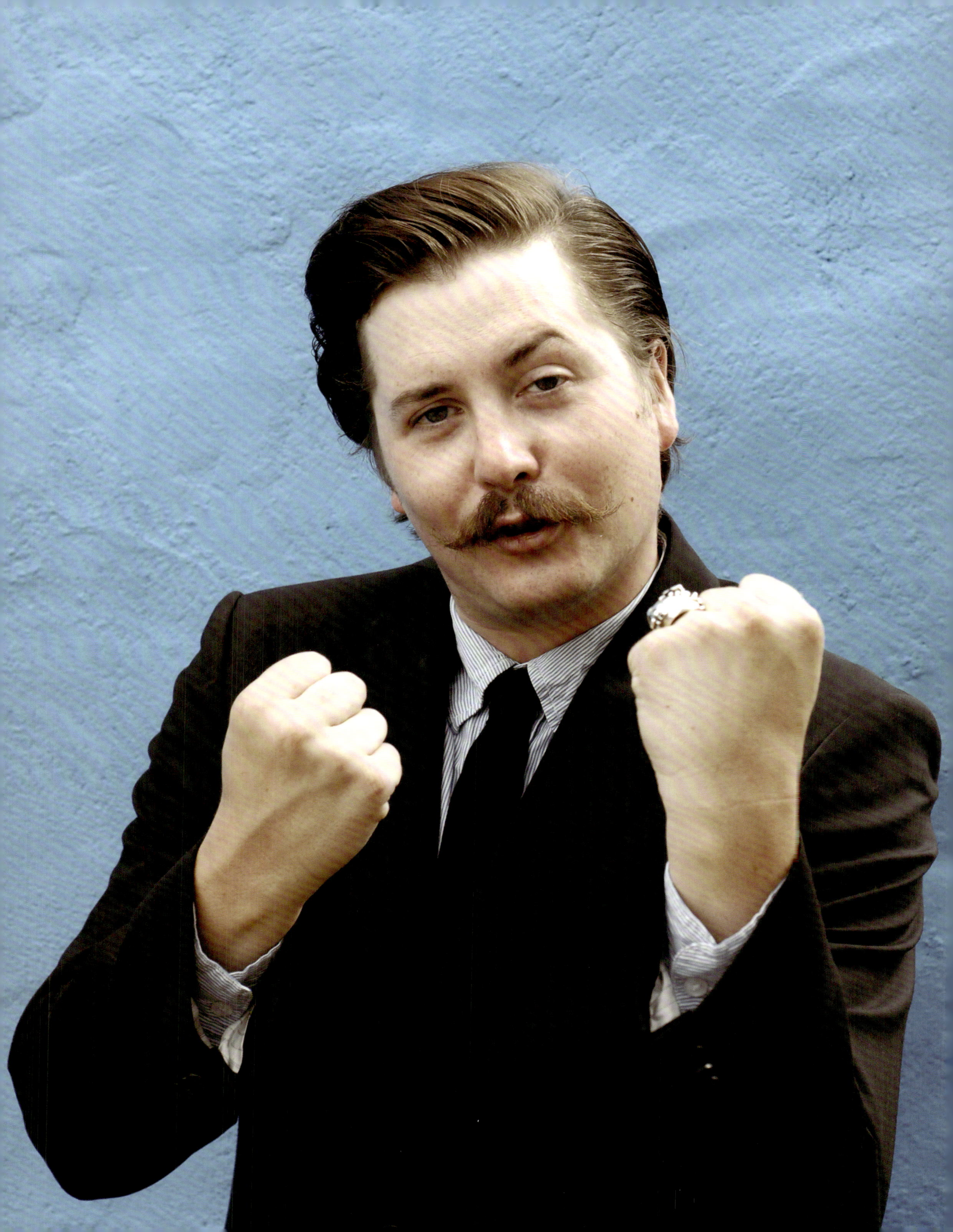

Nic Armstrong

Shakey Graves

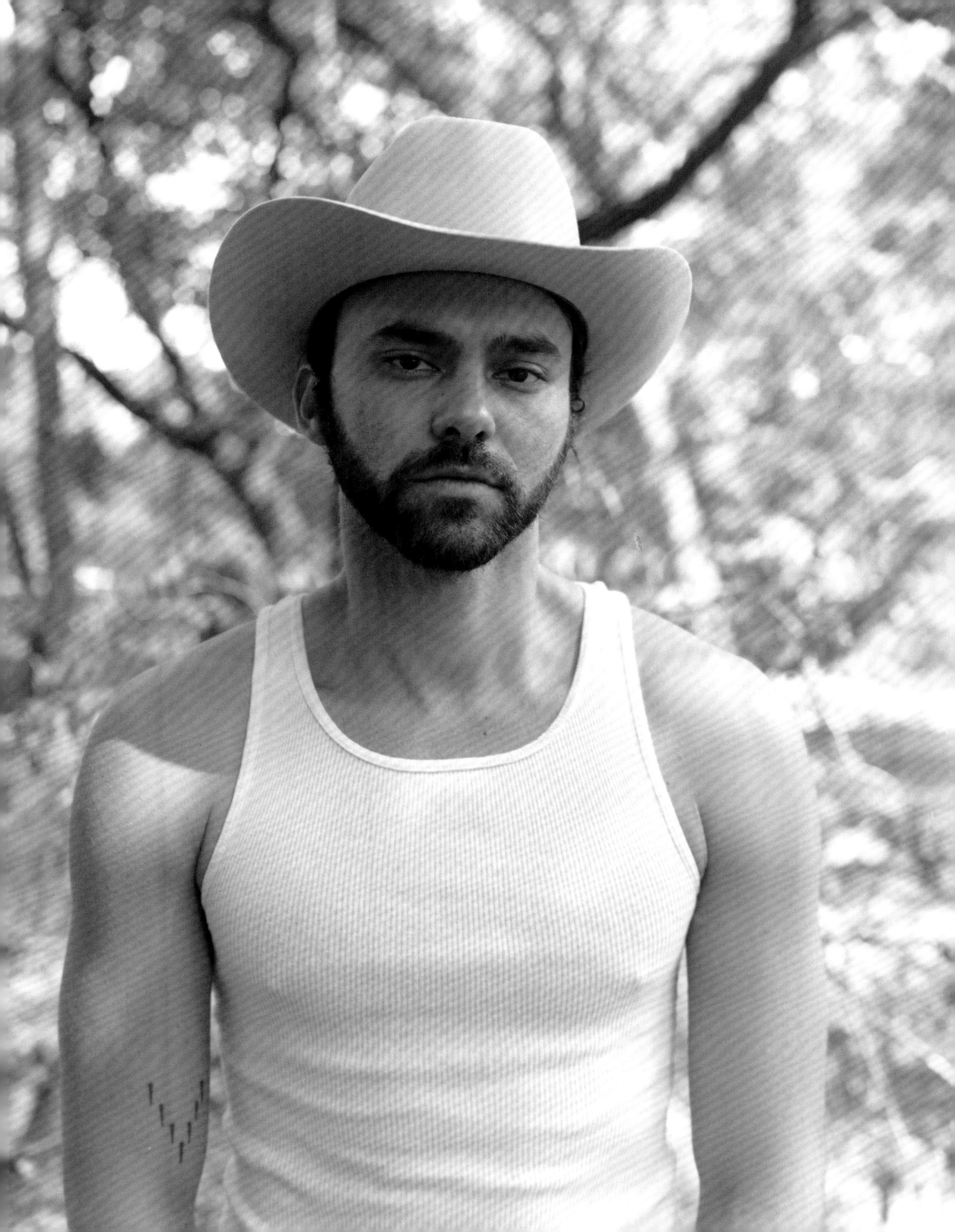

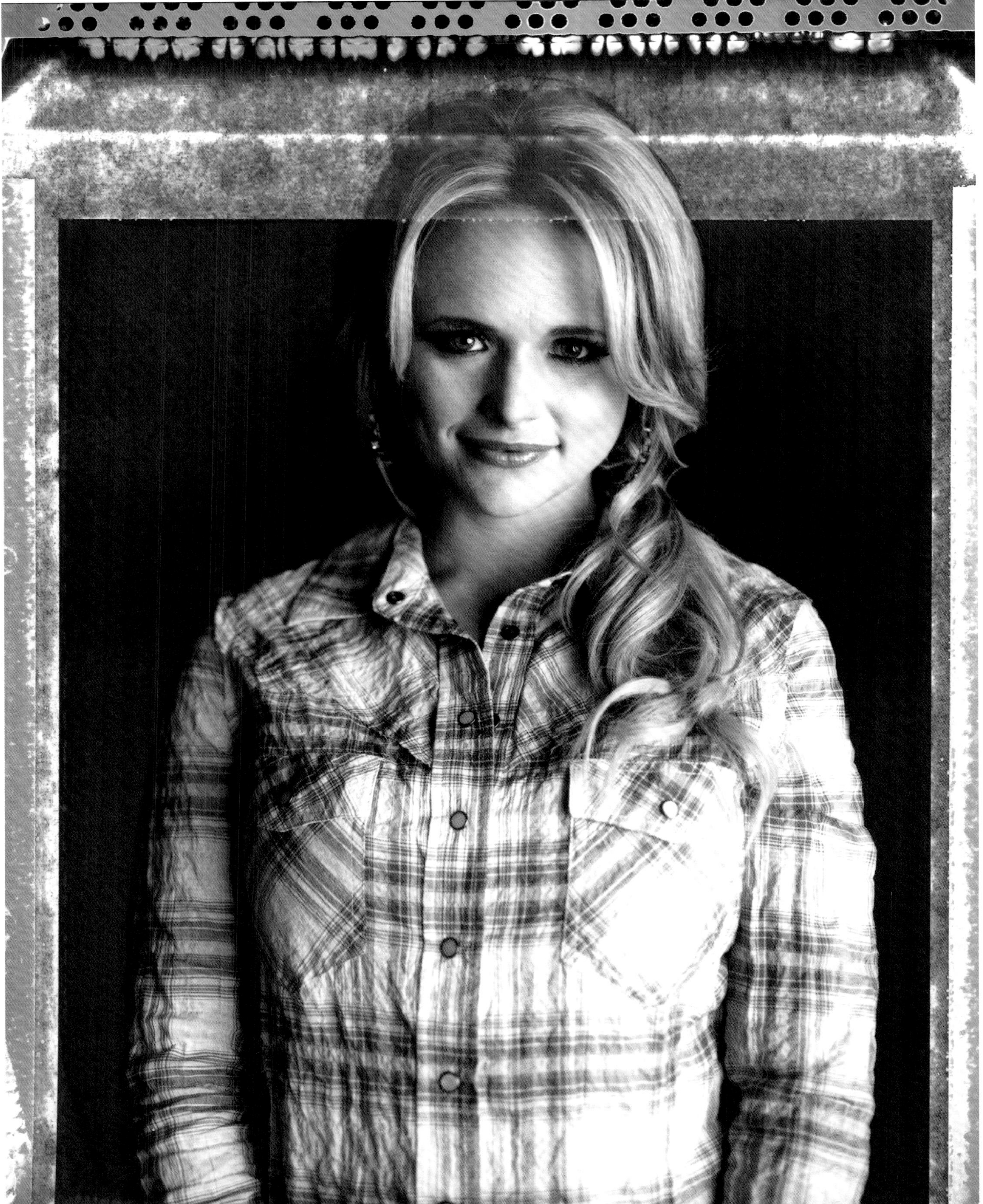

Miranda Lambert

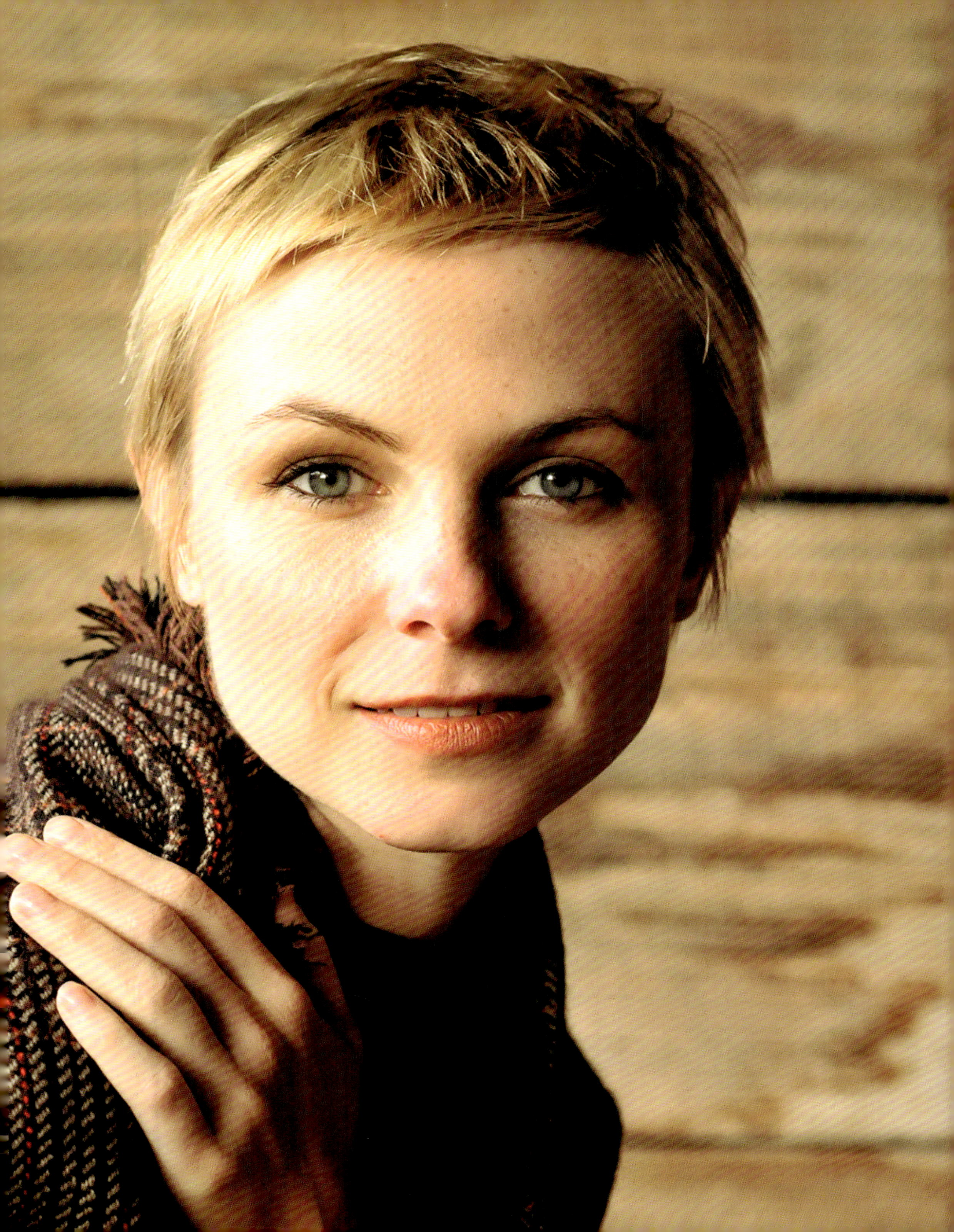

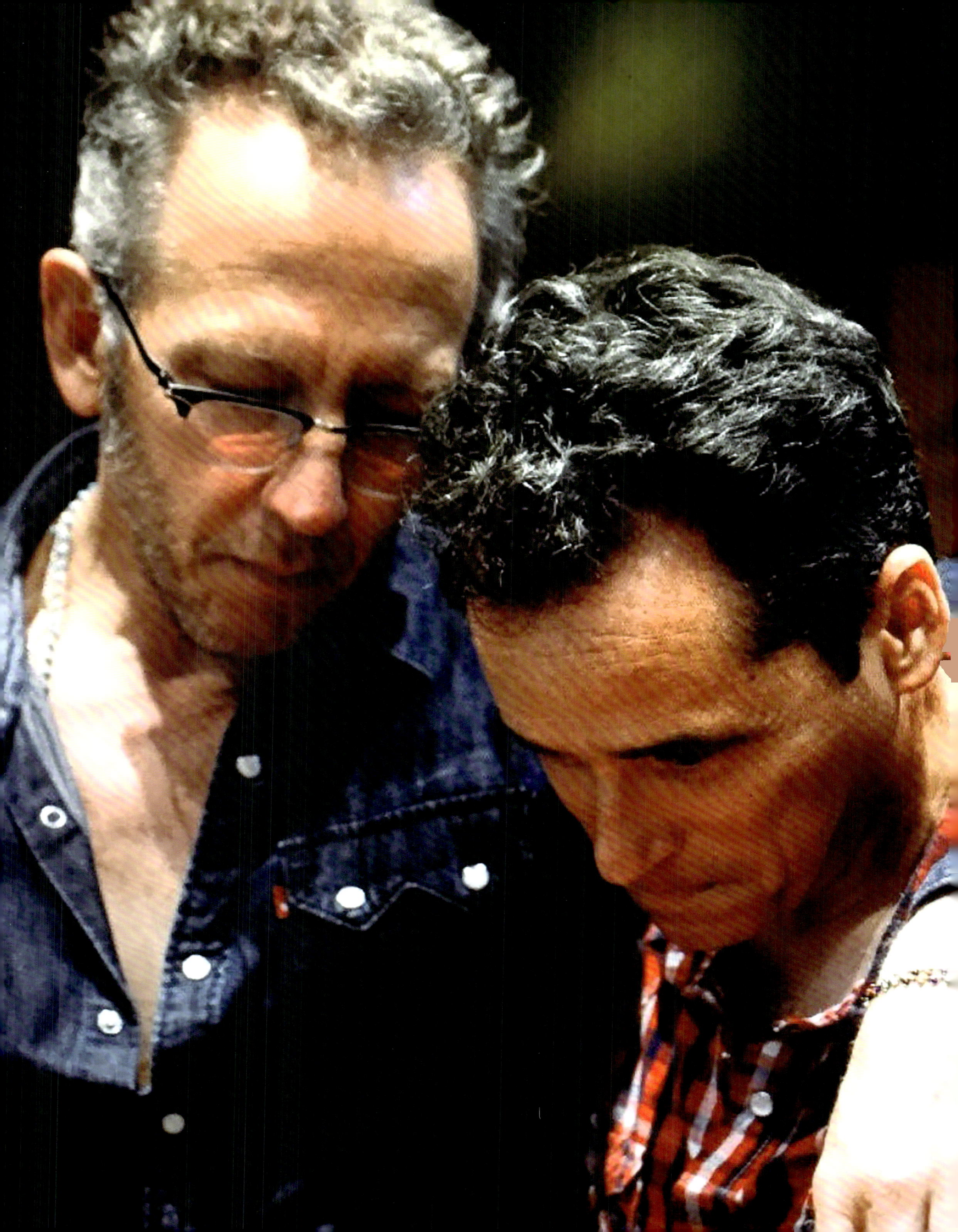

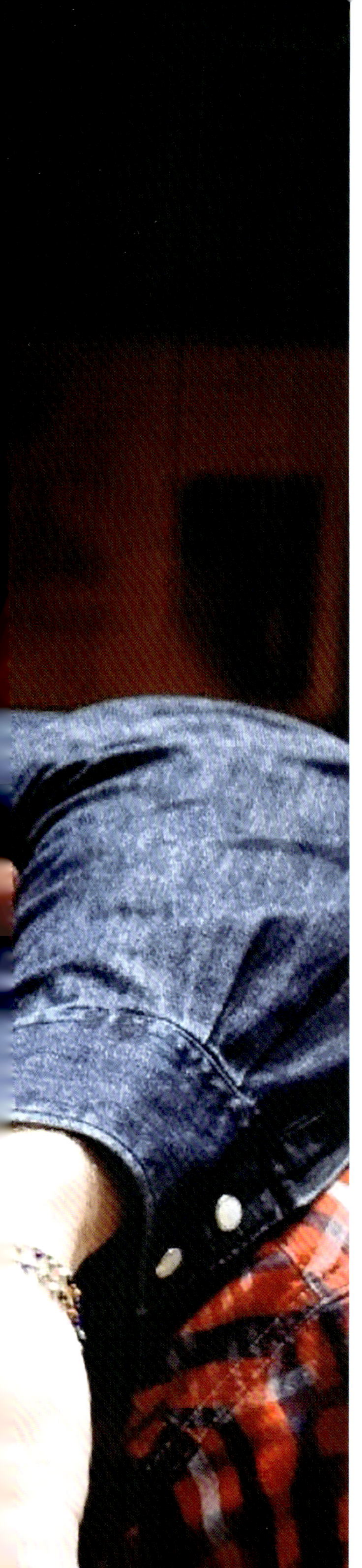

Darden Smith and **Monte** Warden

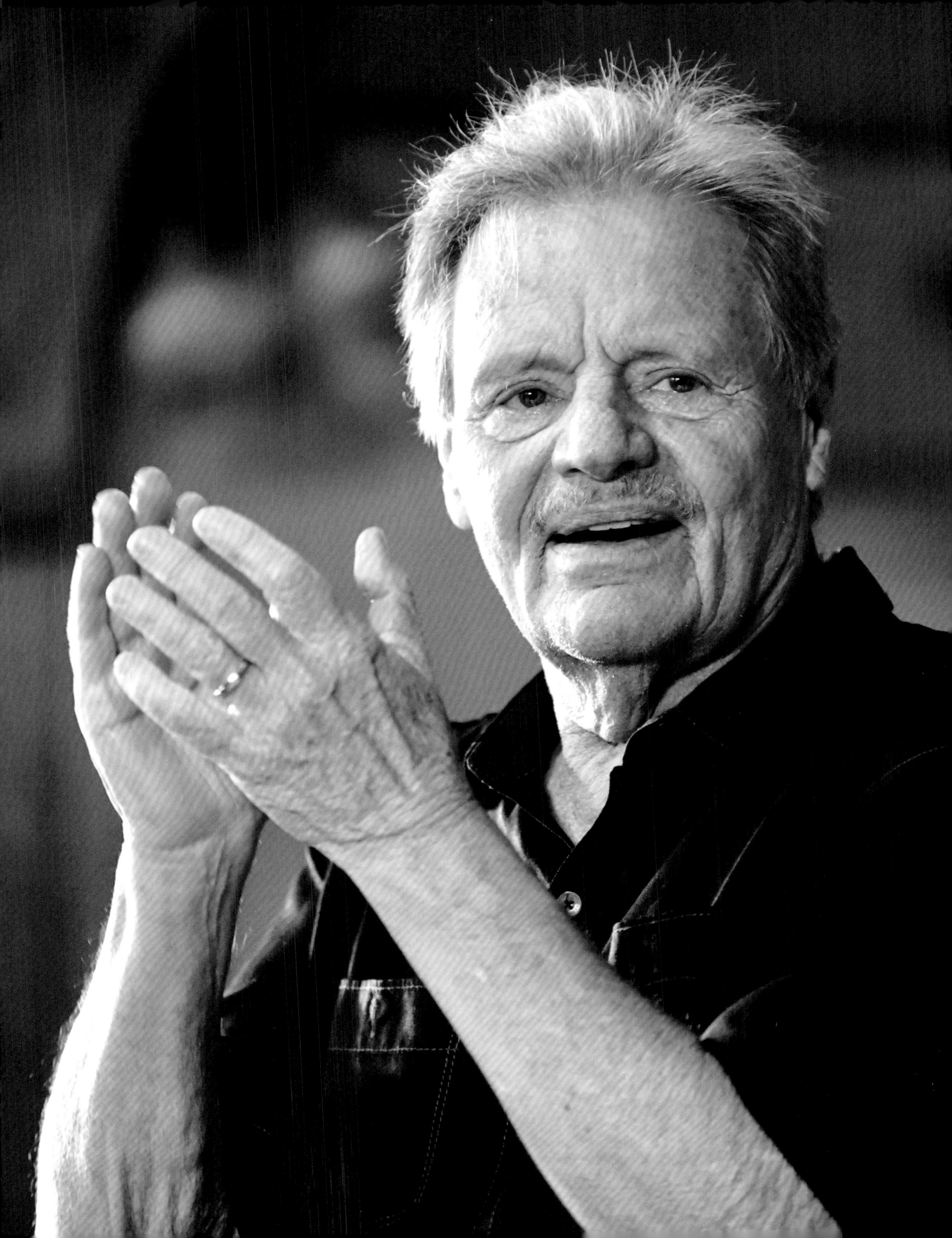

Delbert McClinton

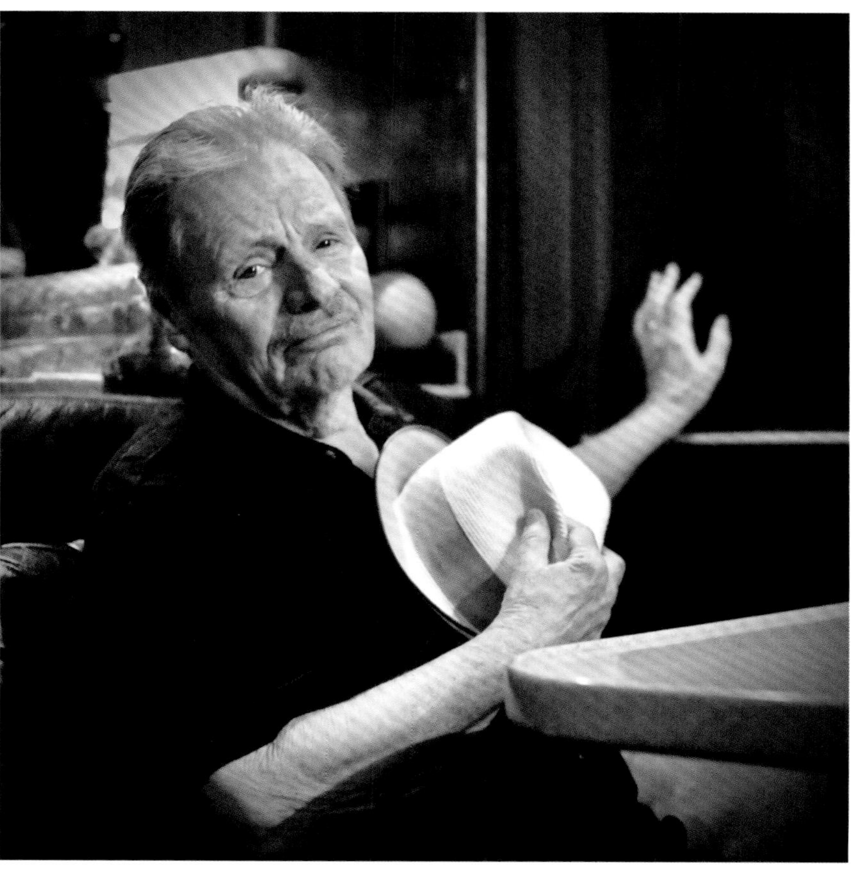

Calder Allen

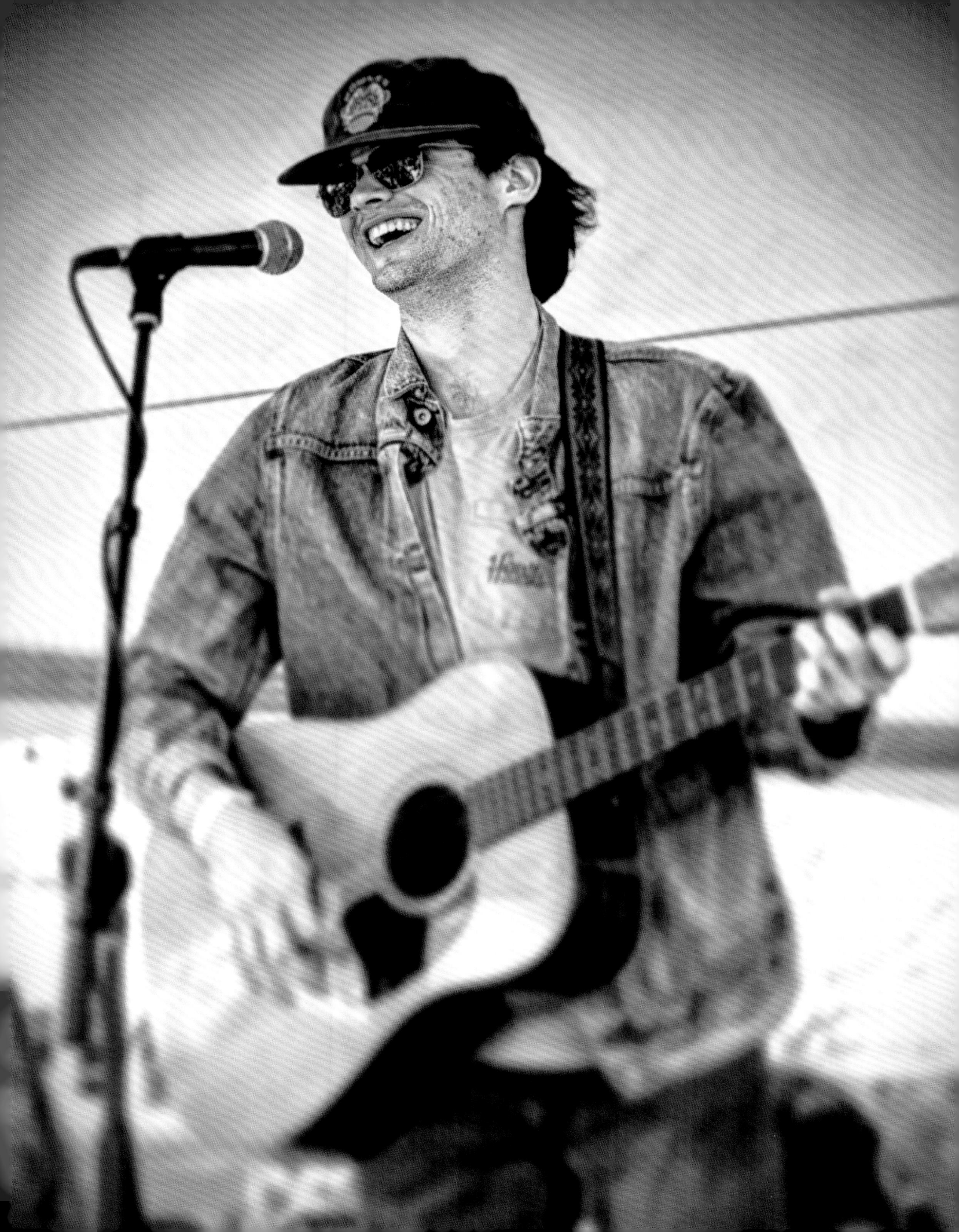

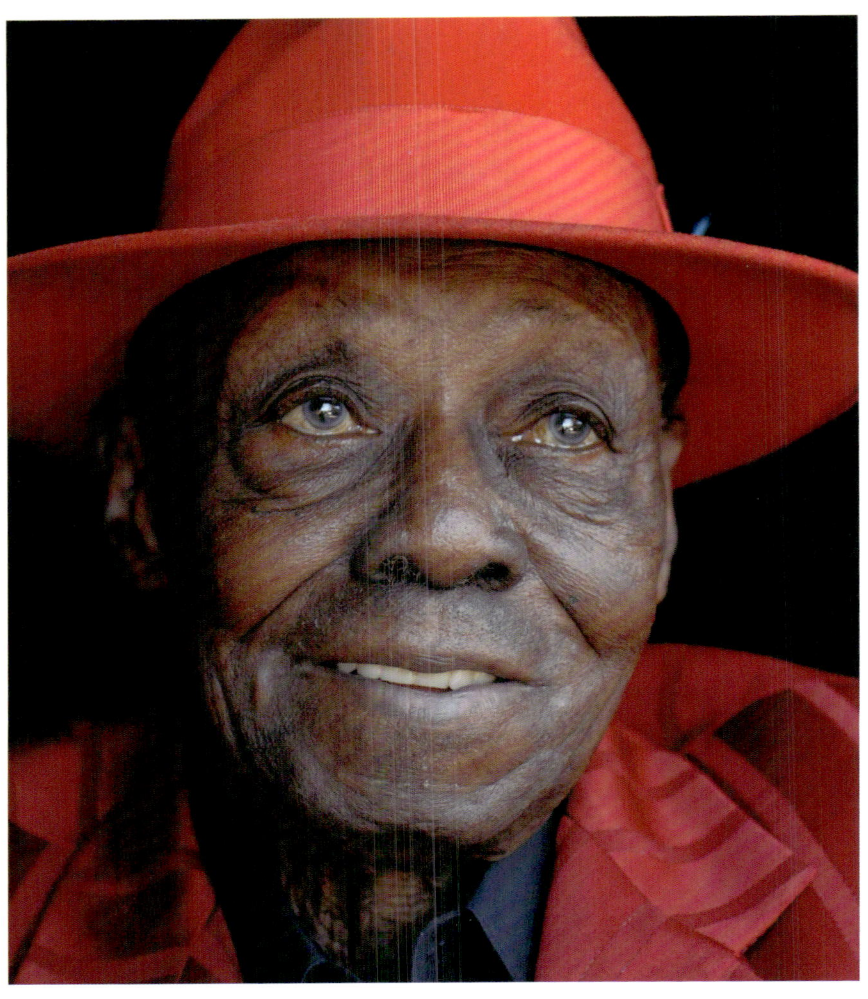

Pinetop Perkins

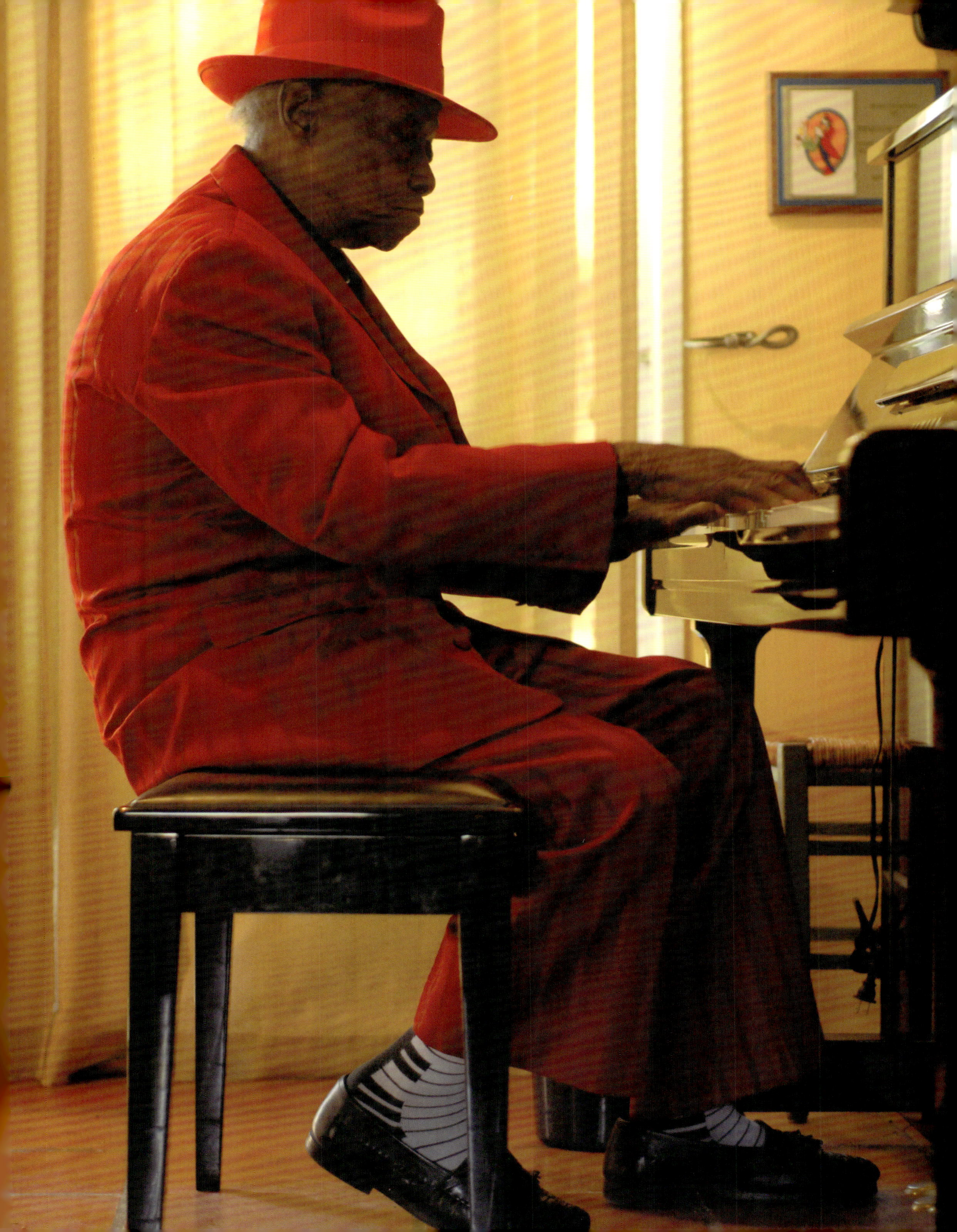

Ruby Jane

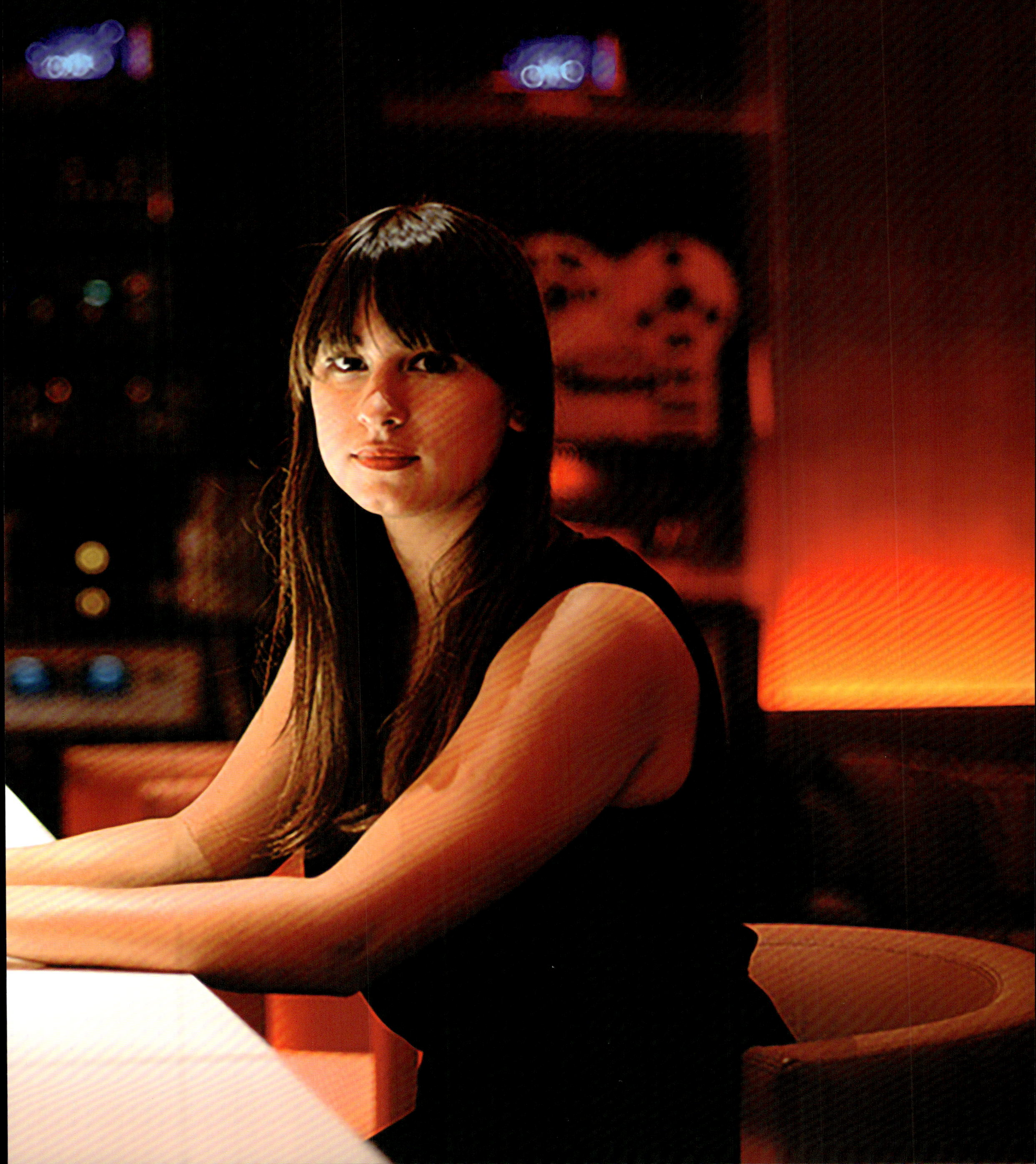

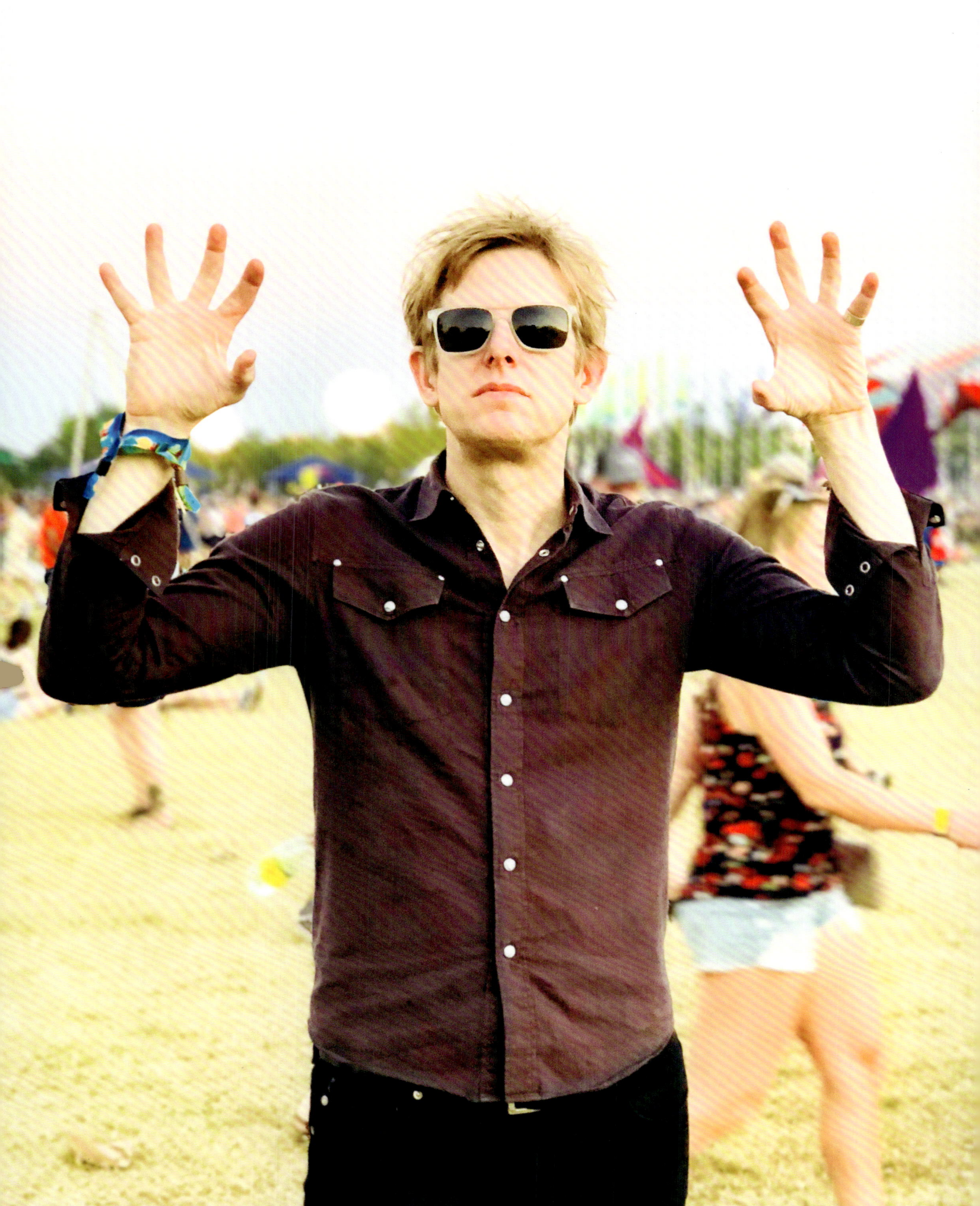

Britt Daniel

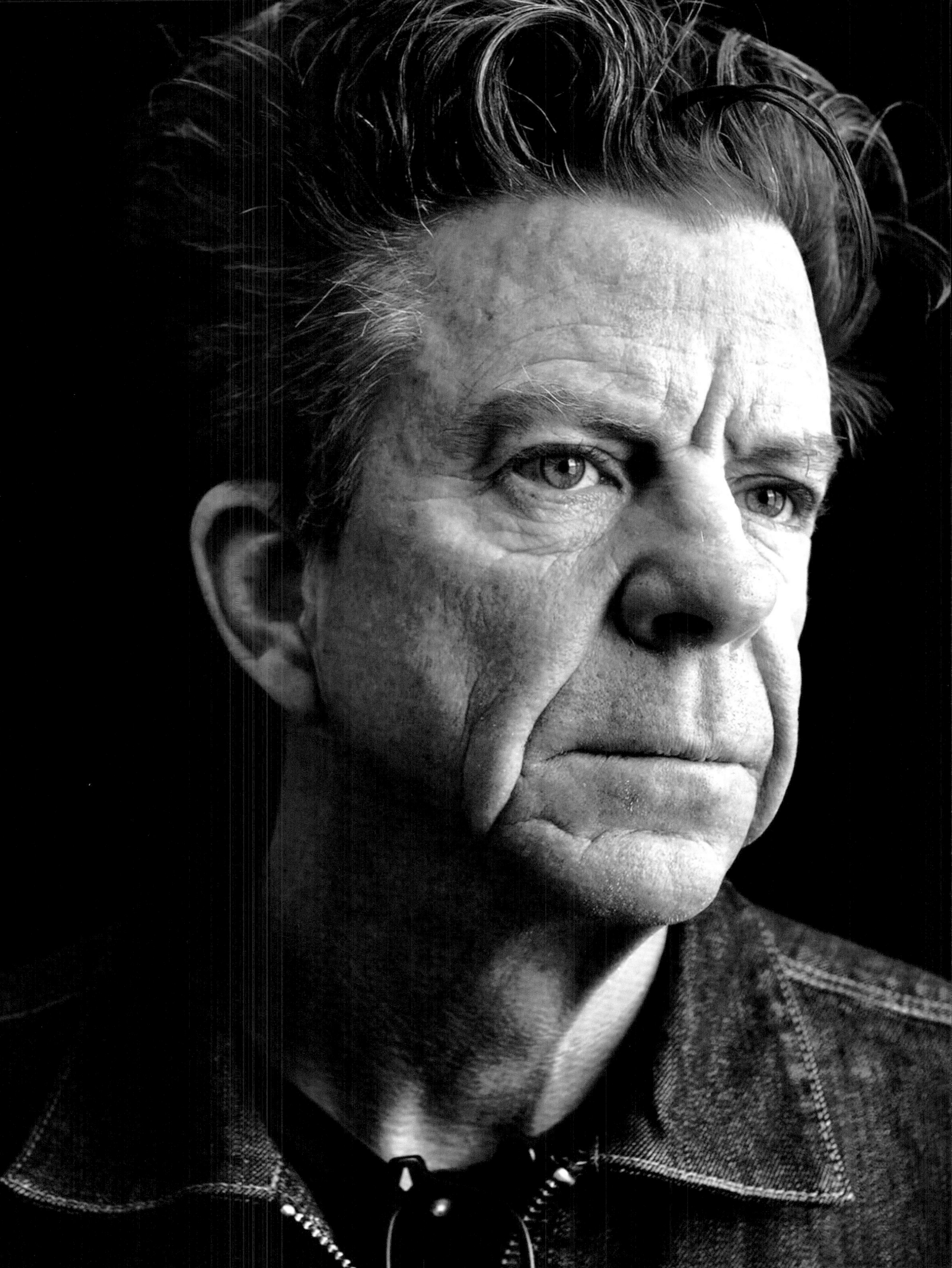

Chris Layton

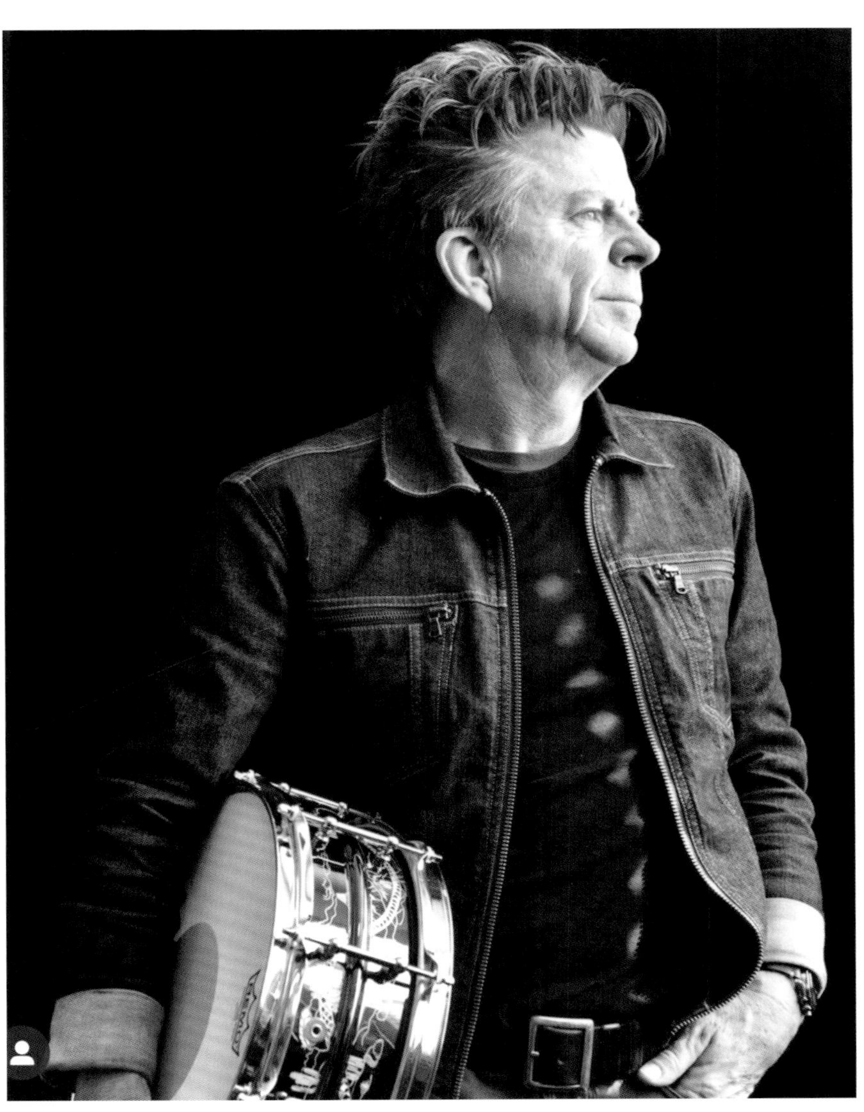

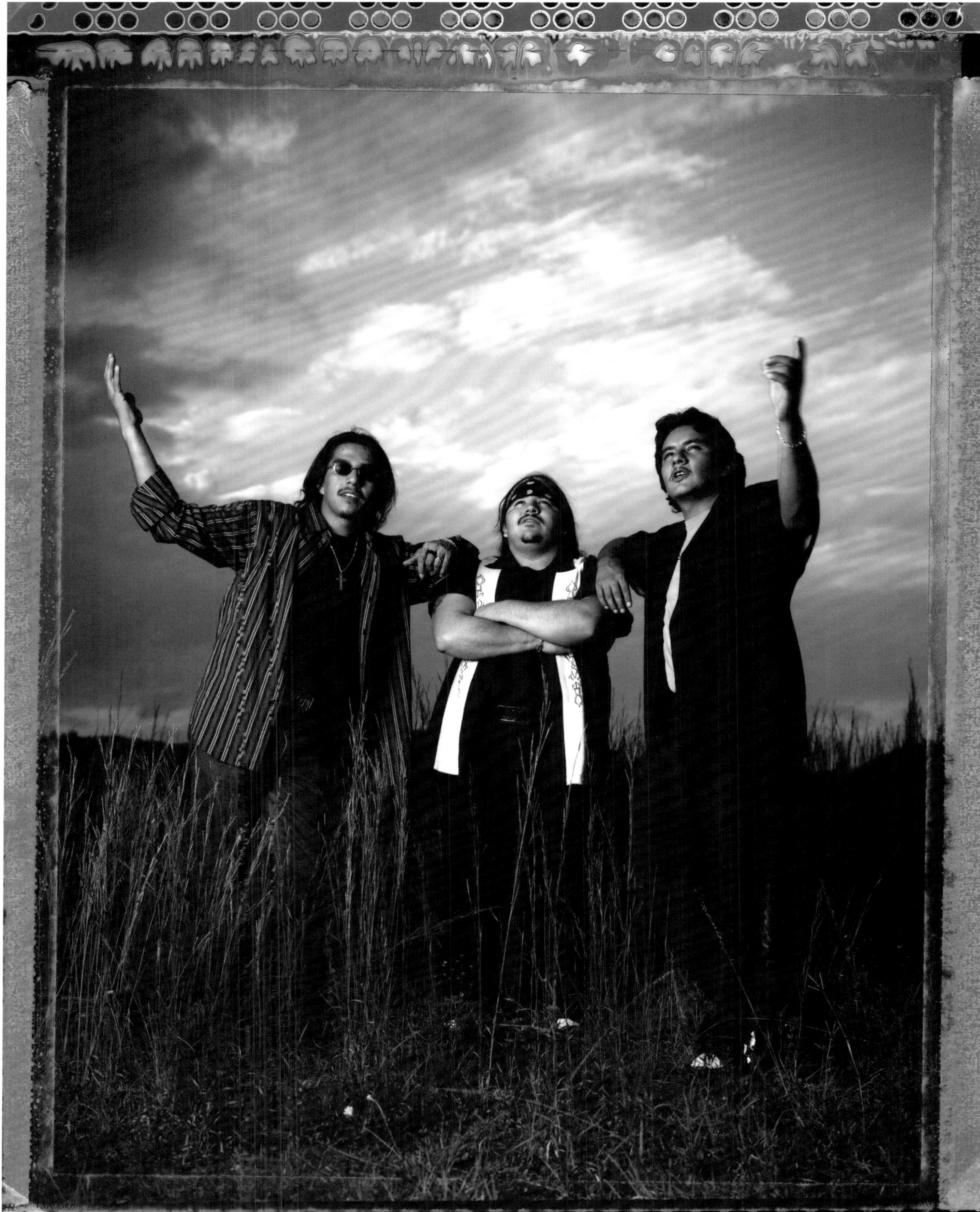

Los **Lonely Boys**

Avril Lavigne

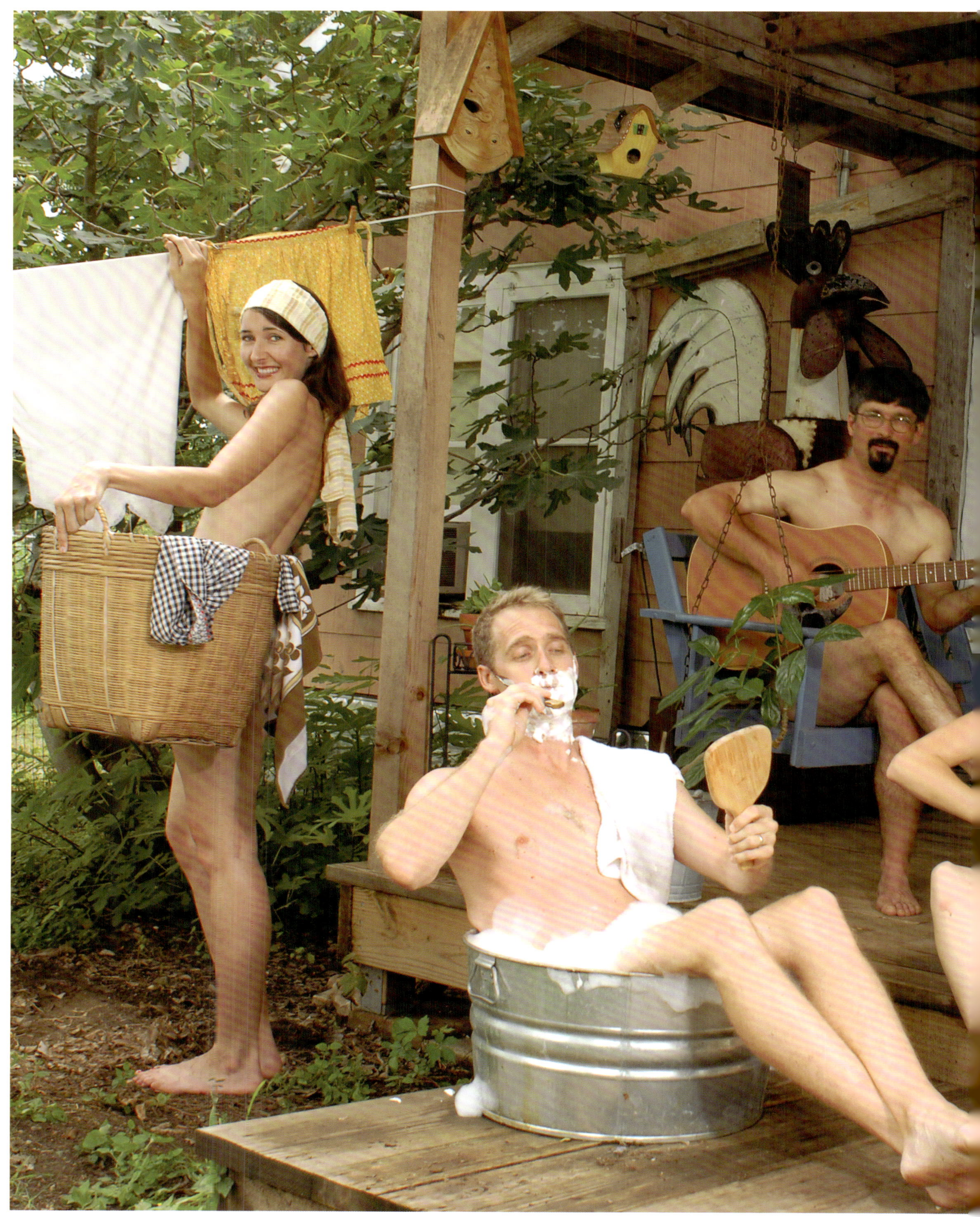

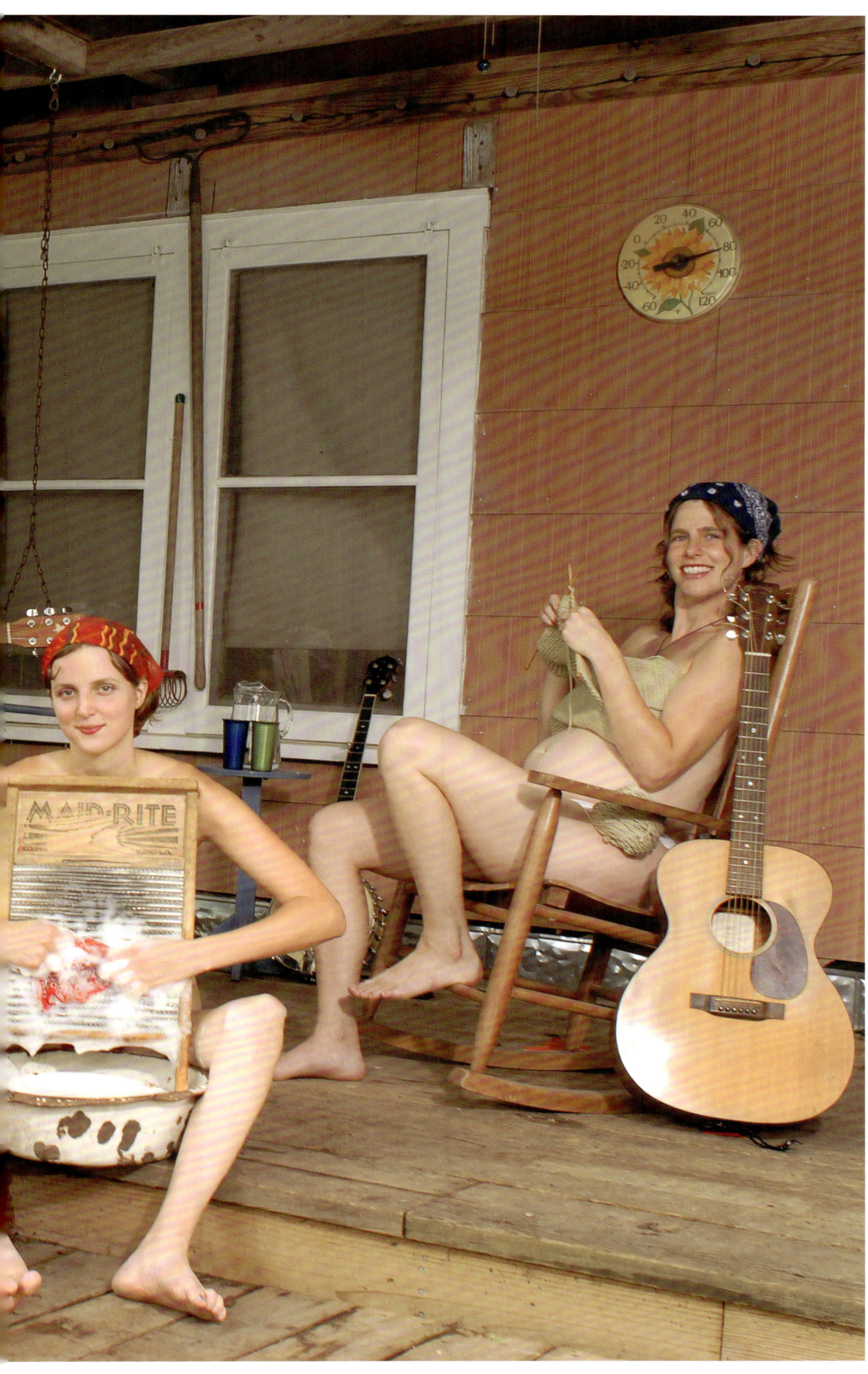

Austin **Family Jewels**

Robert Rodriguez
and
Patricia Vonne

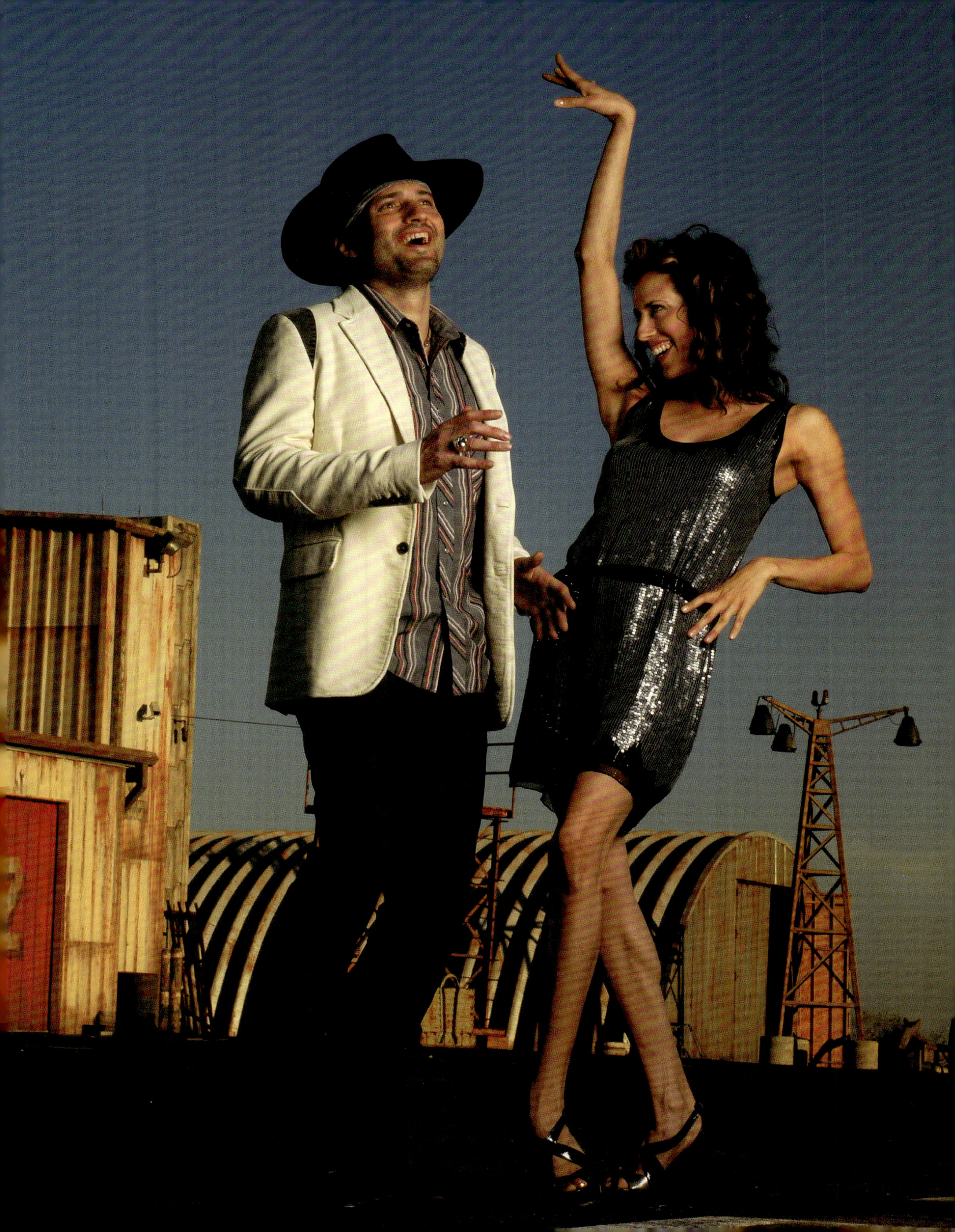

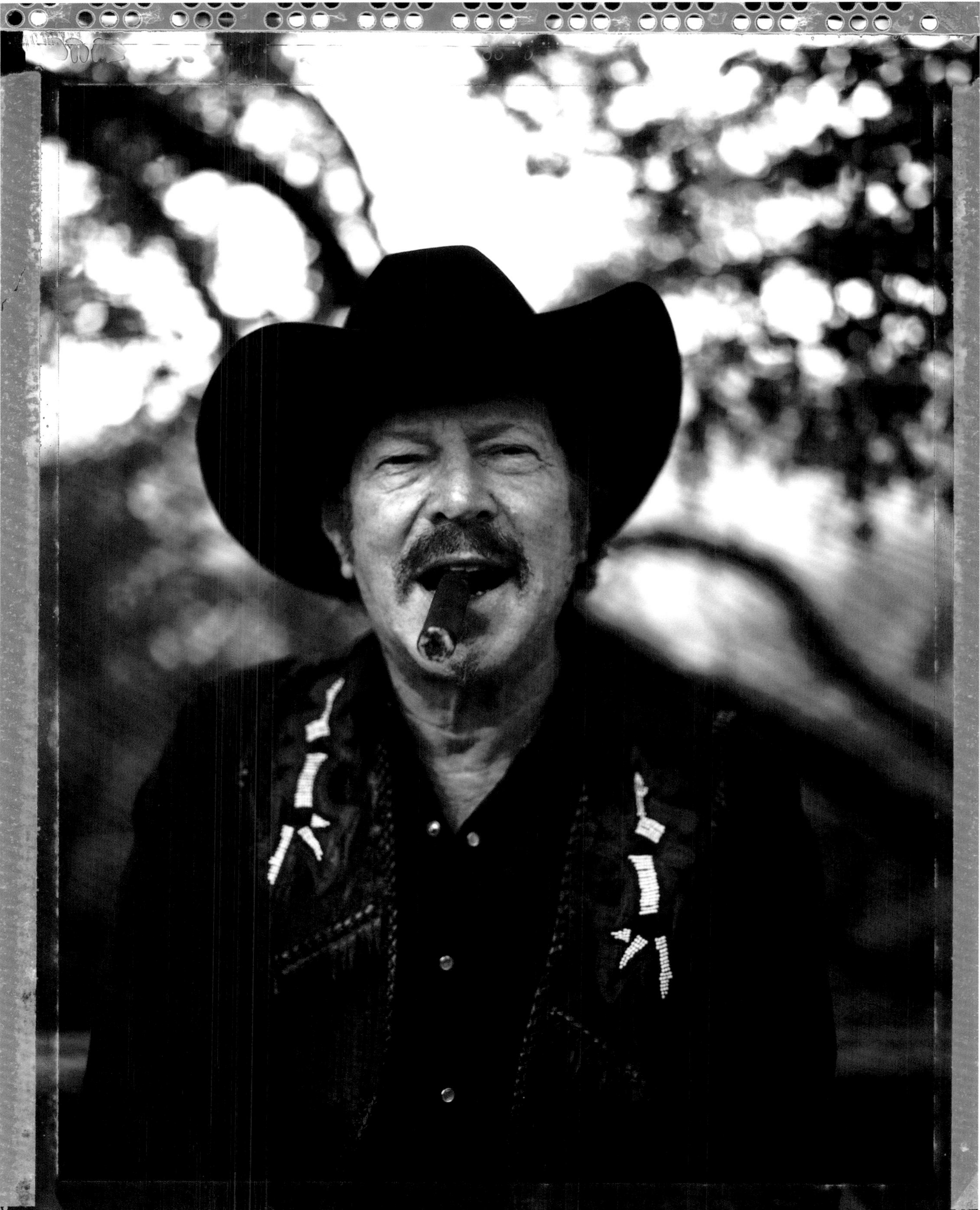

Kinky Friedman

Bob Schneider

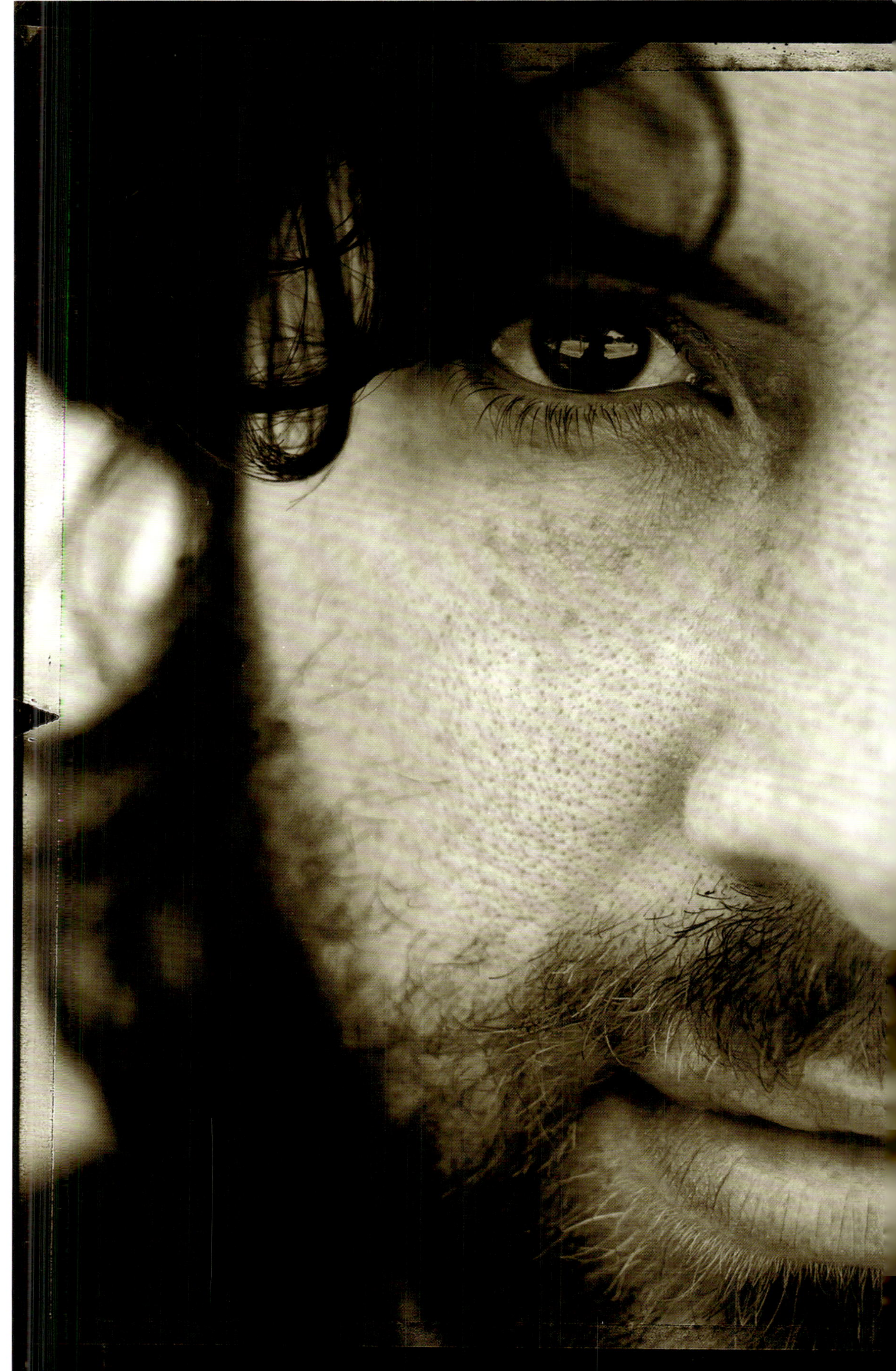

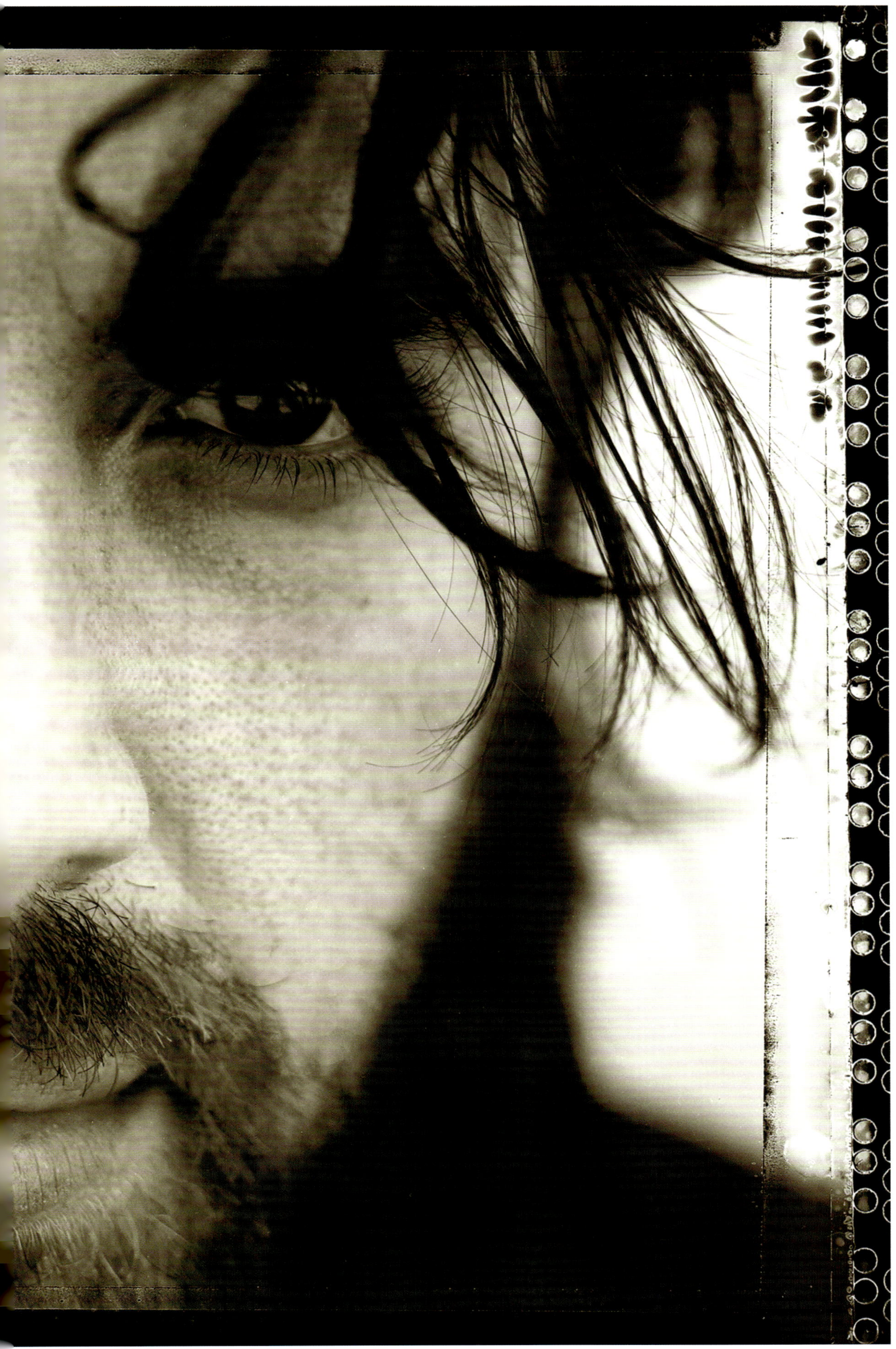

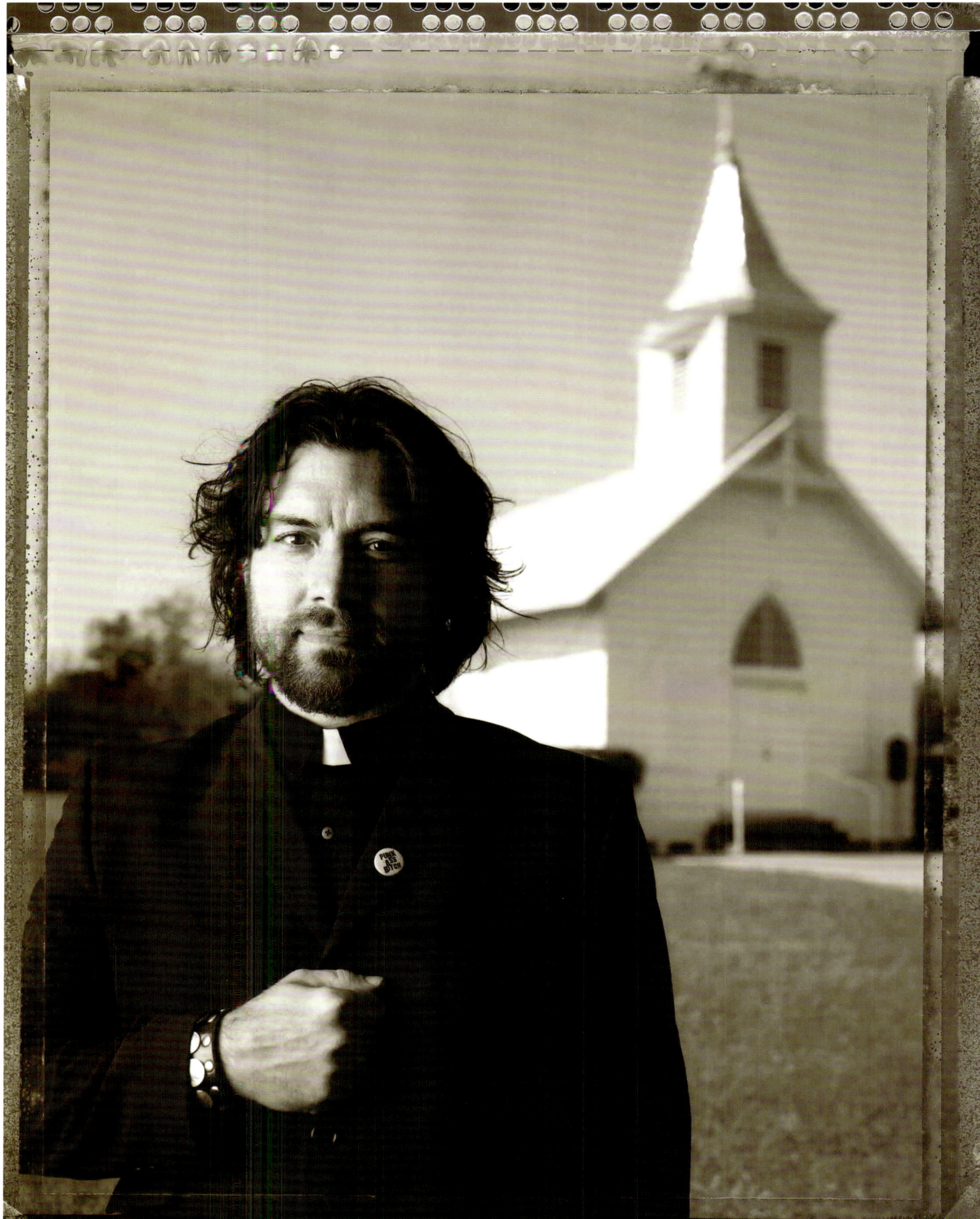
PUNK
ASS
BITCH

Bob Schneider

Charlie Sexton

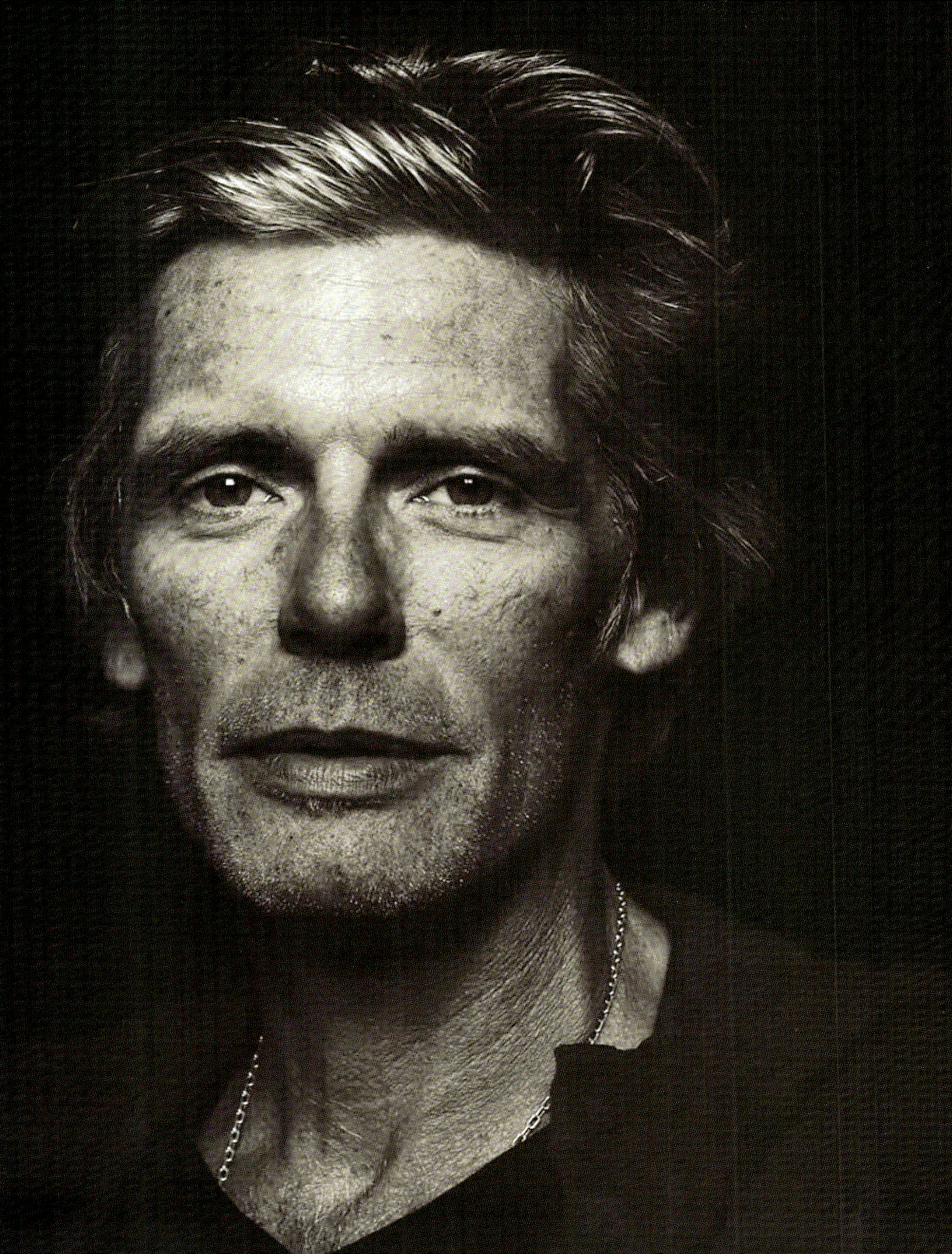

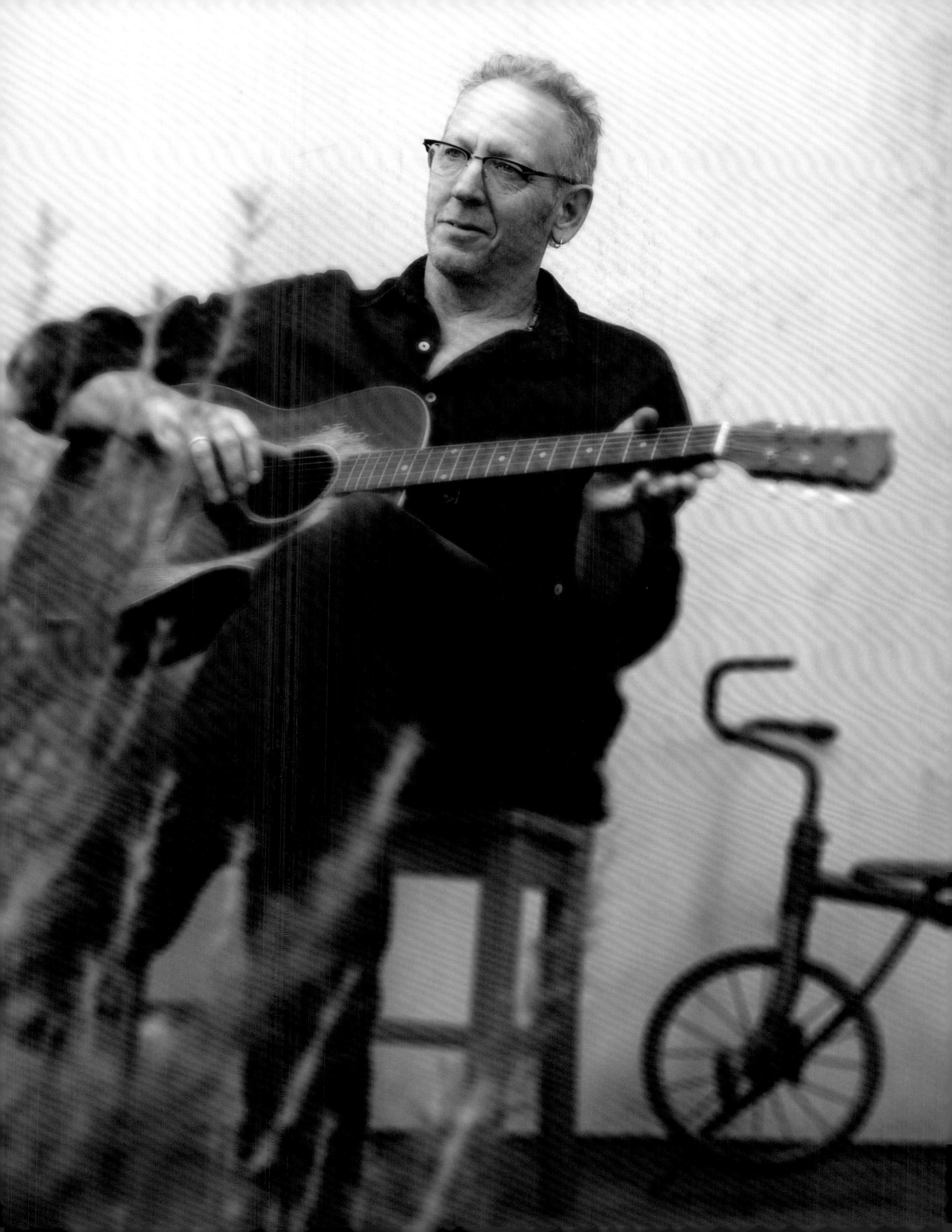

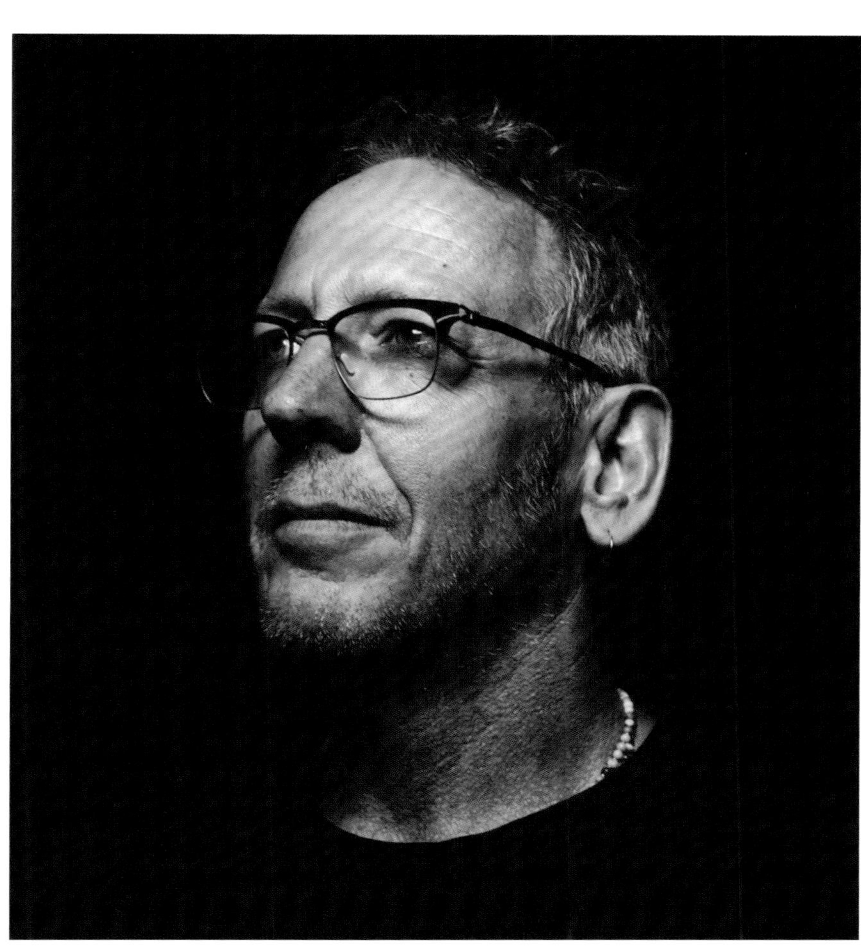

Darden Smith

Butch Hancock, **Jimmie Dale** Gilmore, and **Joe** Ely

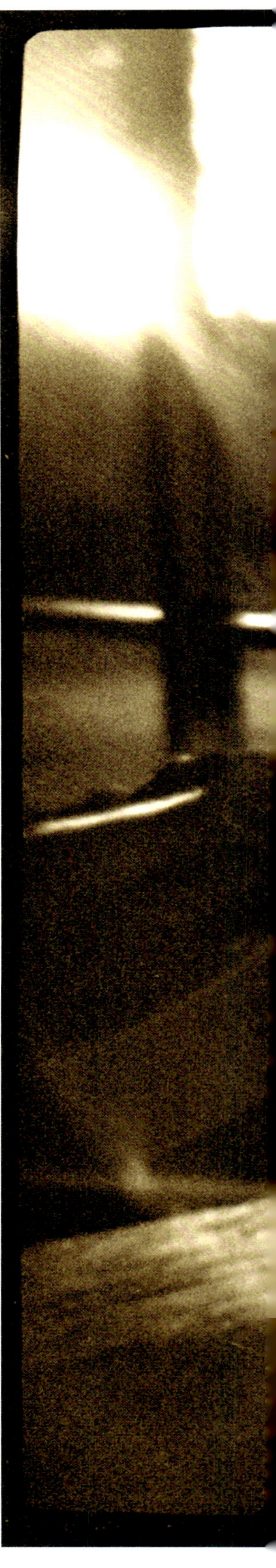

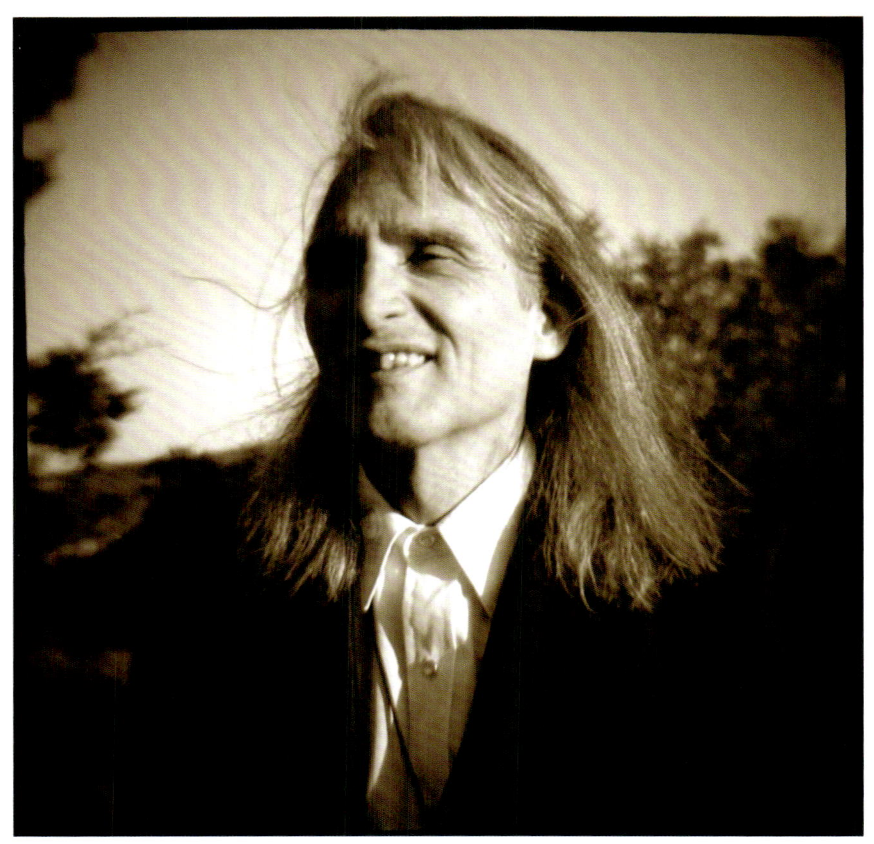

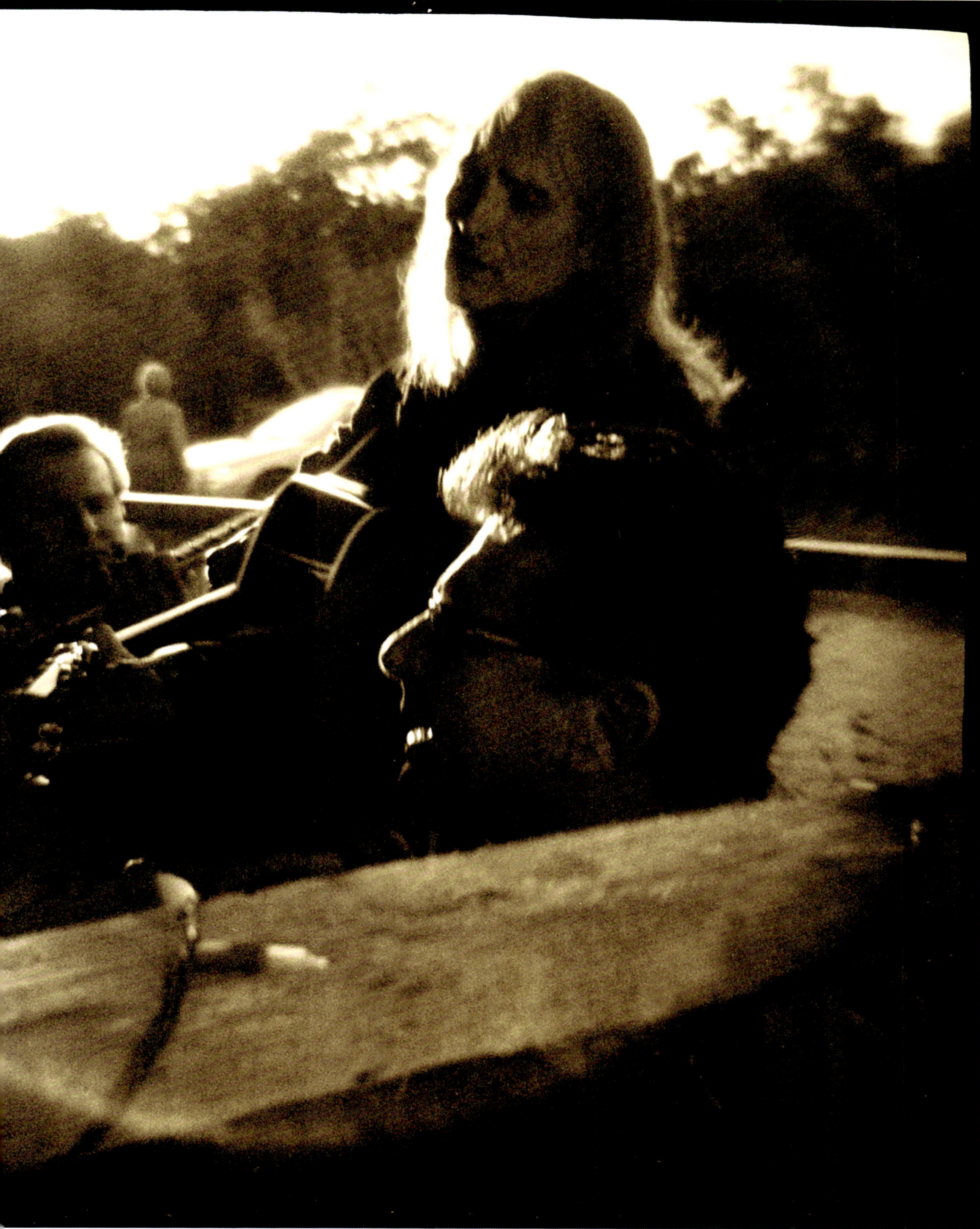

Billy Joe Shaver

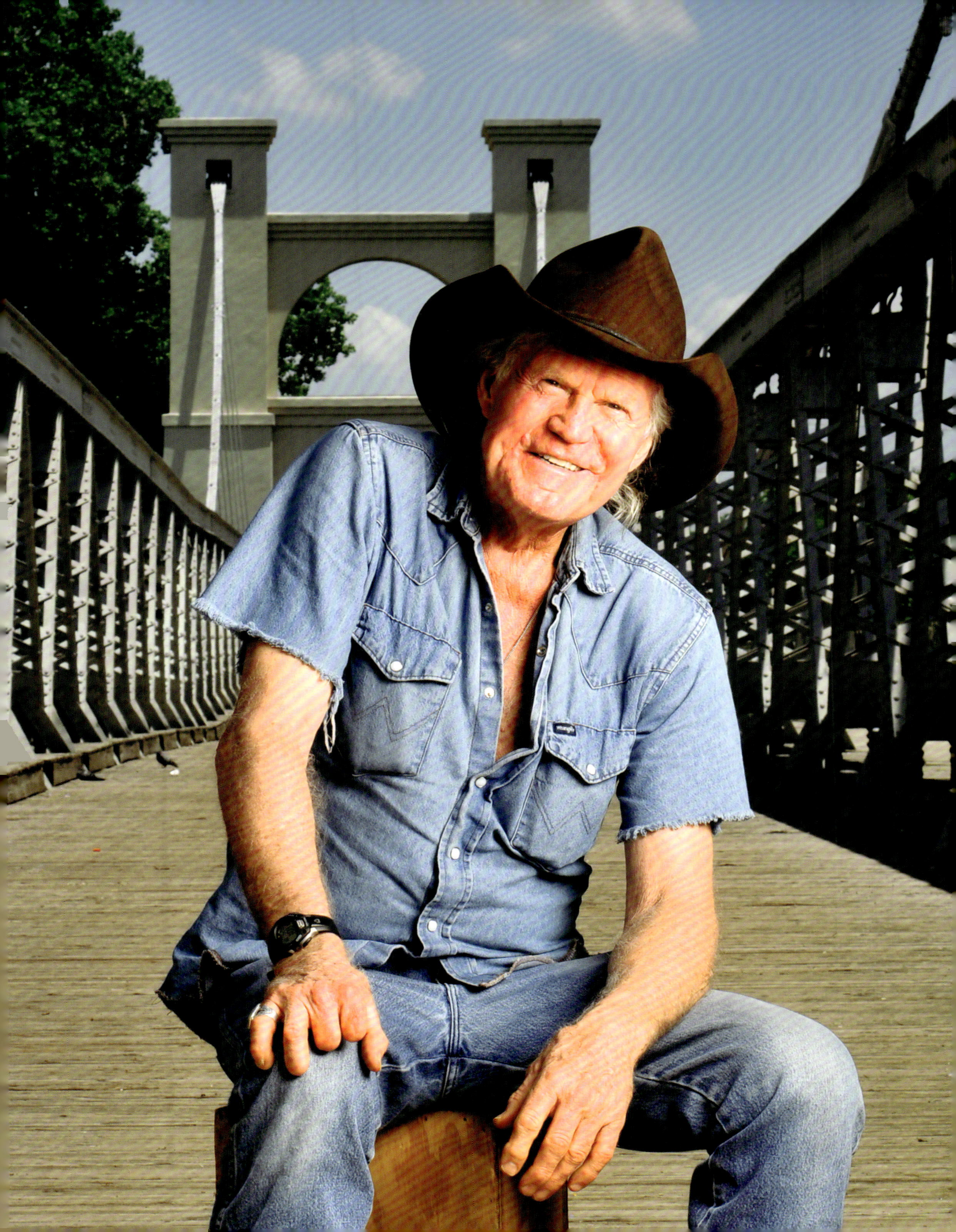

Billy Joe Shaver

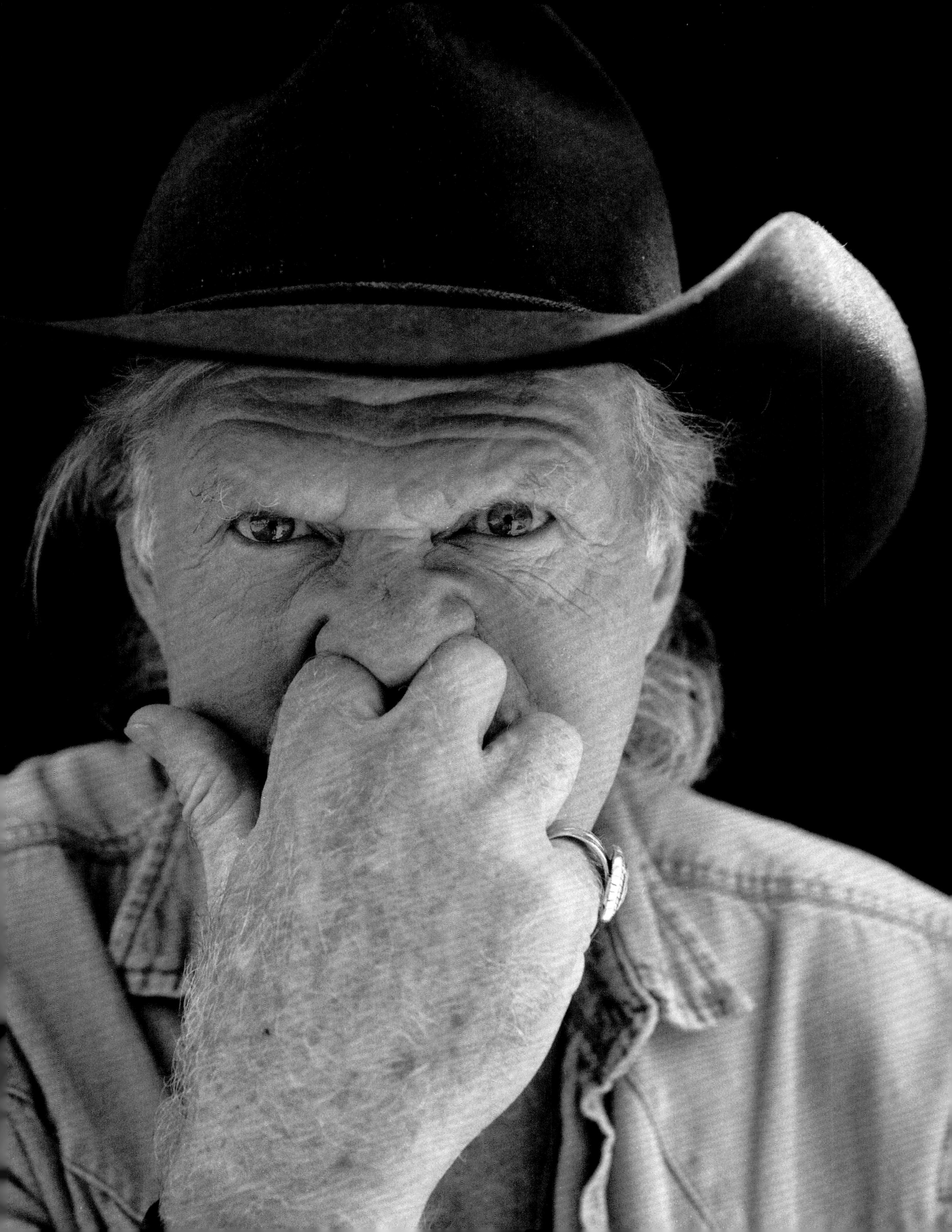

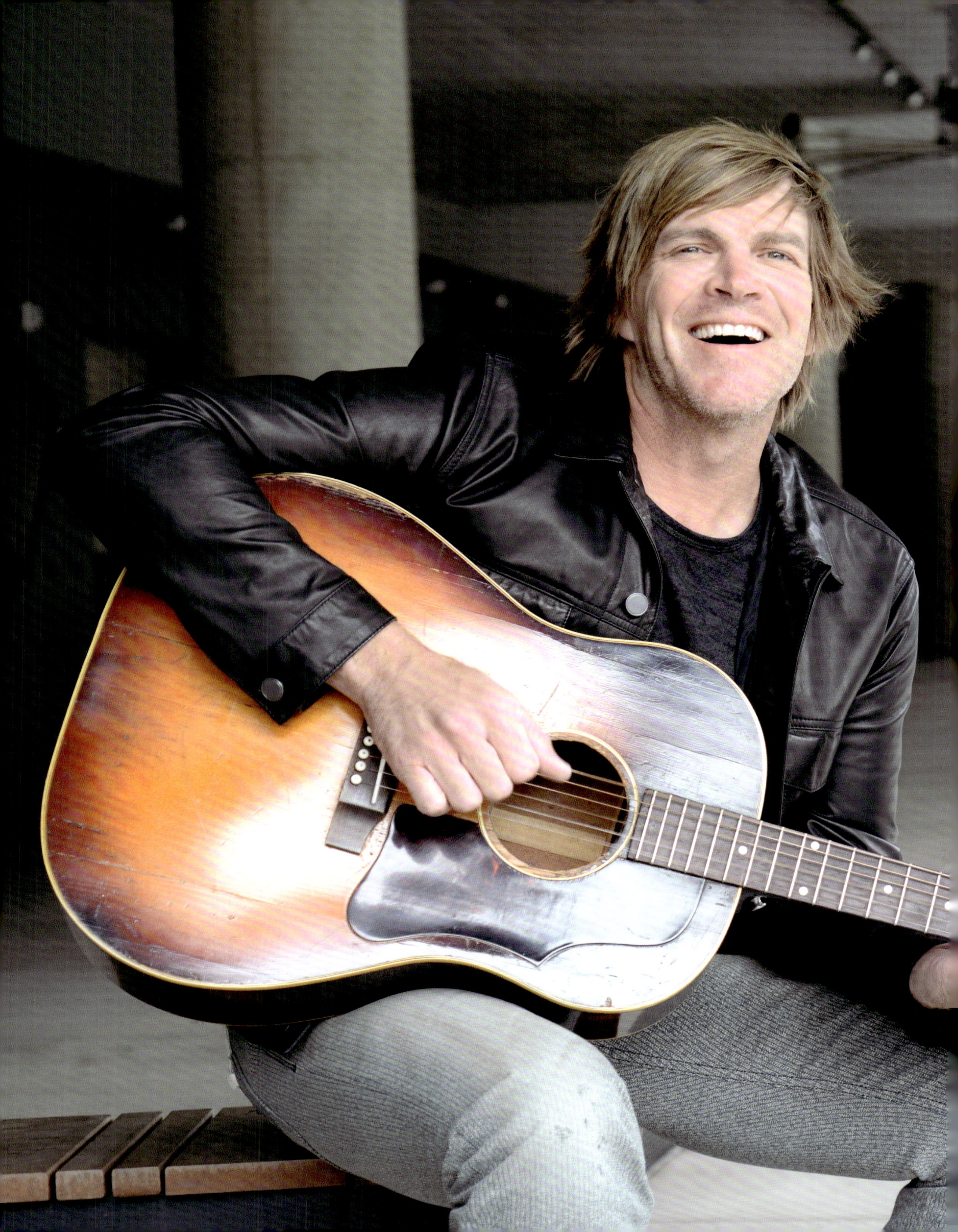

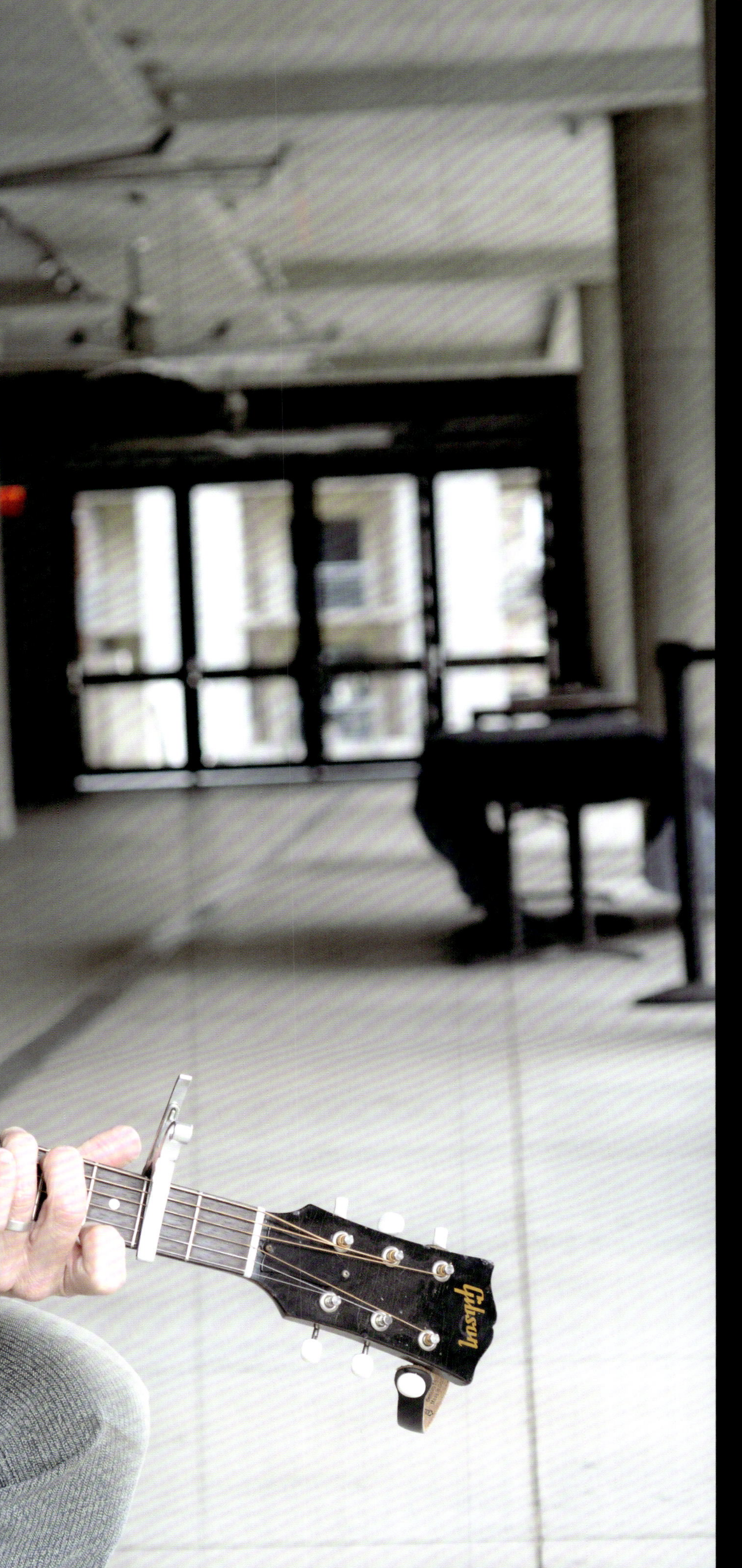

Jack Ingram

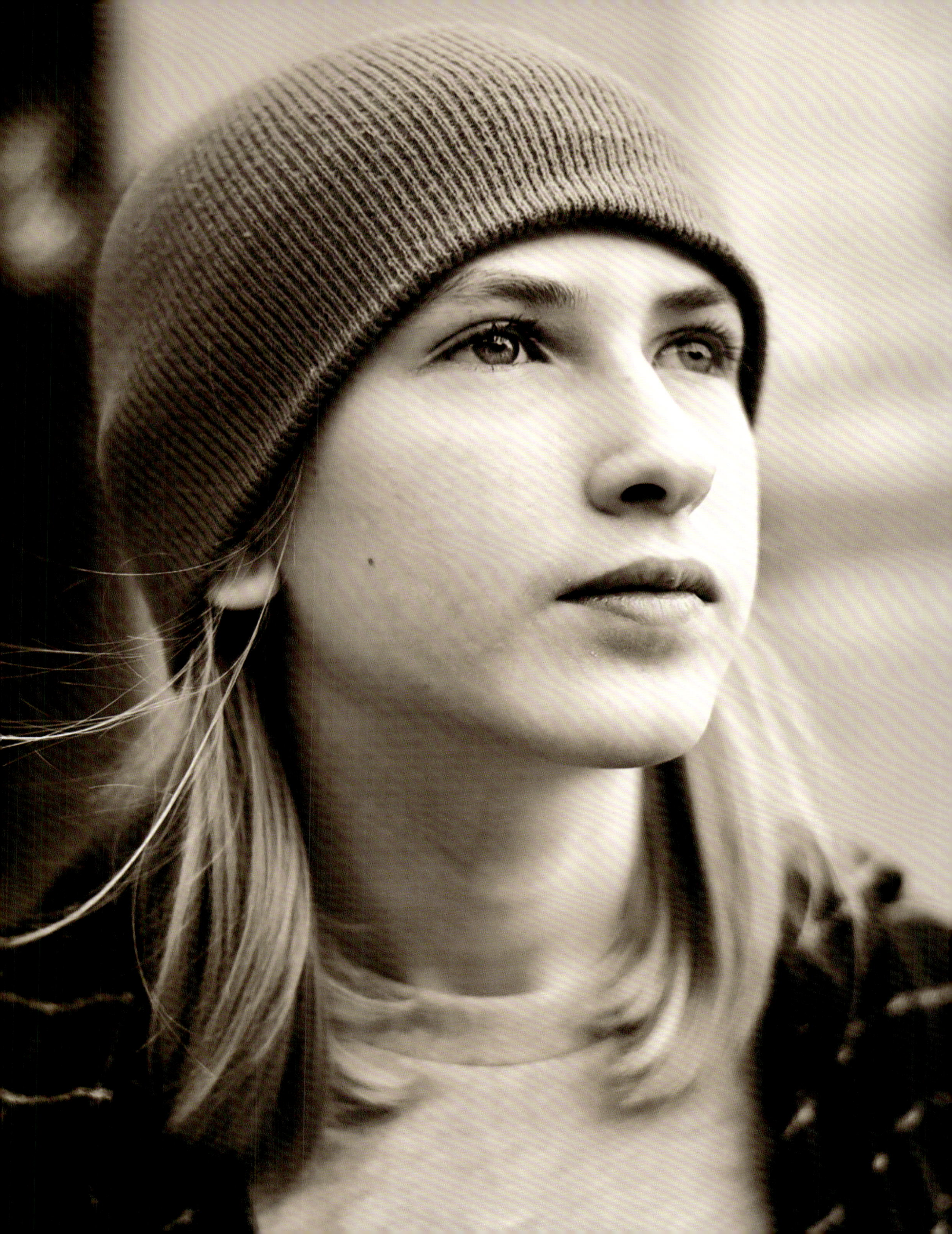

Jack Barksdale

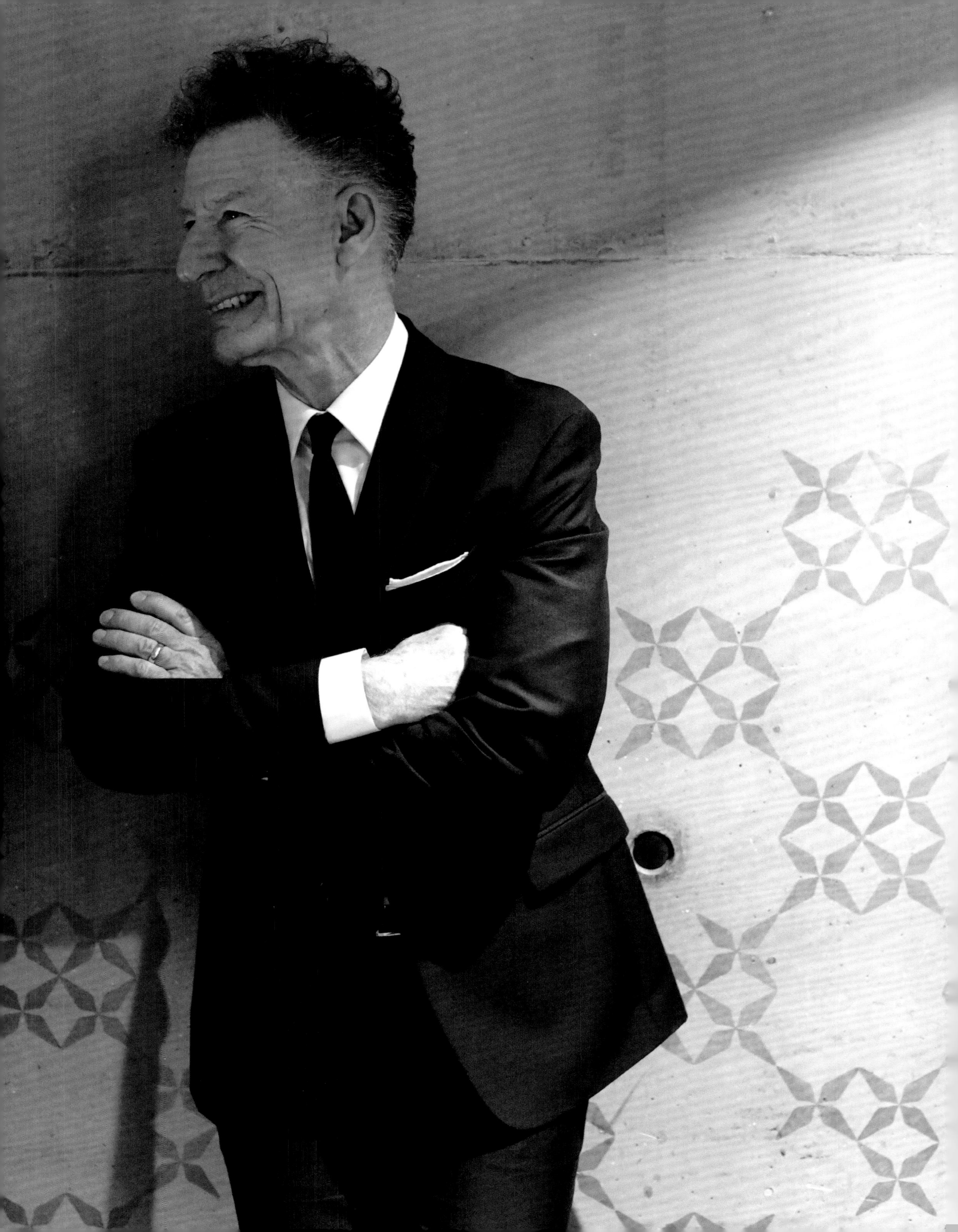

Lyle Lovett

Lyle Lovett

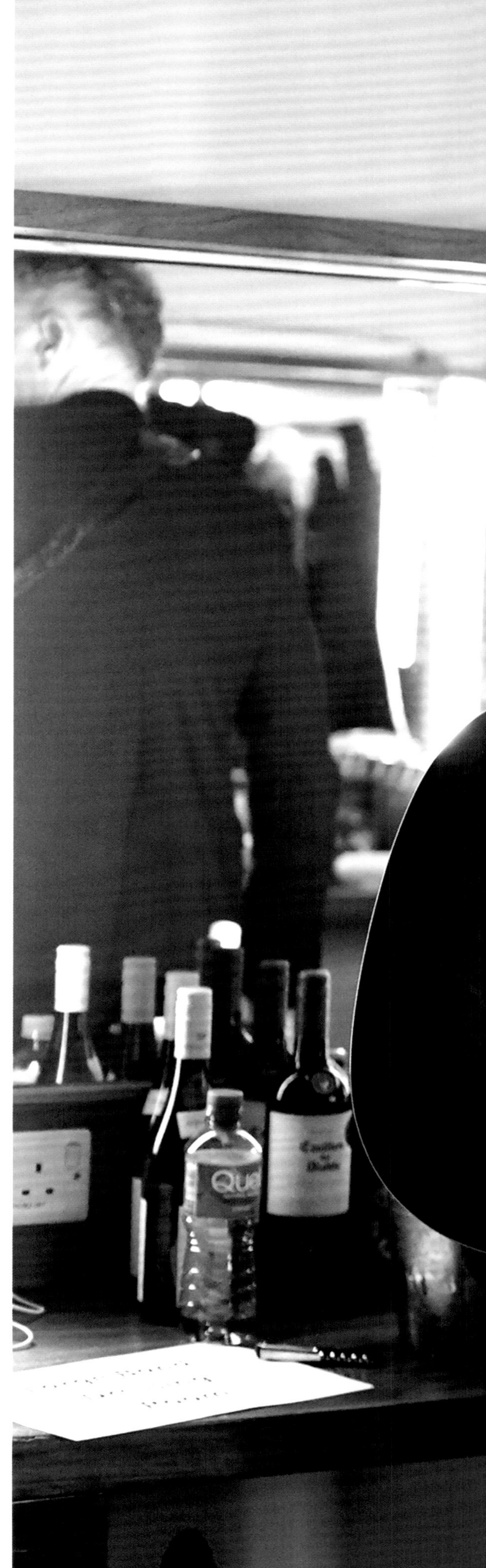

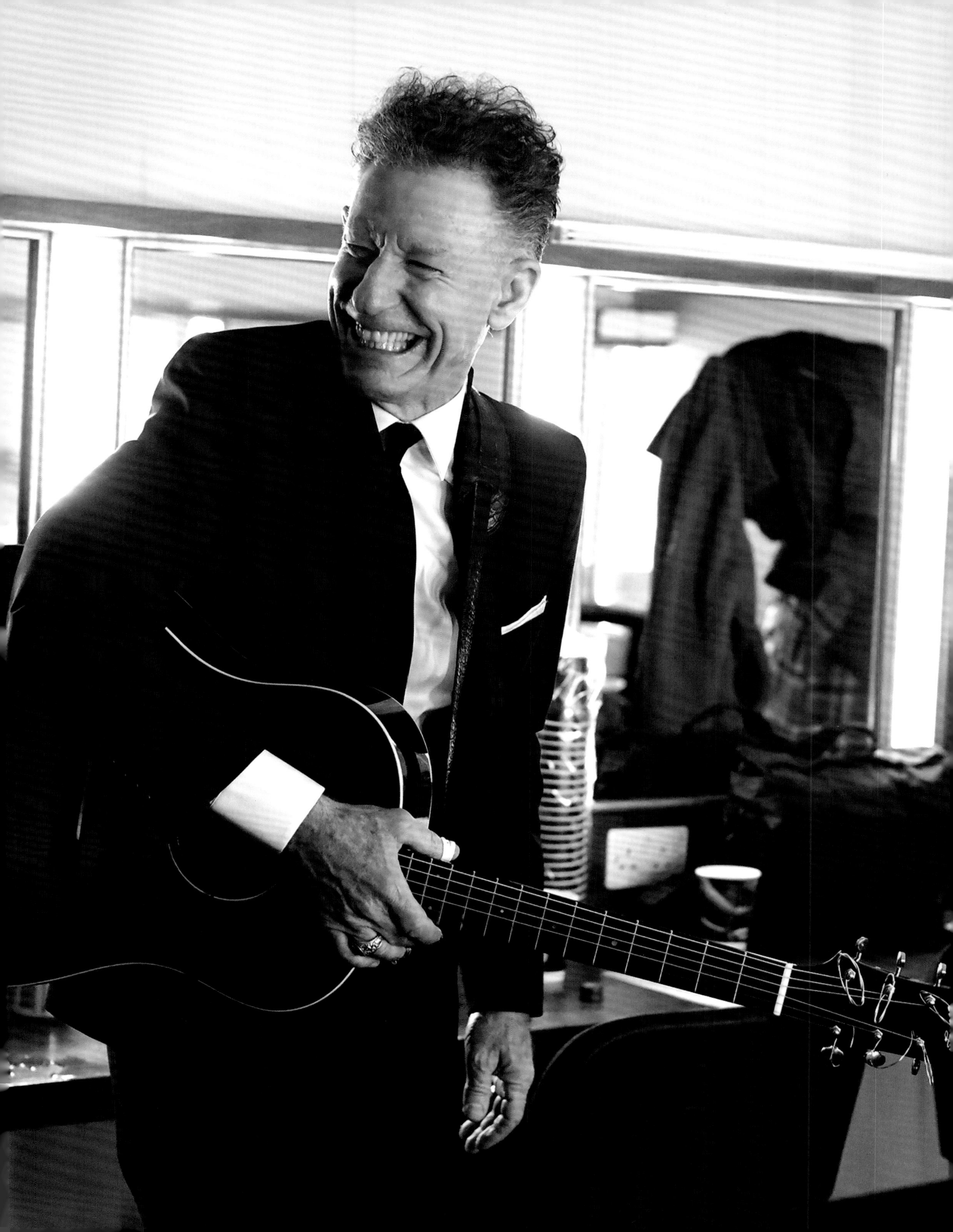

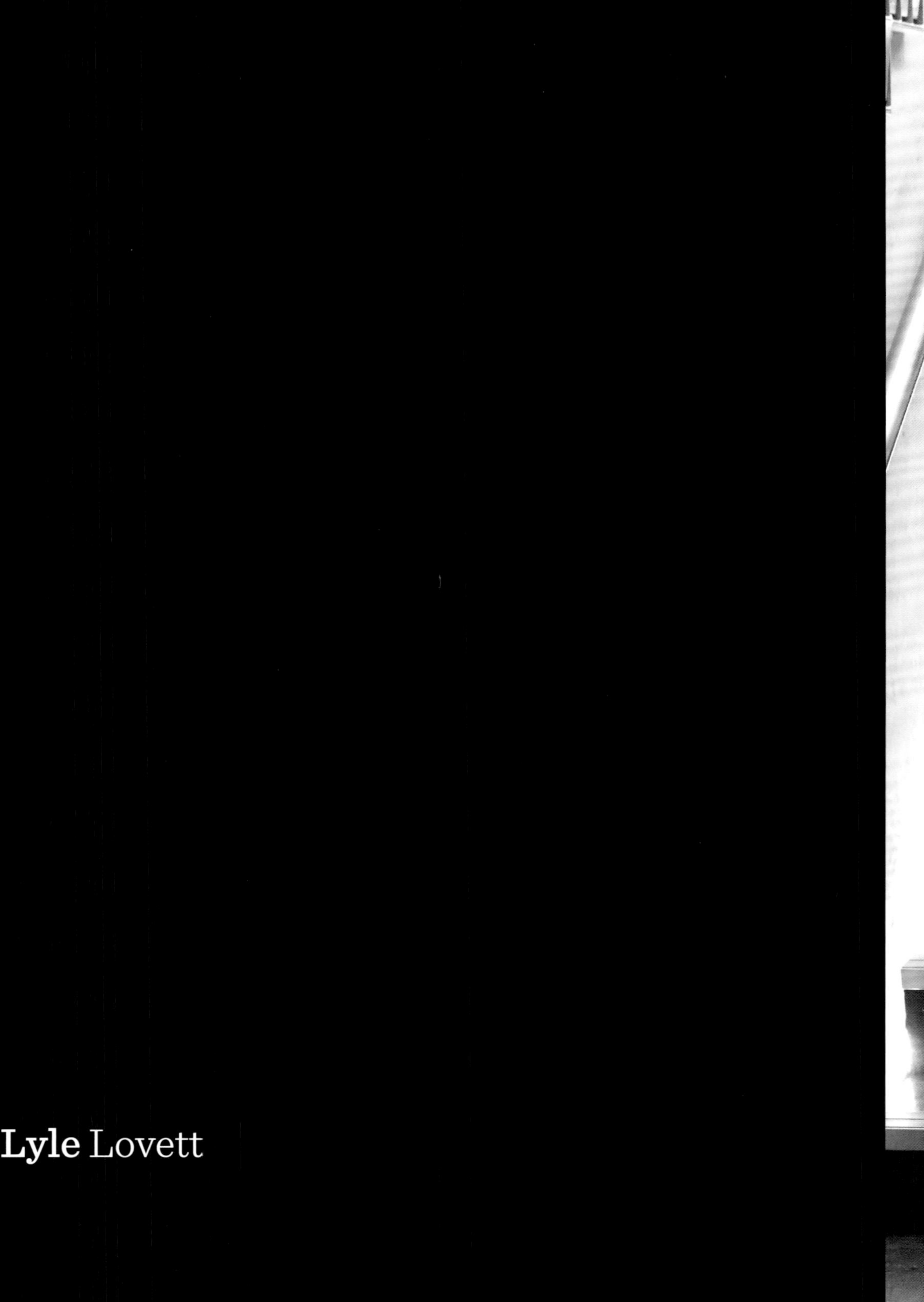

Lyle Lovett

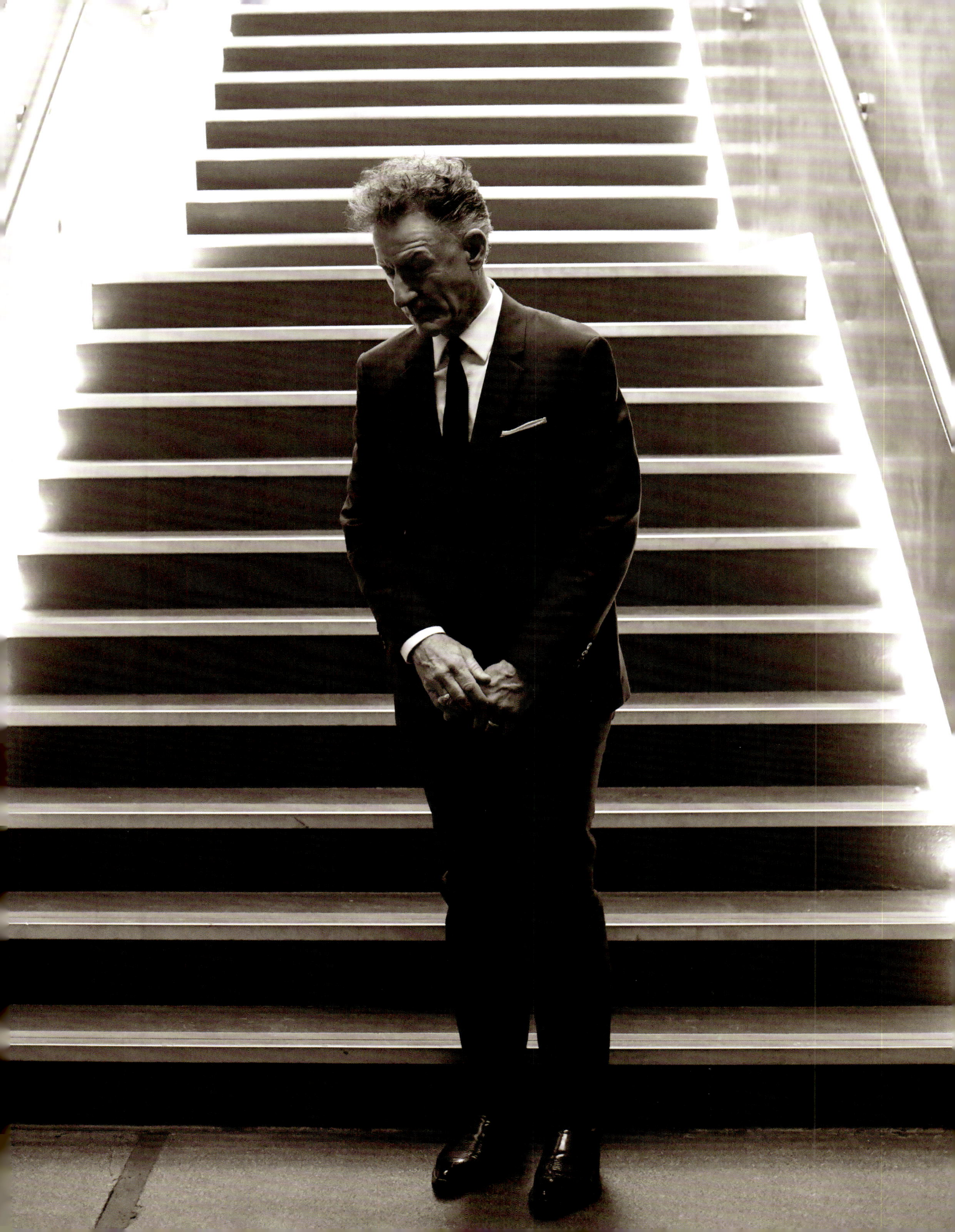

Family and **Friends**

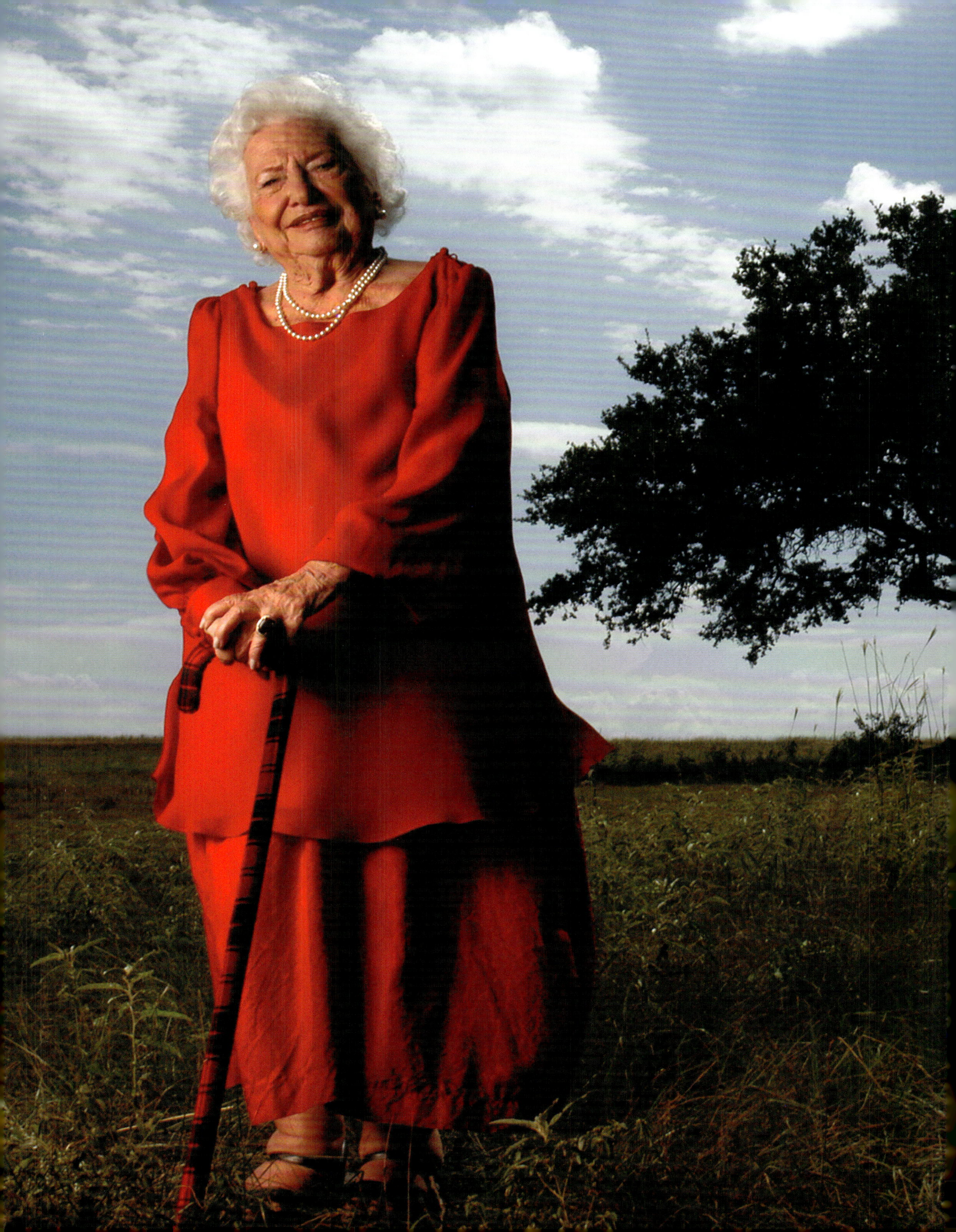

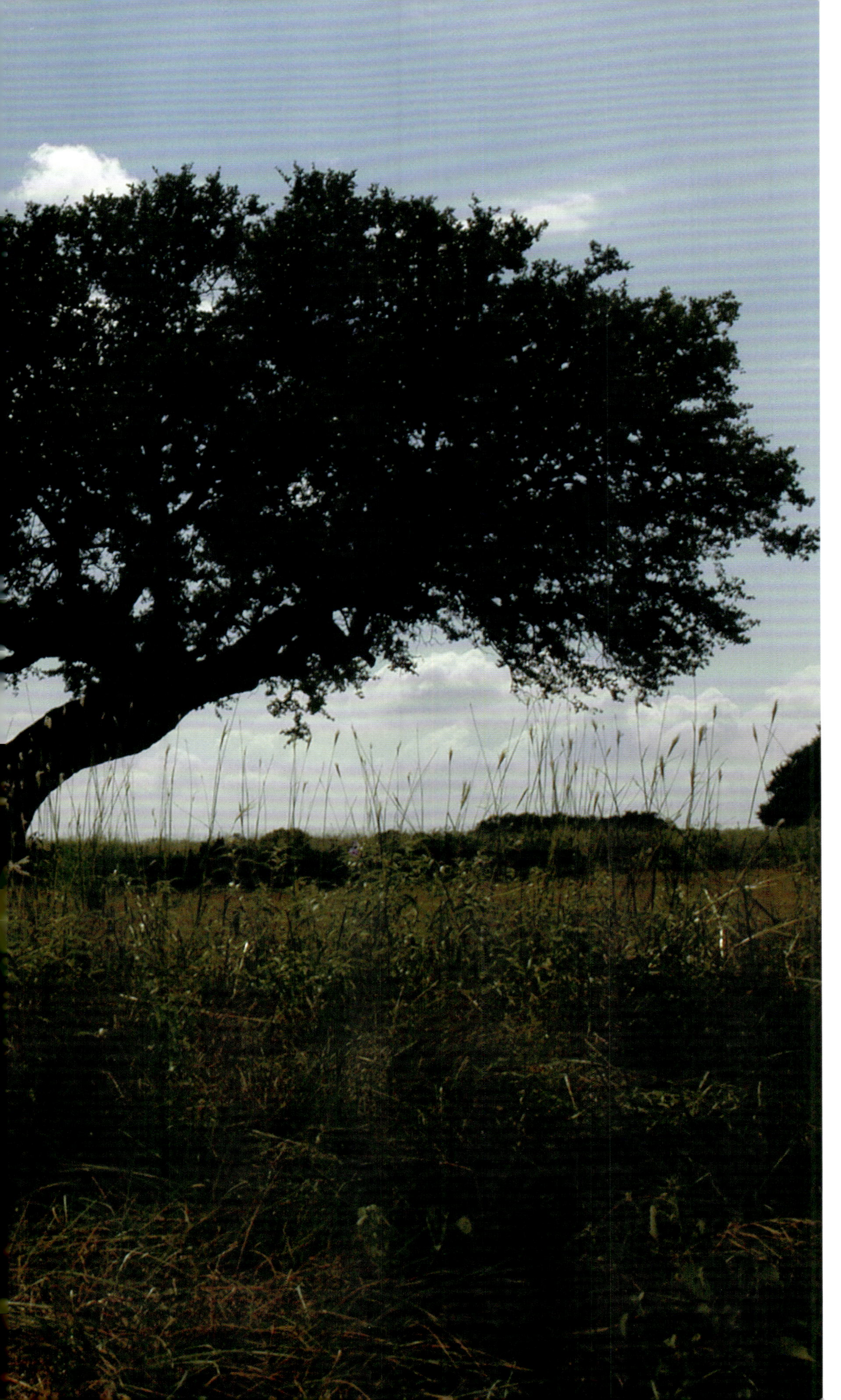

Liz
Carpenter

Molly Ivins, **Liz** Carpenter, and **Sarah** Weddington

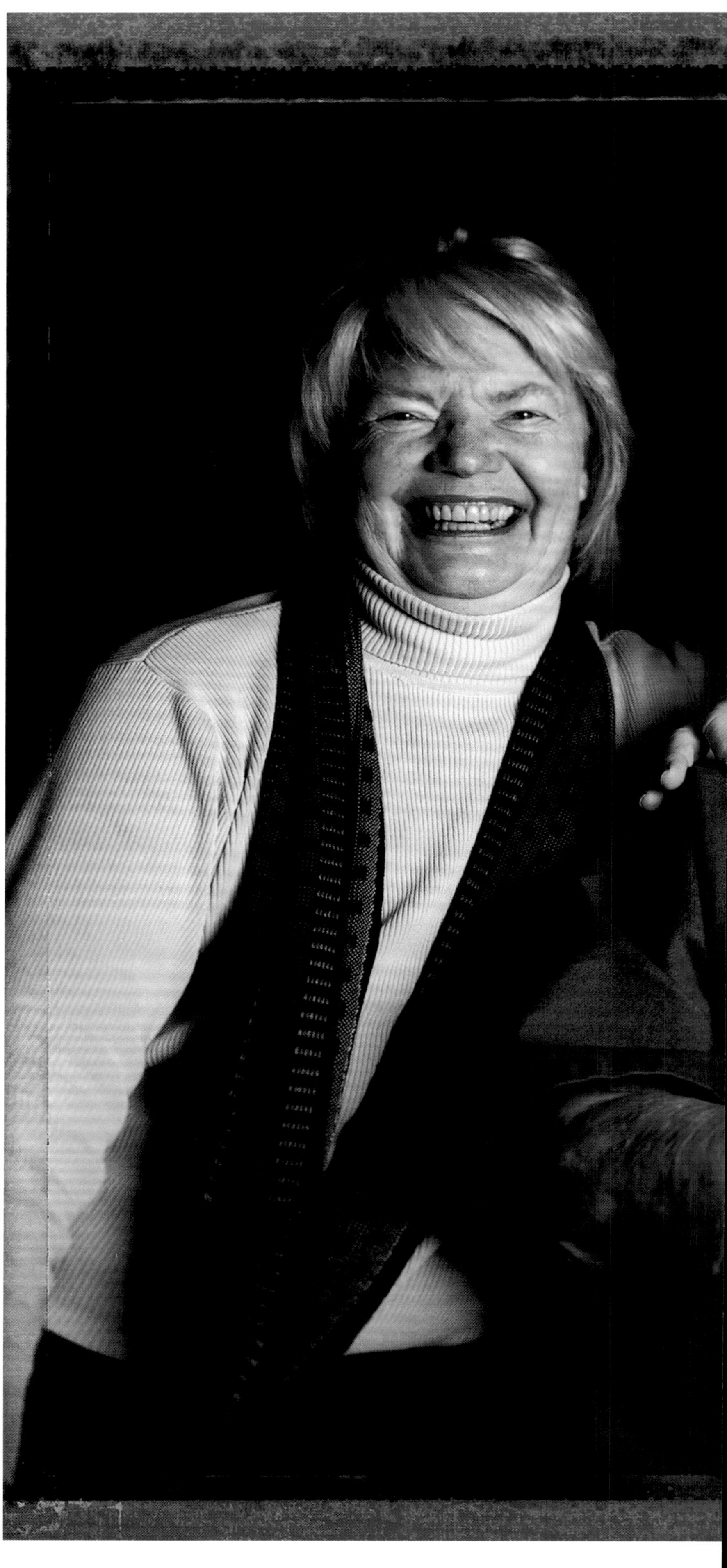

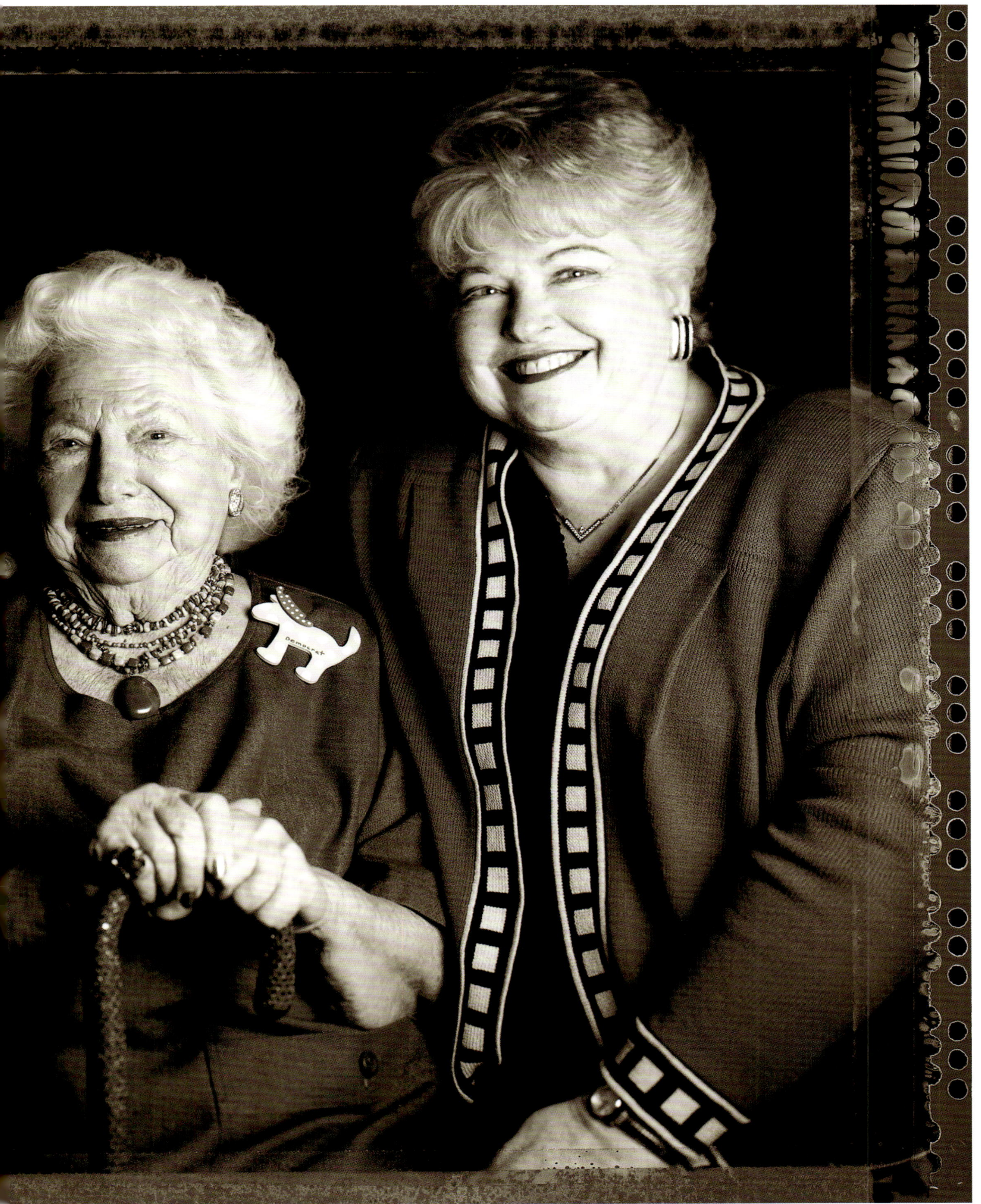
Democrat

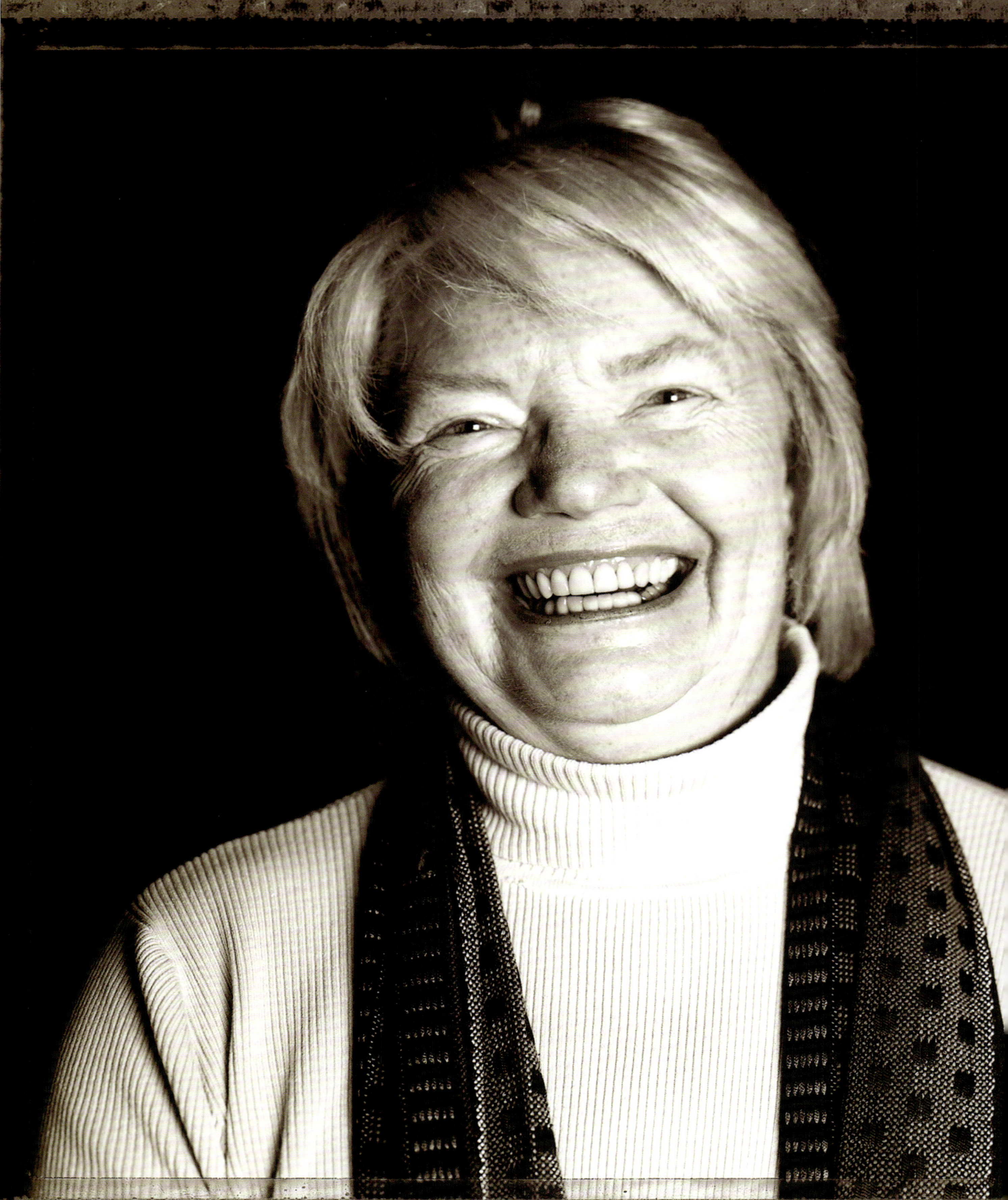

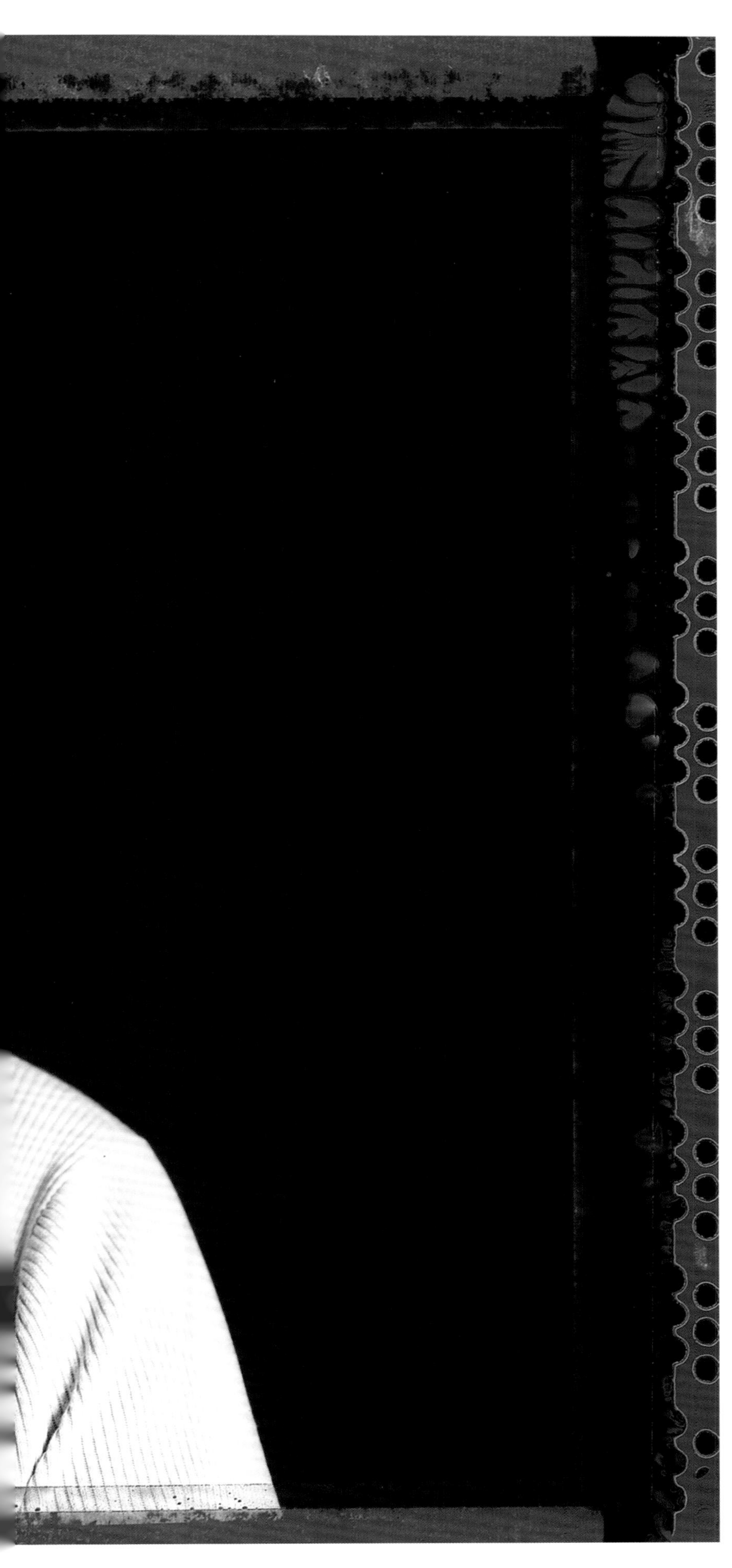

Molly Ivins

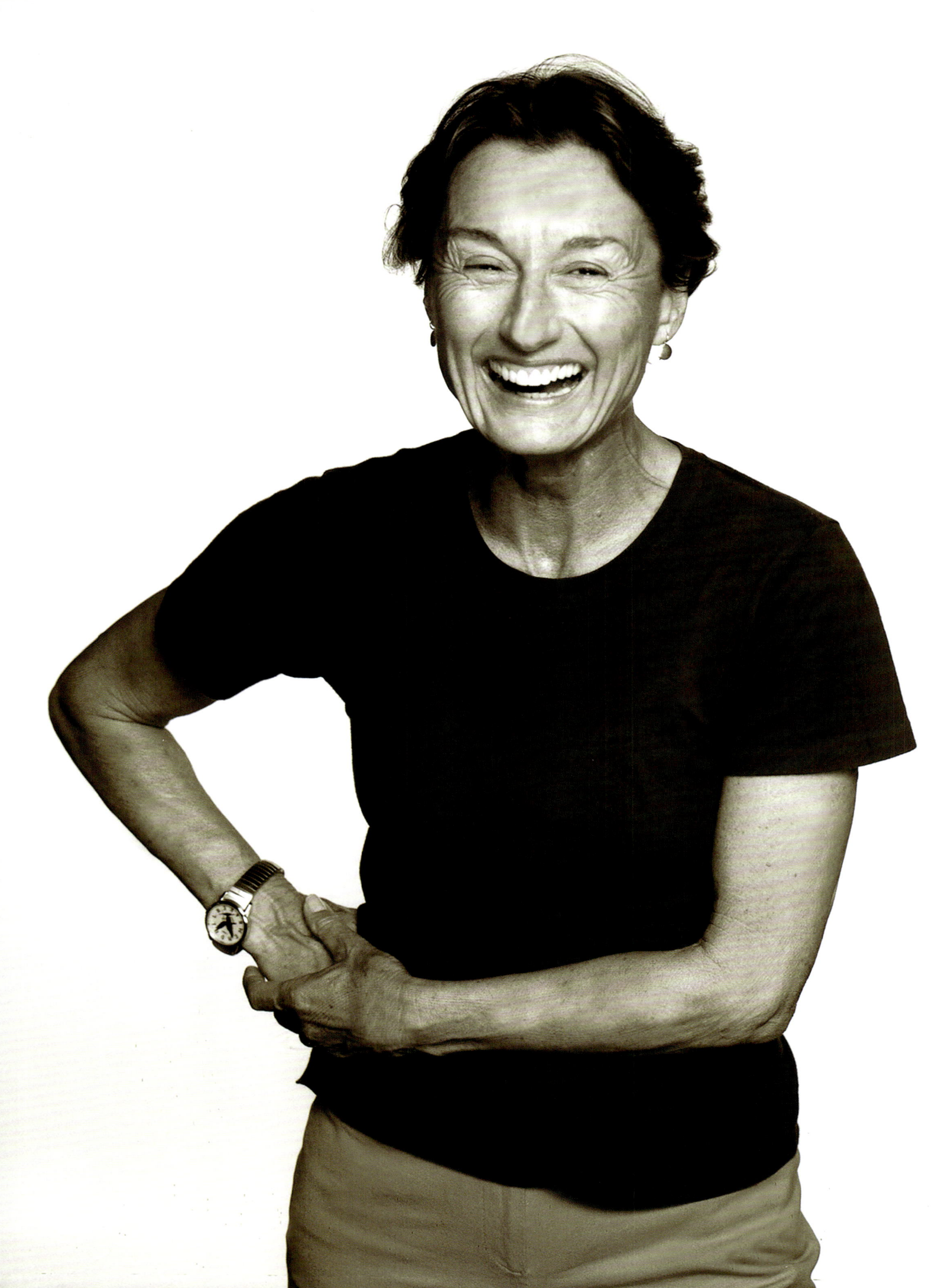

Laura Wilson

Adrian Whipp

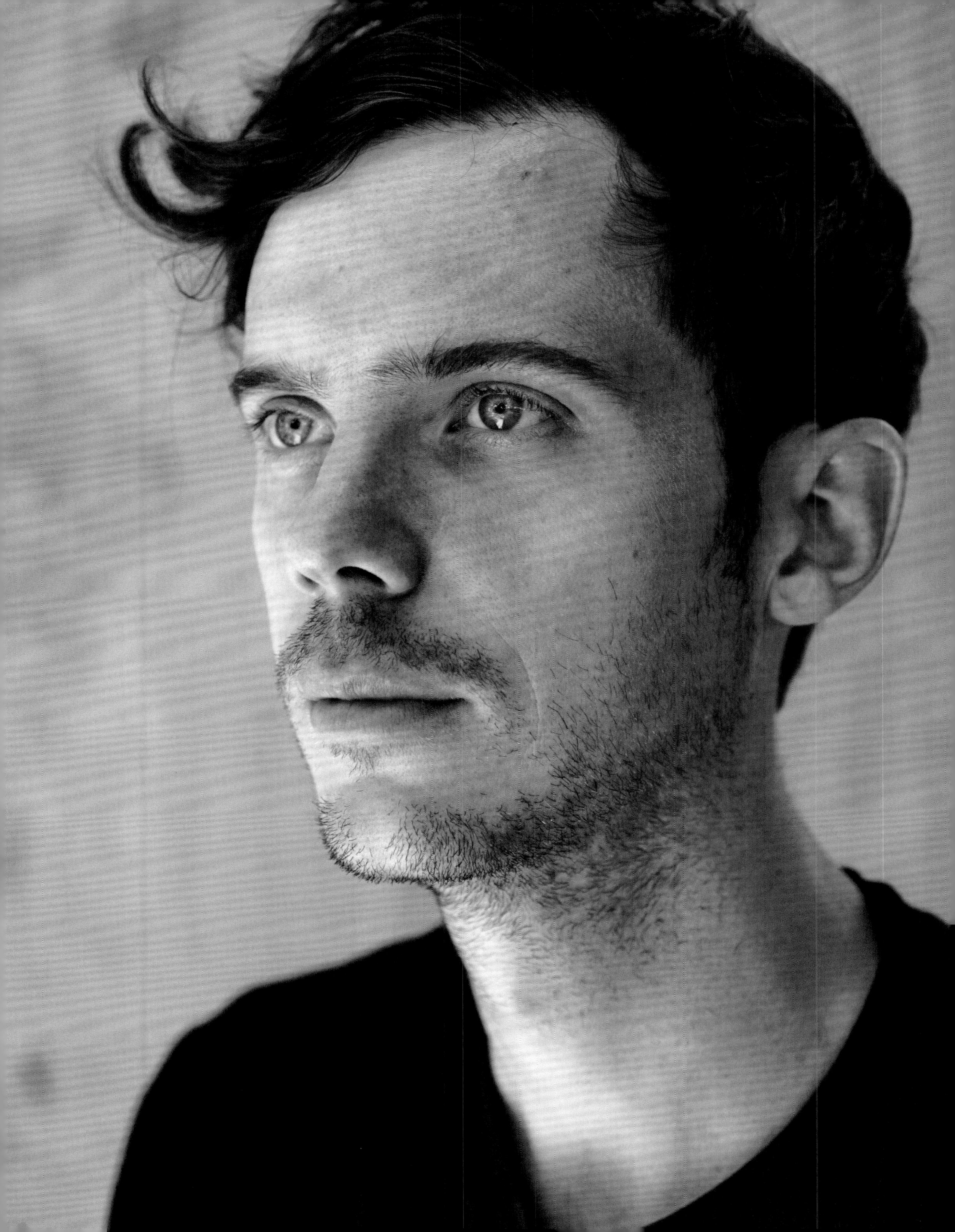

Lisl Friday

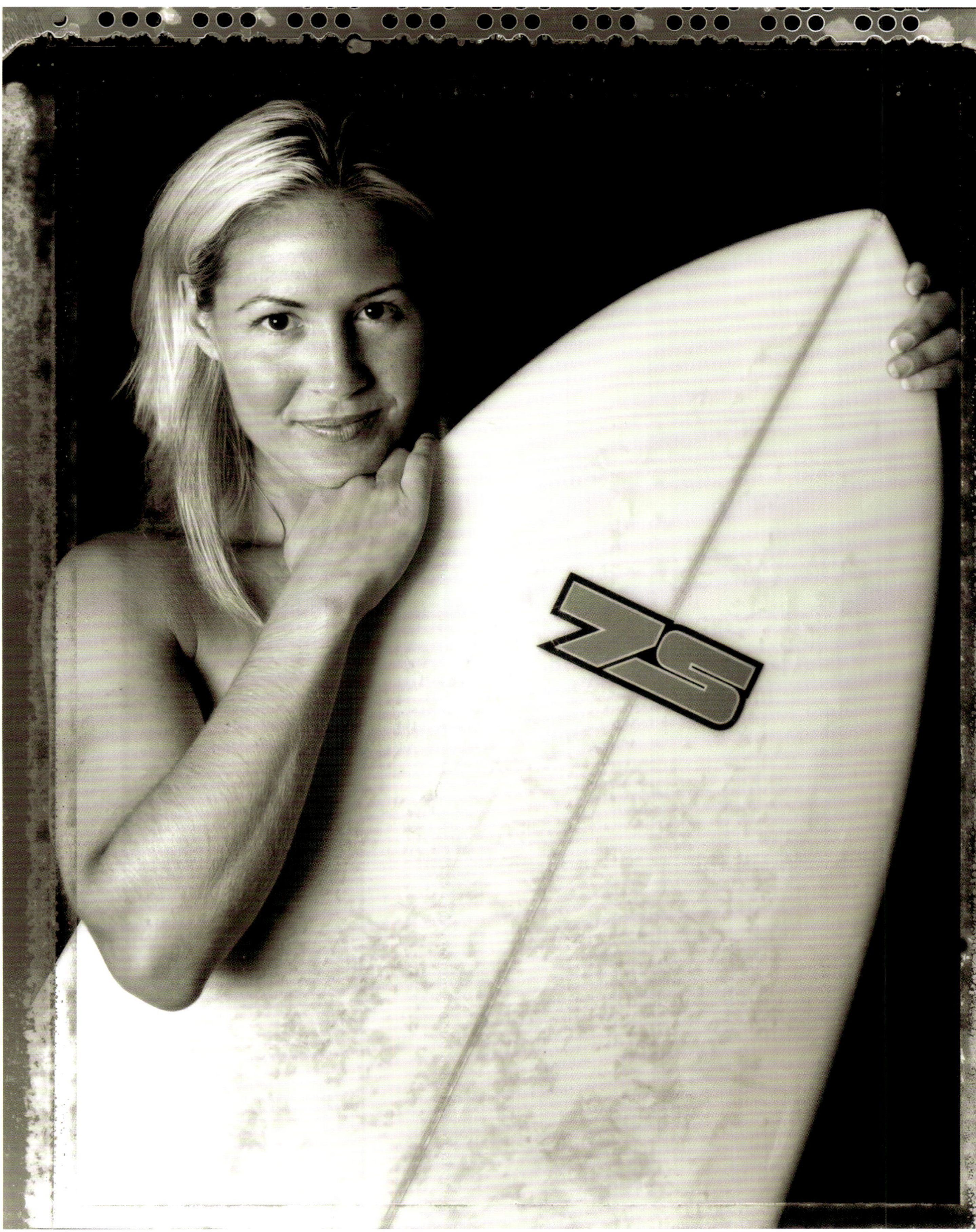
7S

Turk Pipkin

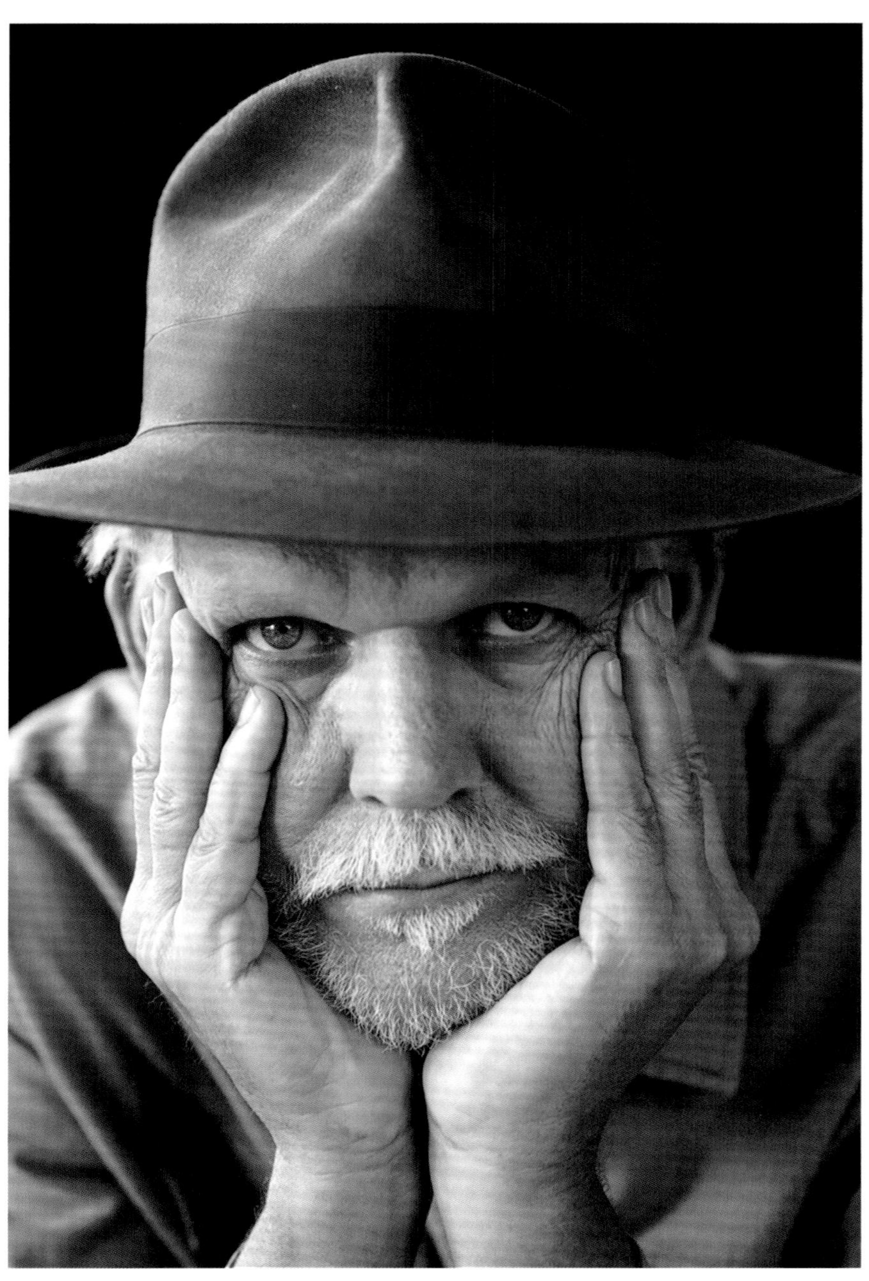

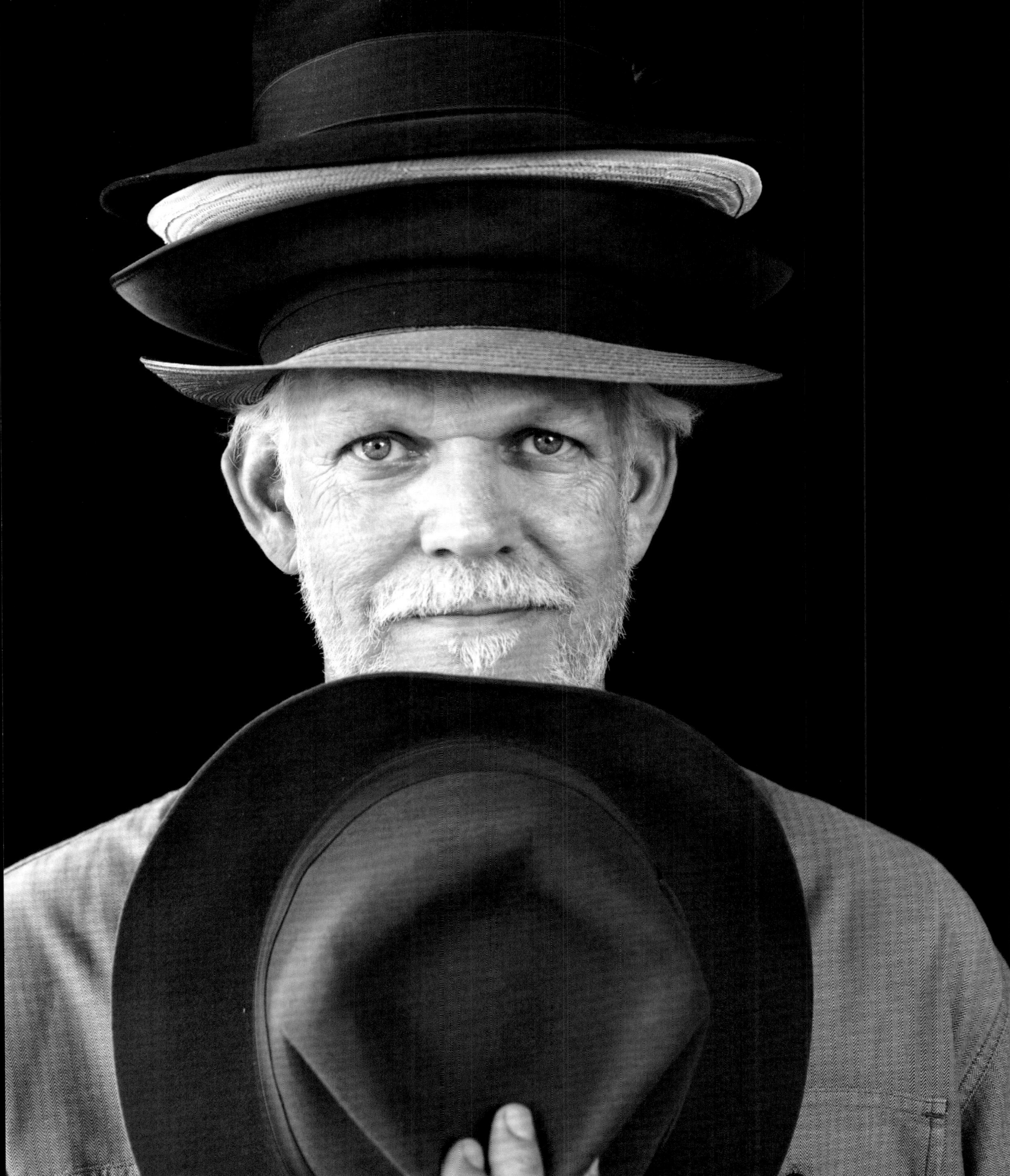

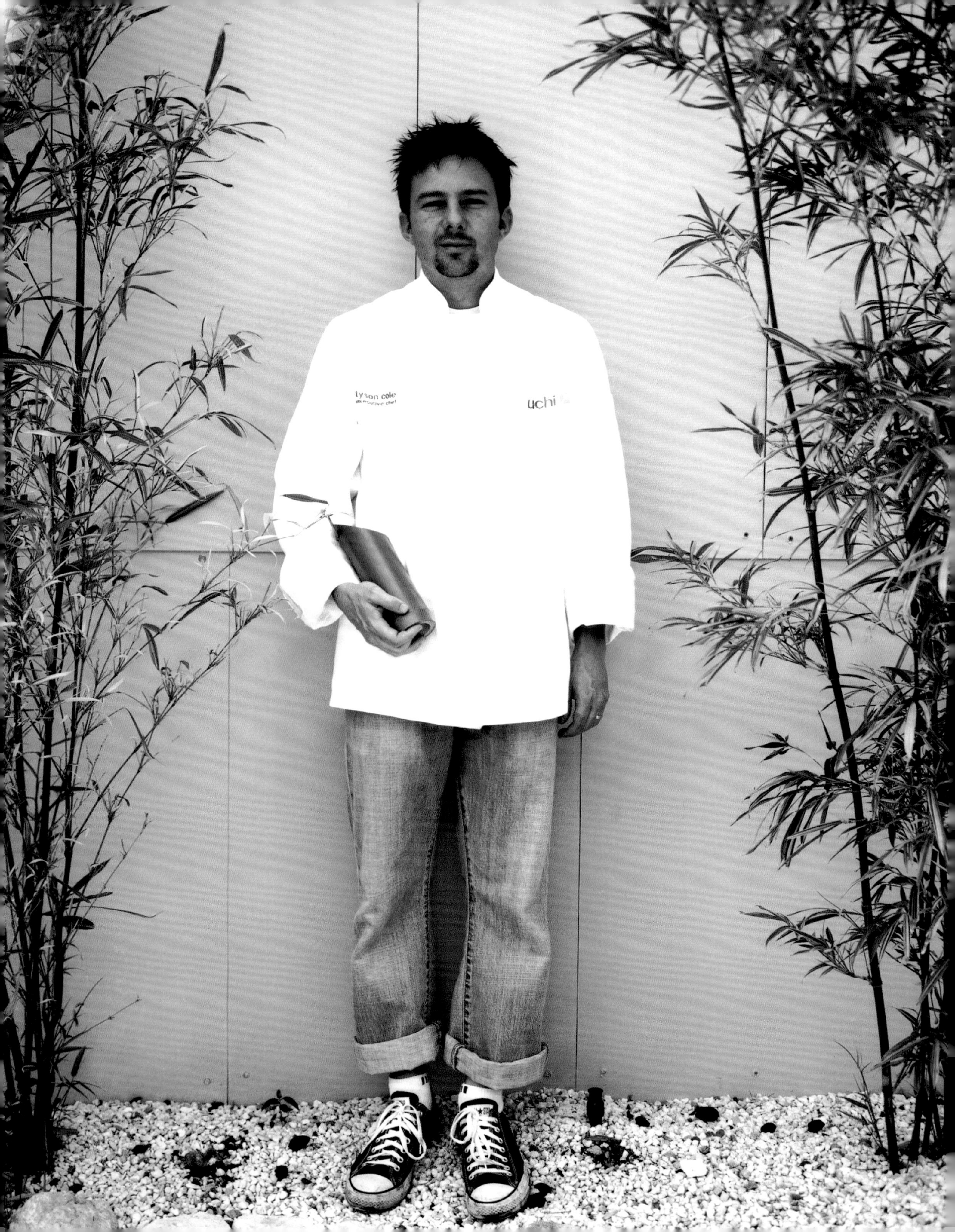
tyson cole
uchi

Tyson Cole

Yoshi Okai

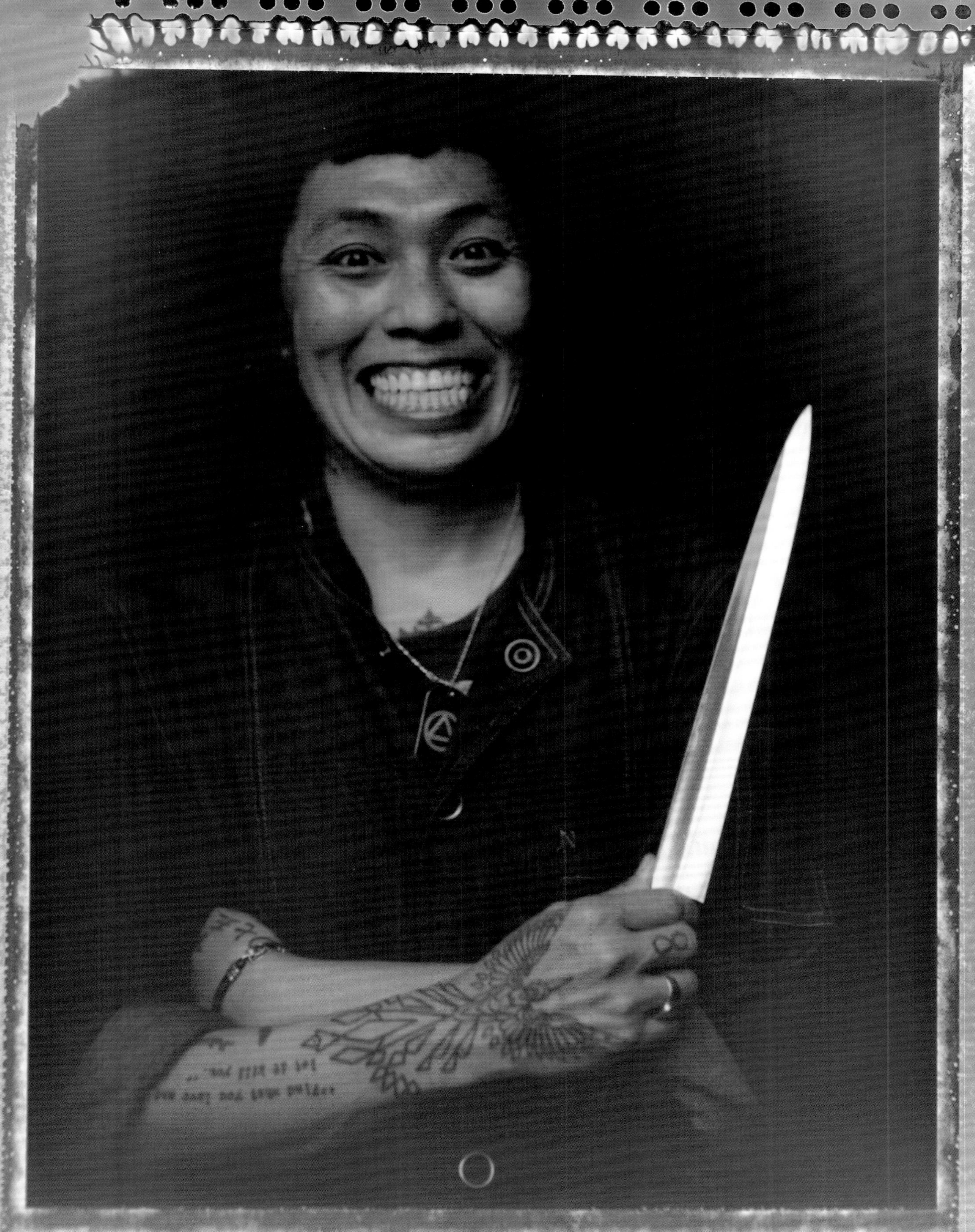

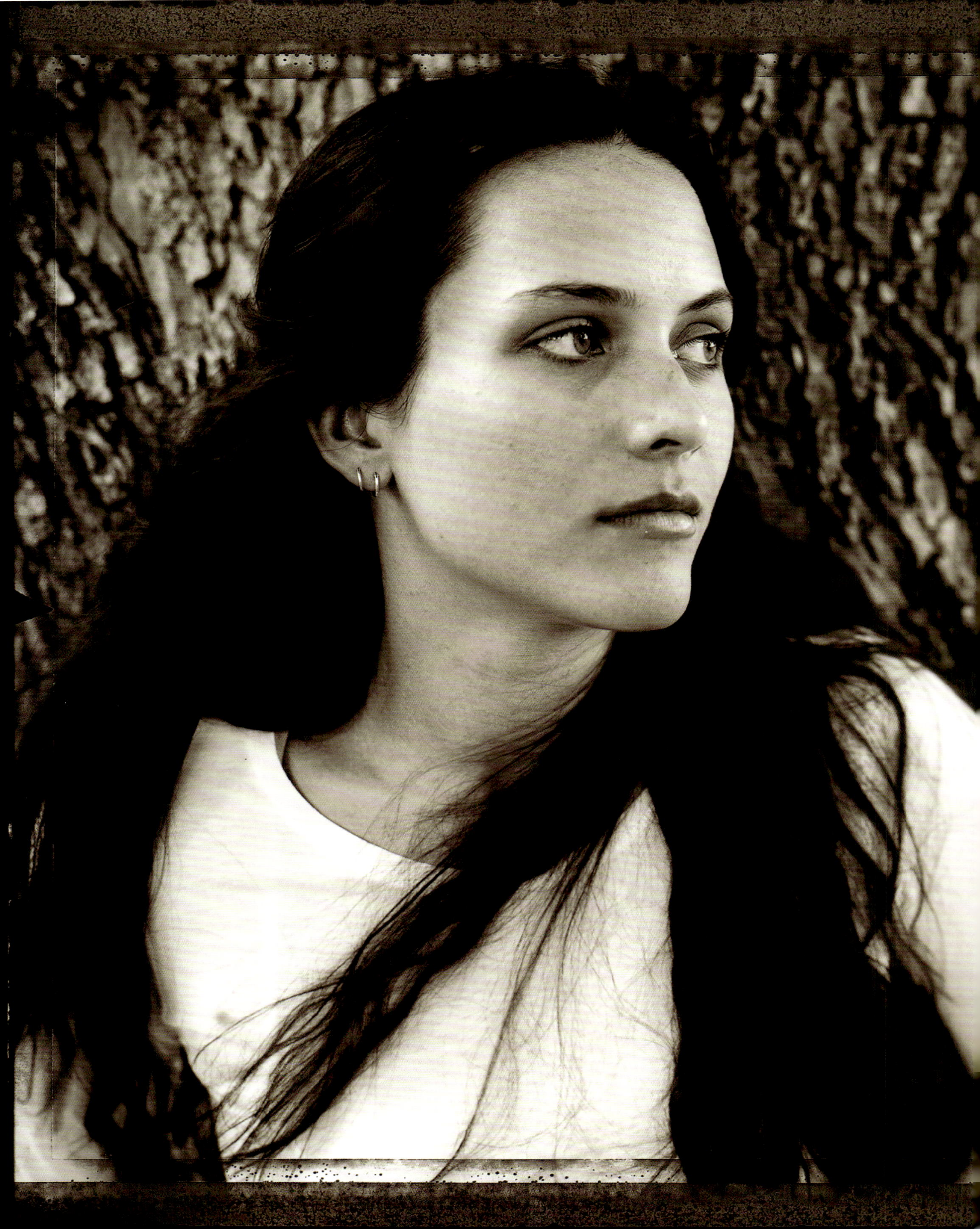

Kelly Hudson

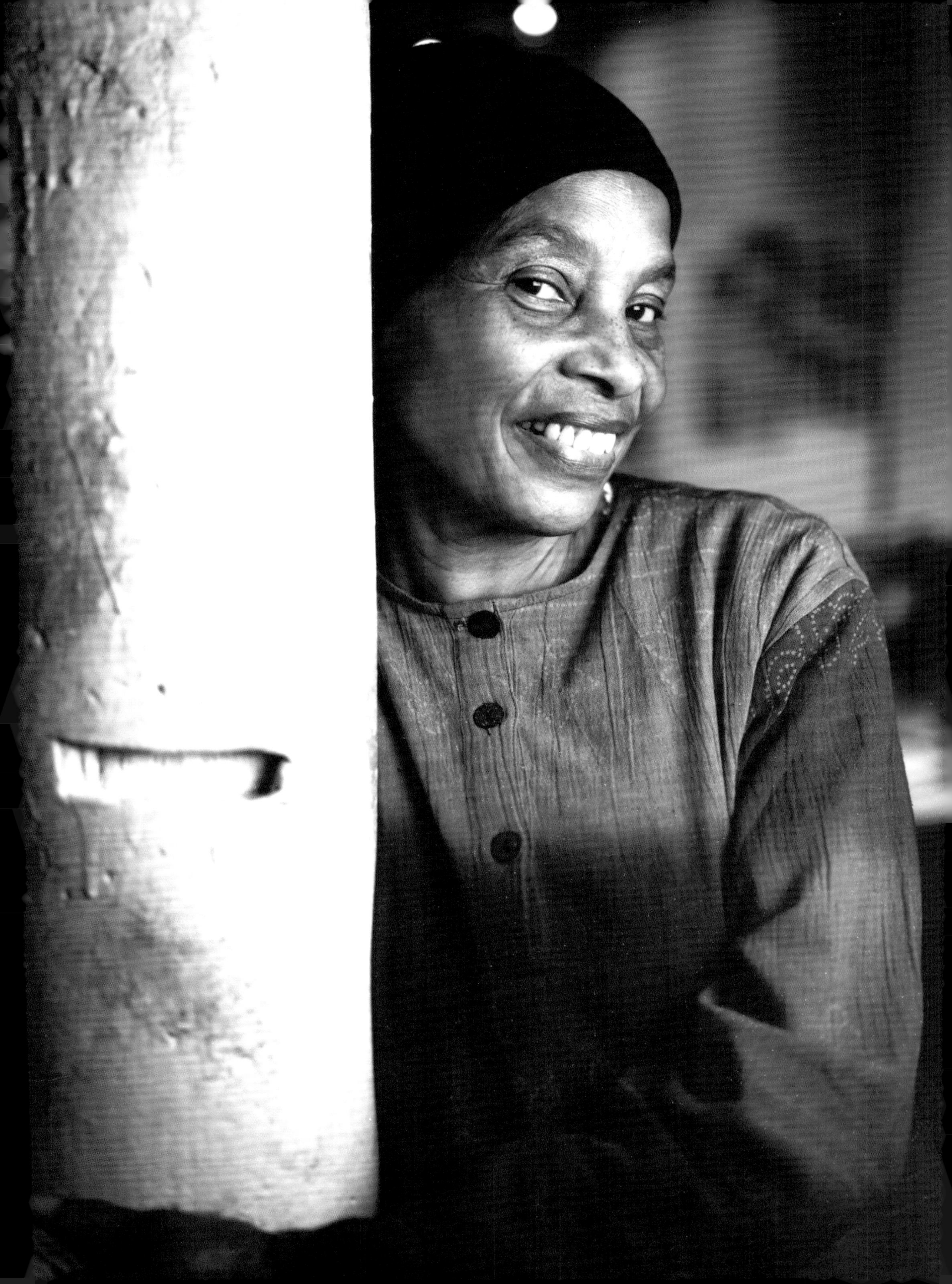

Pearl Griffith Eccles

Shelby and **Shawna**

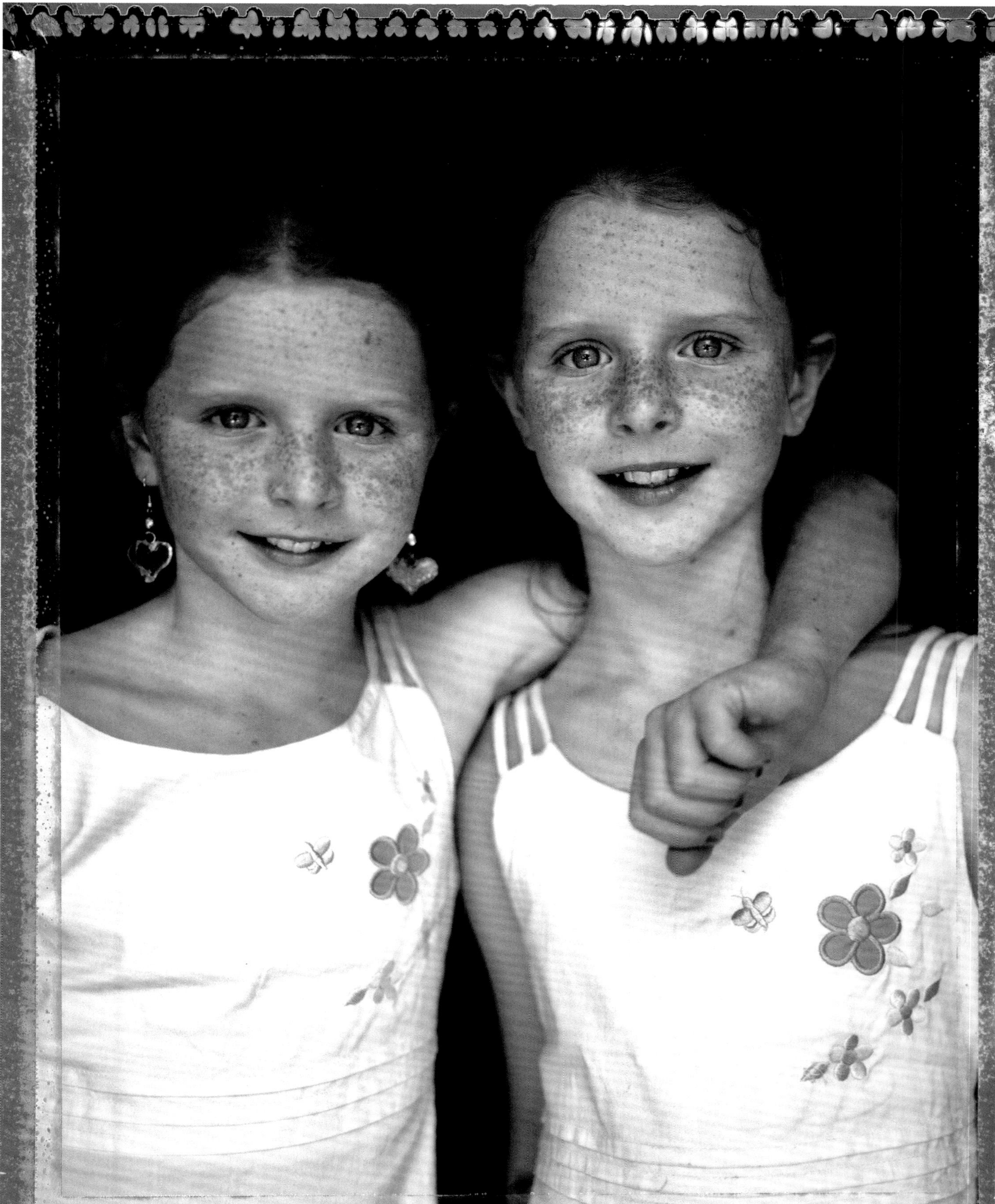

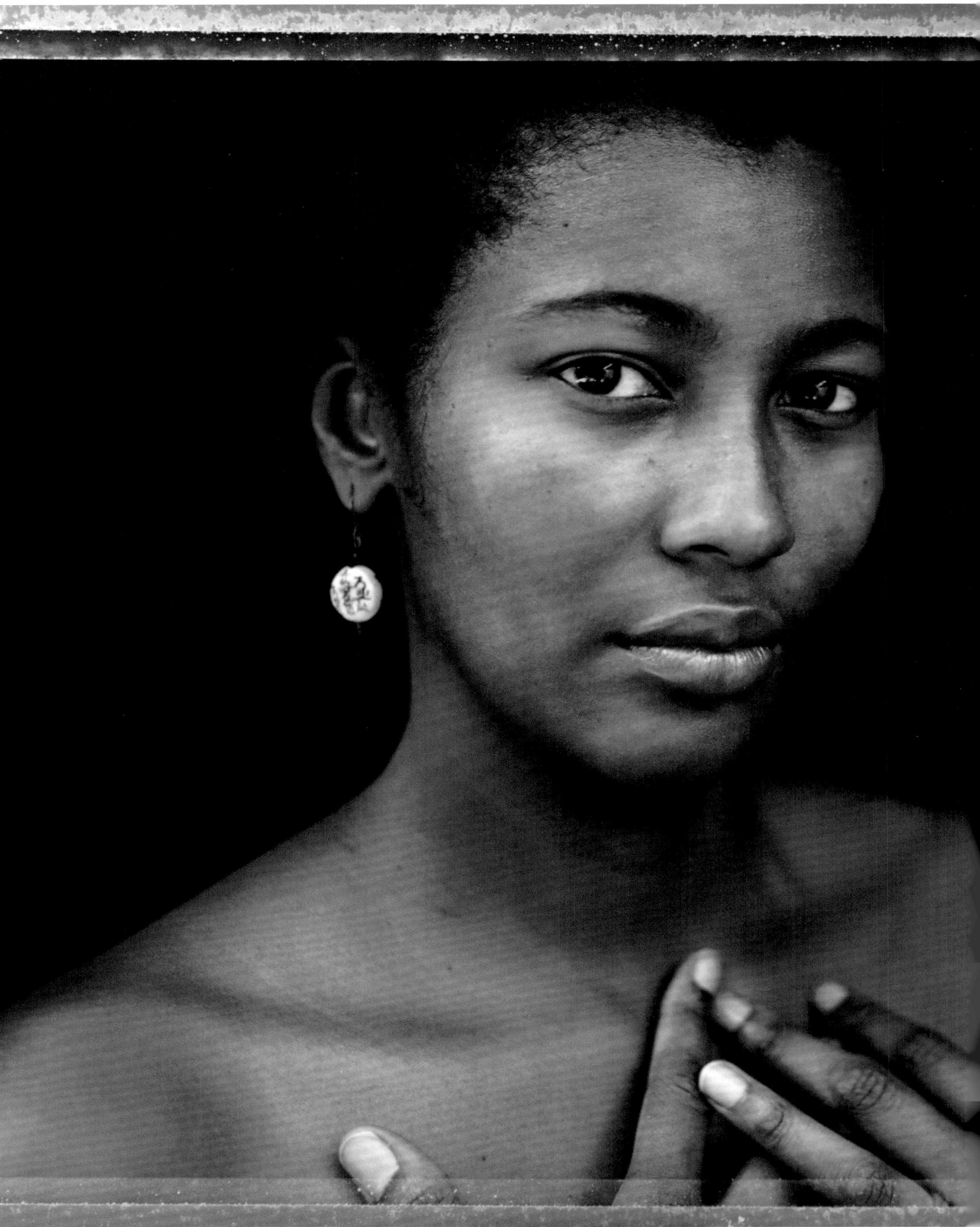

Tracey Beneke

Sutherland

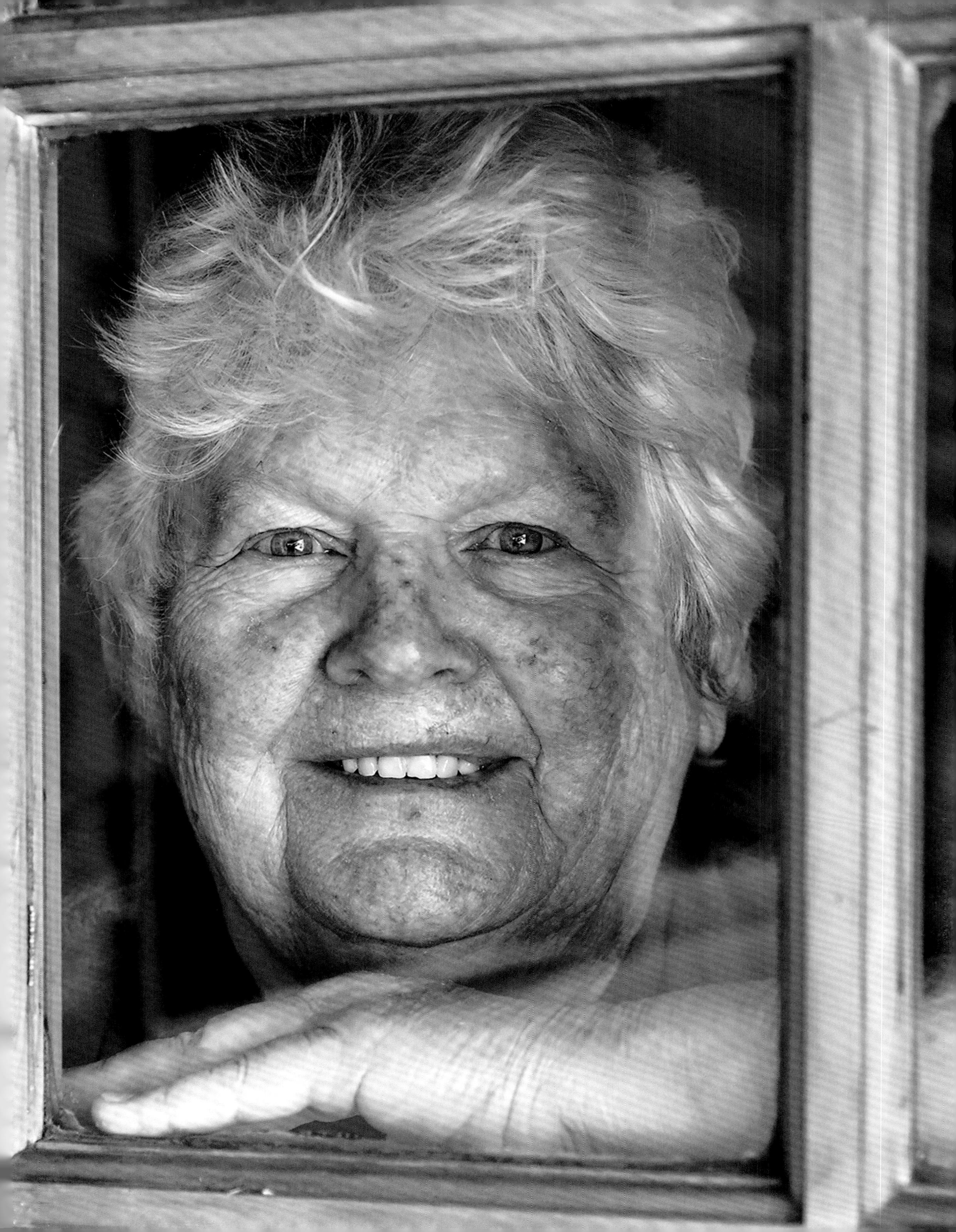

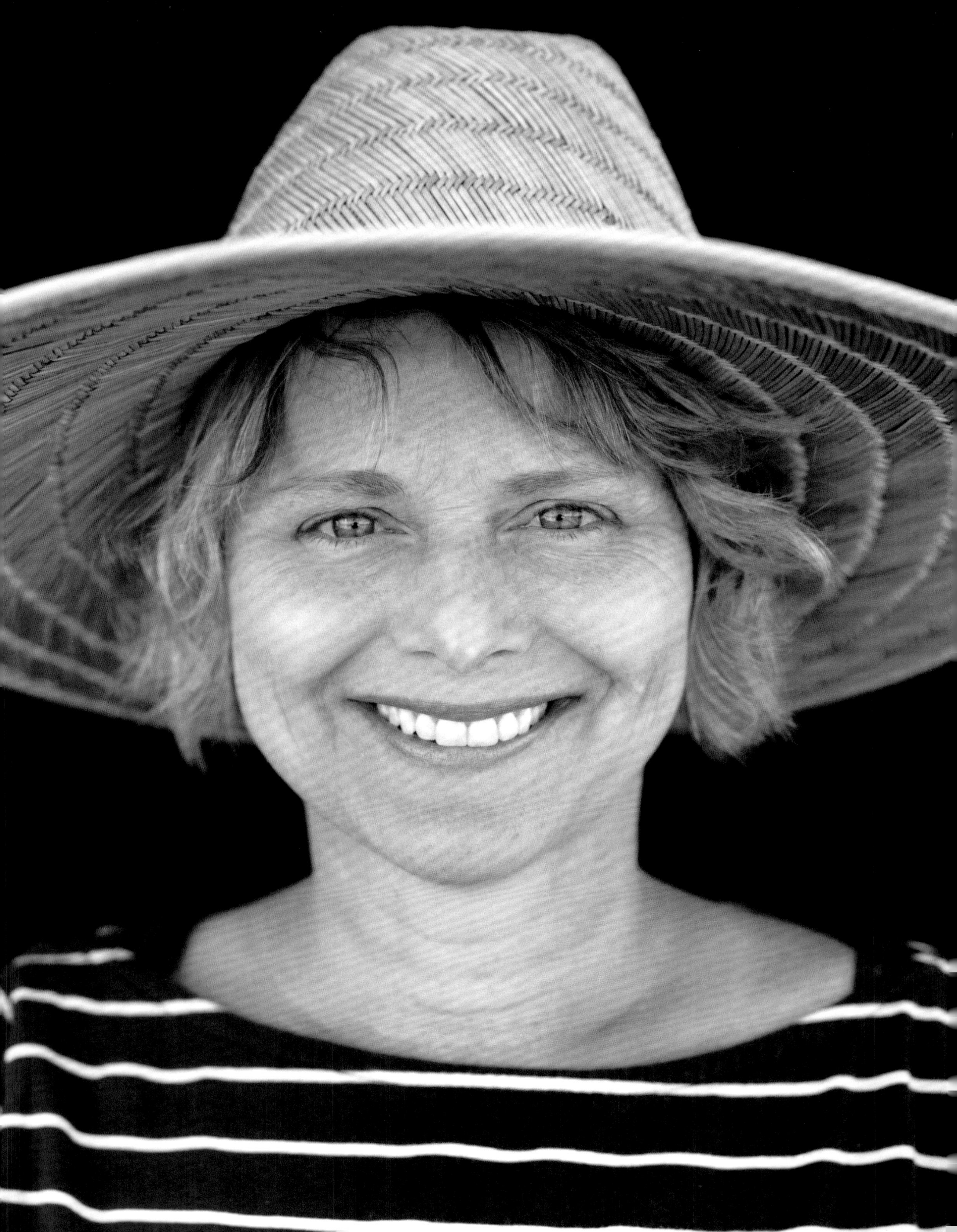

Cathleen Sutherland

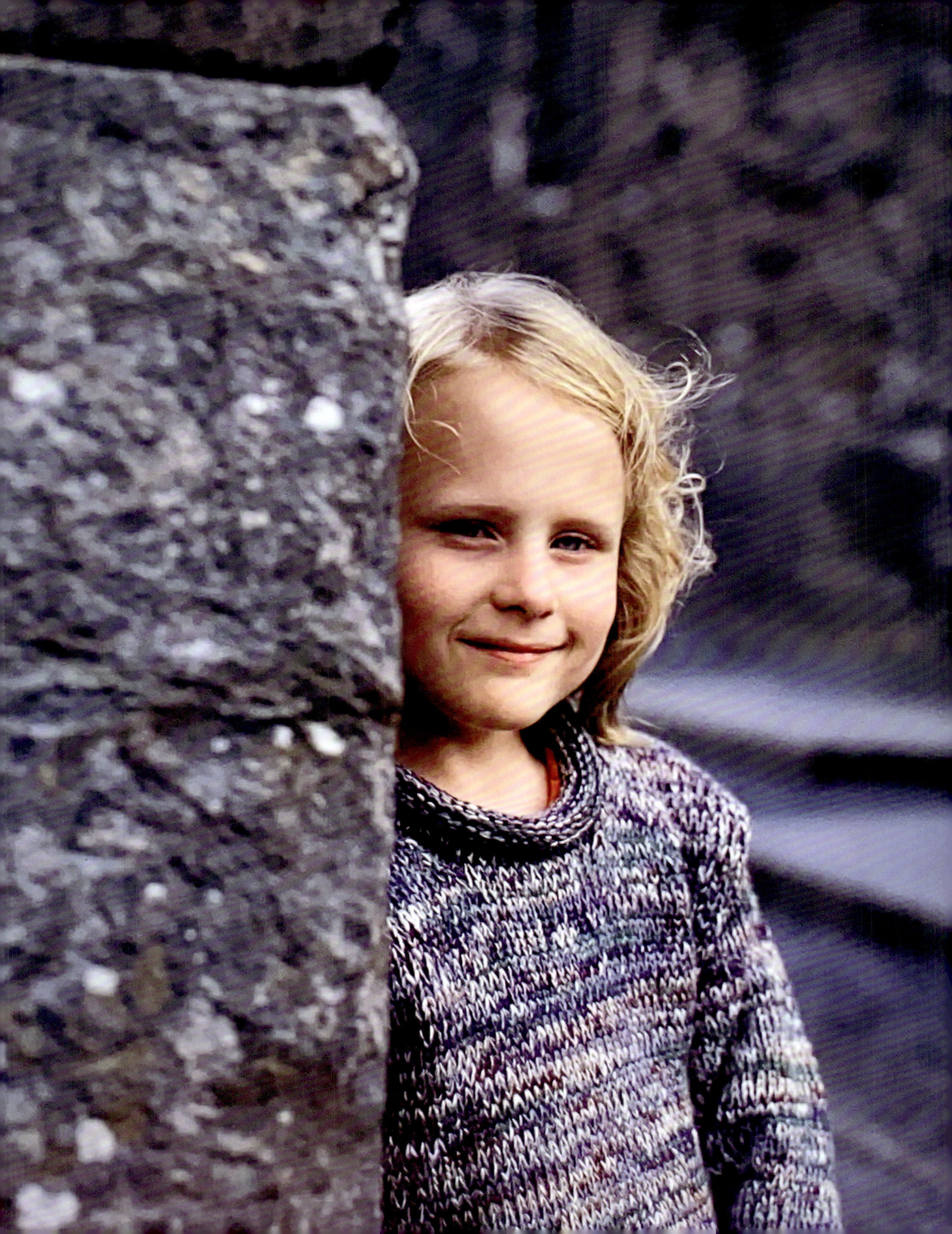

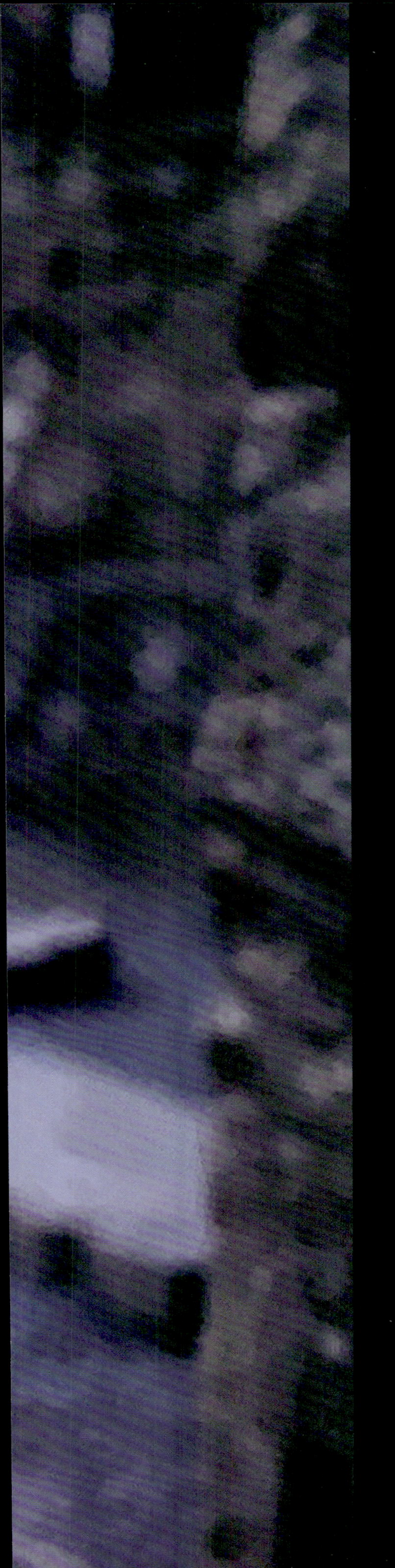

Sinéad Lankes

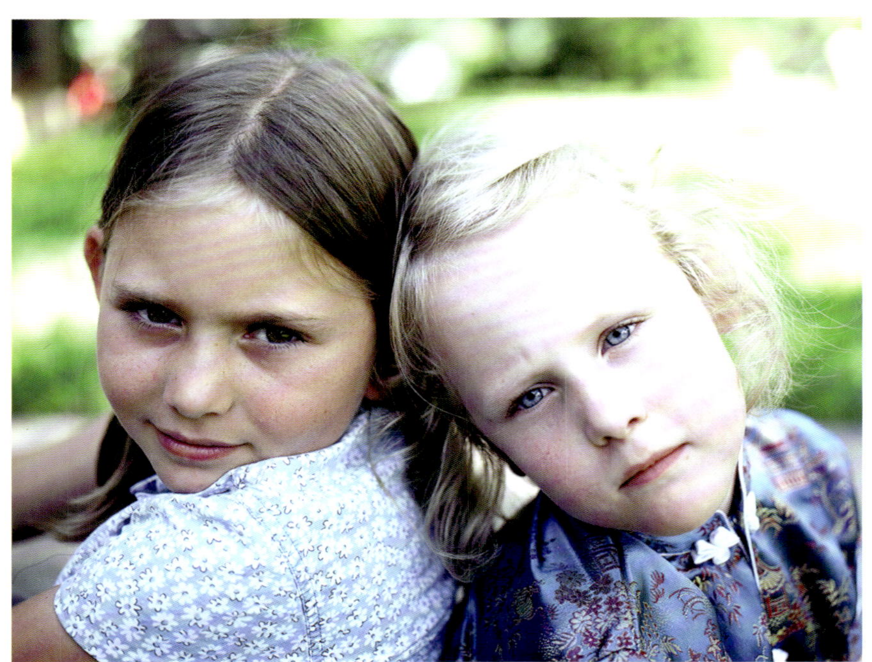

Nicolette and Sinéad

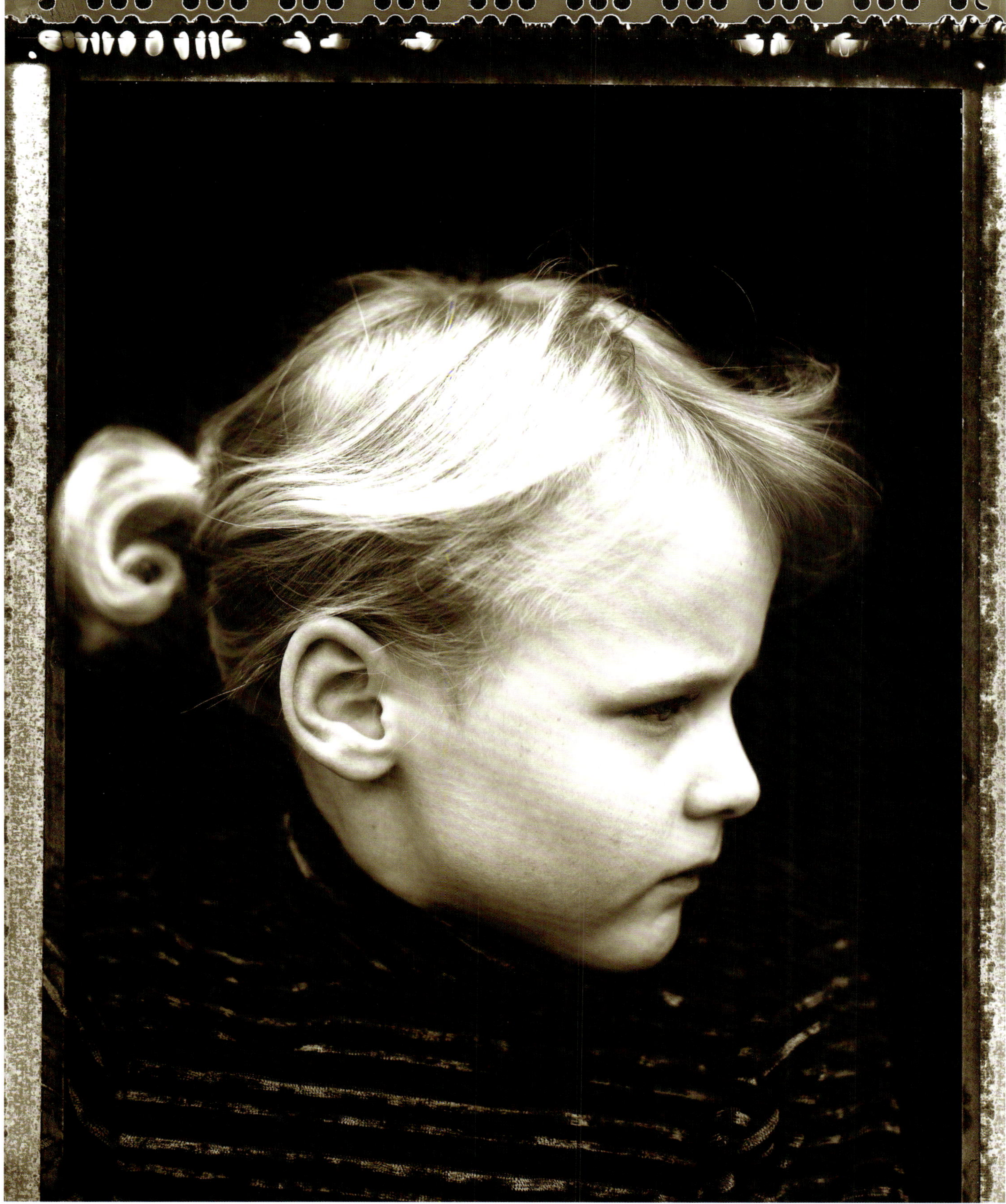

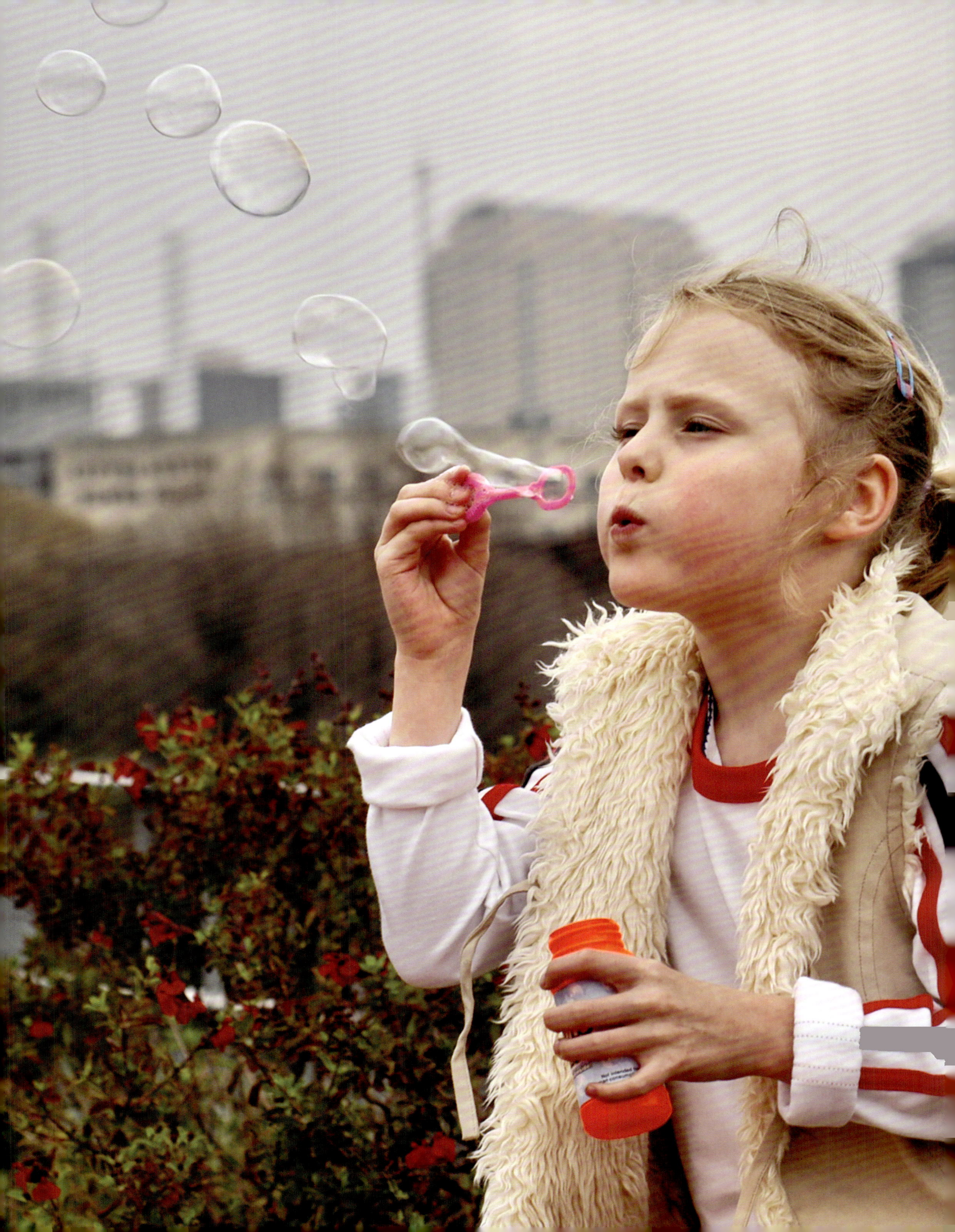

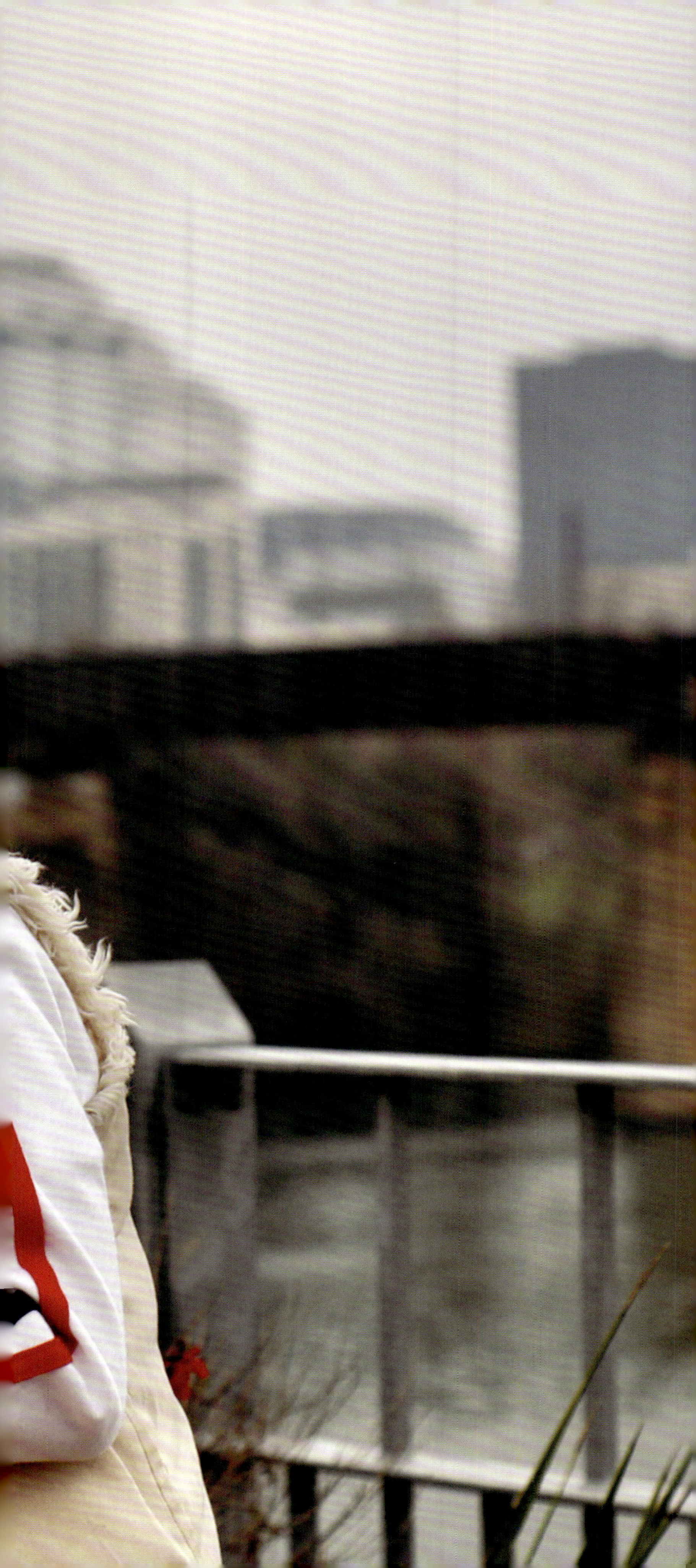

Sinéad

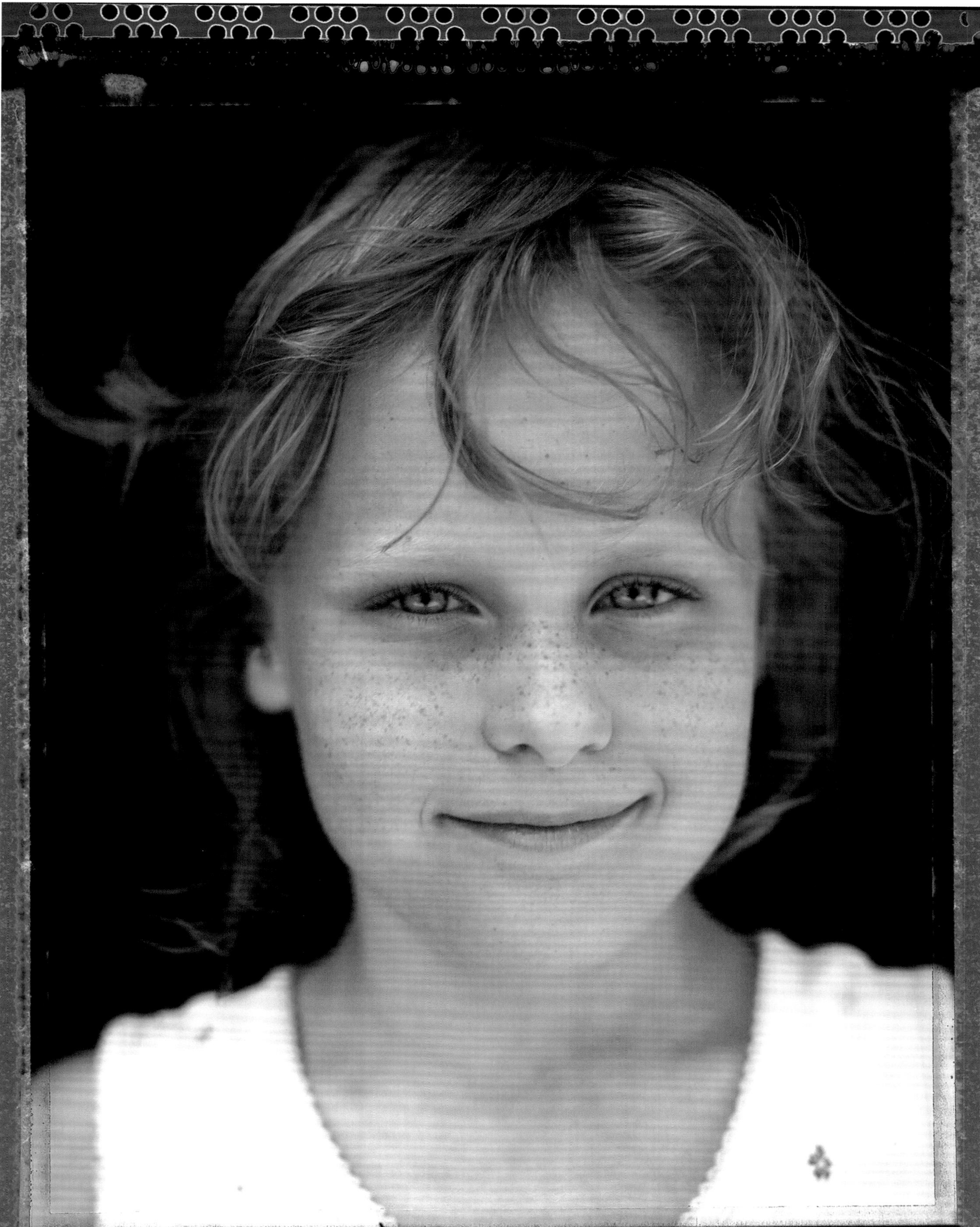

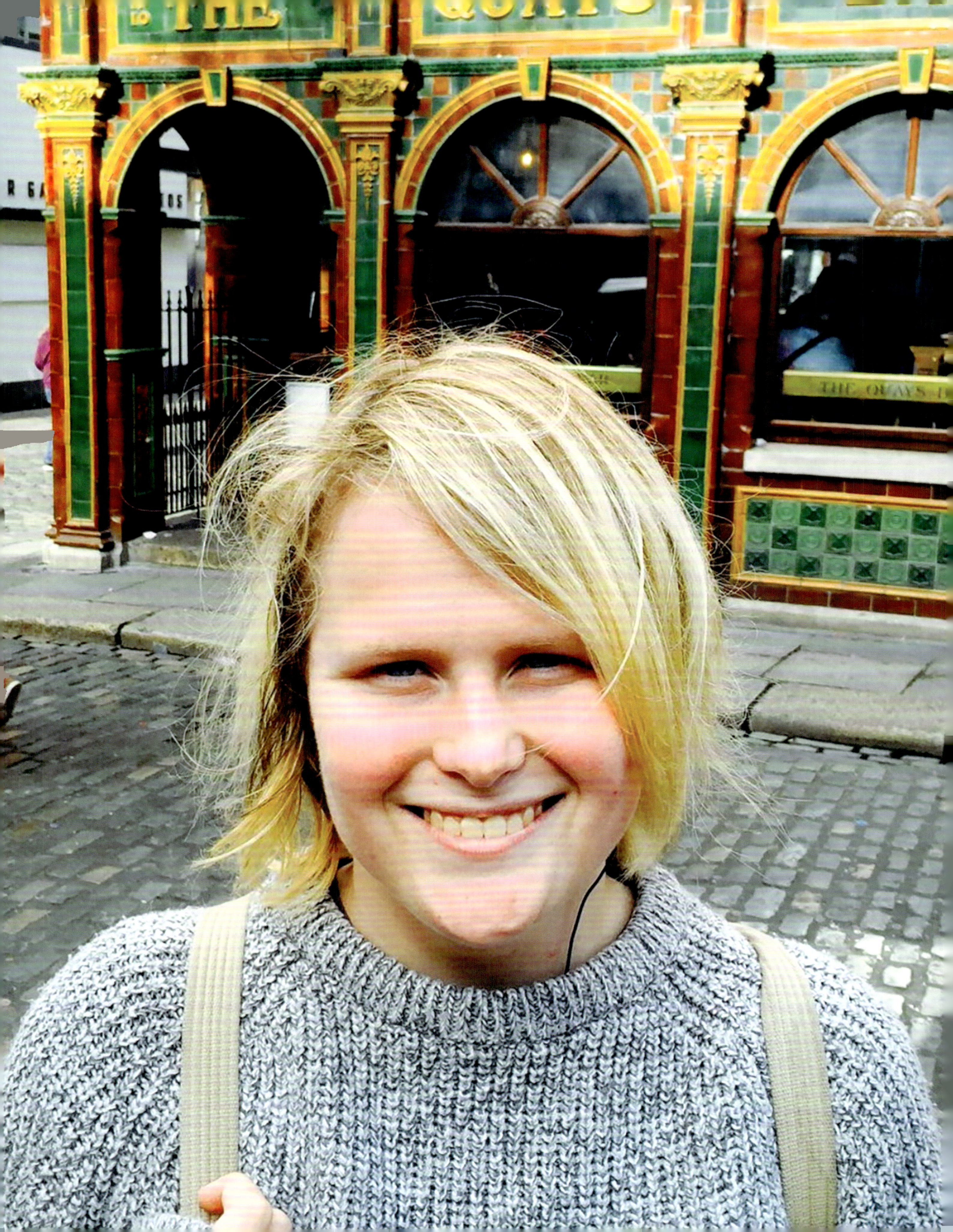
THE
THE QUAYS

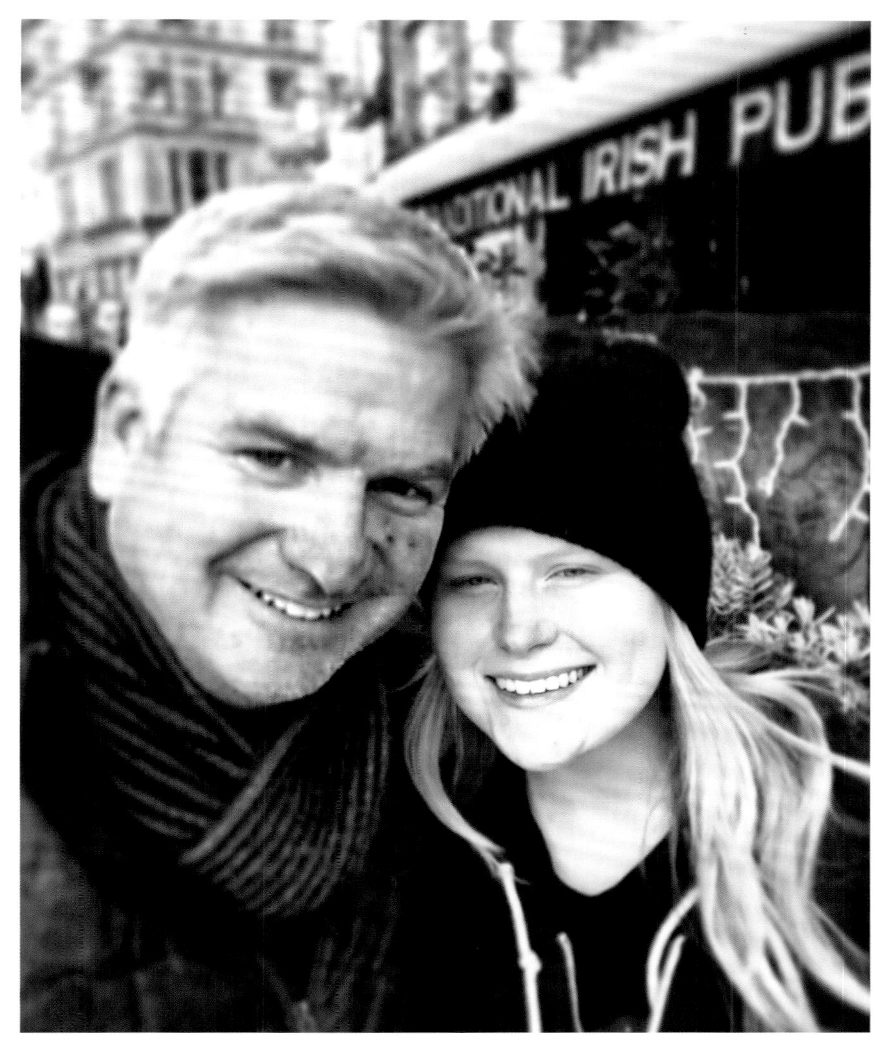

Matt and Sinéad

Sinéad

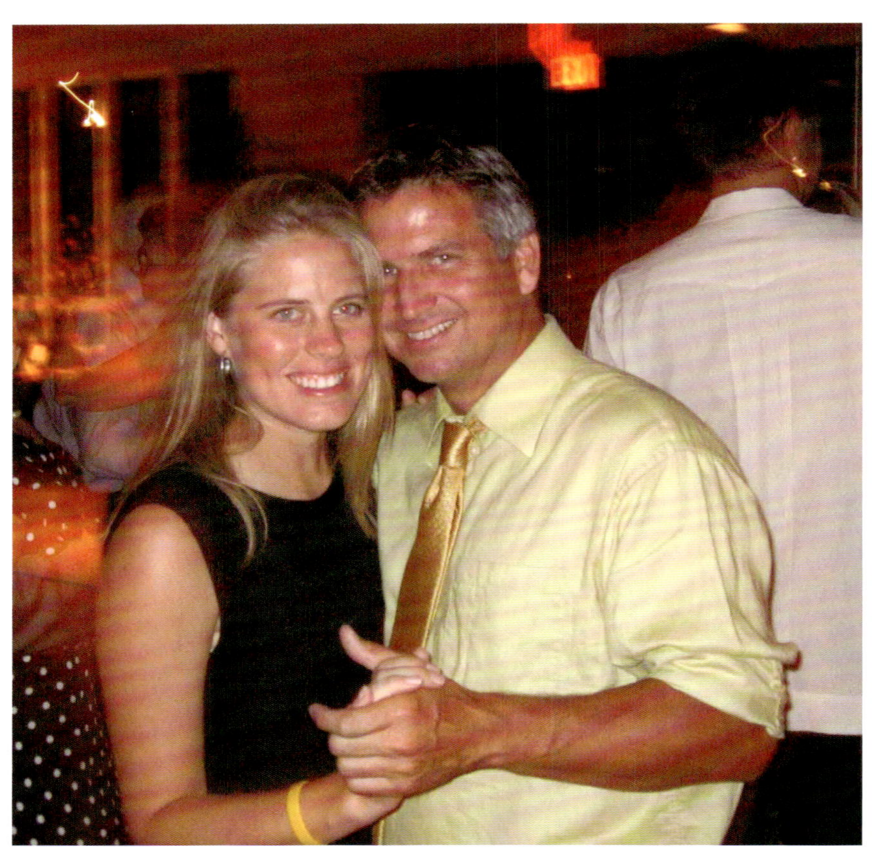

Jamie and Matt

Jamie Nicholson Lankes

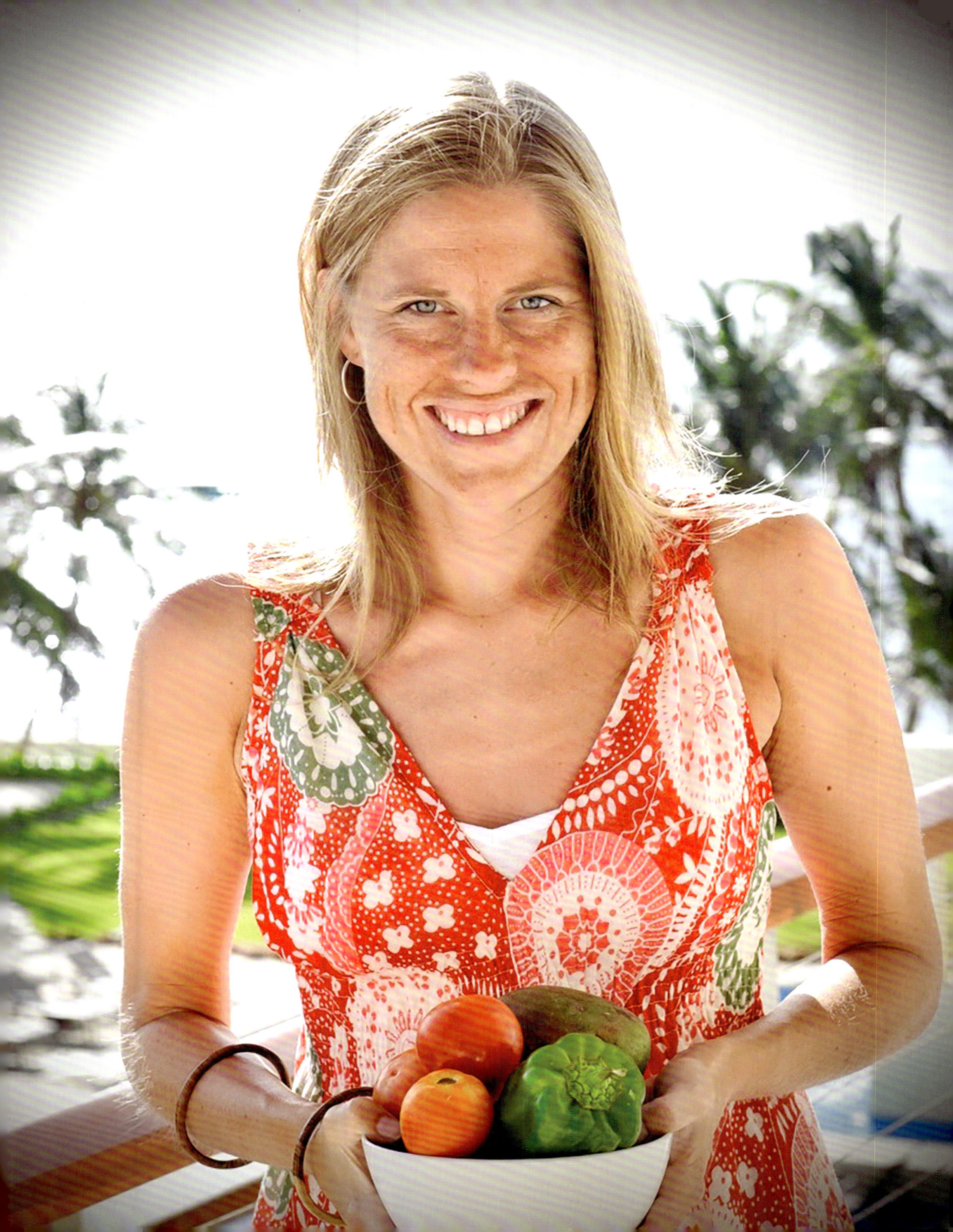

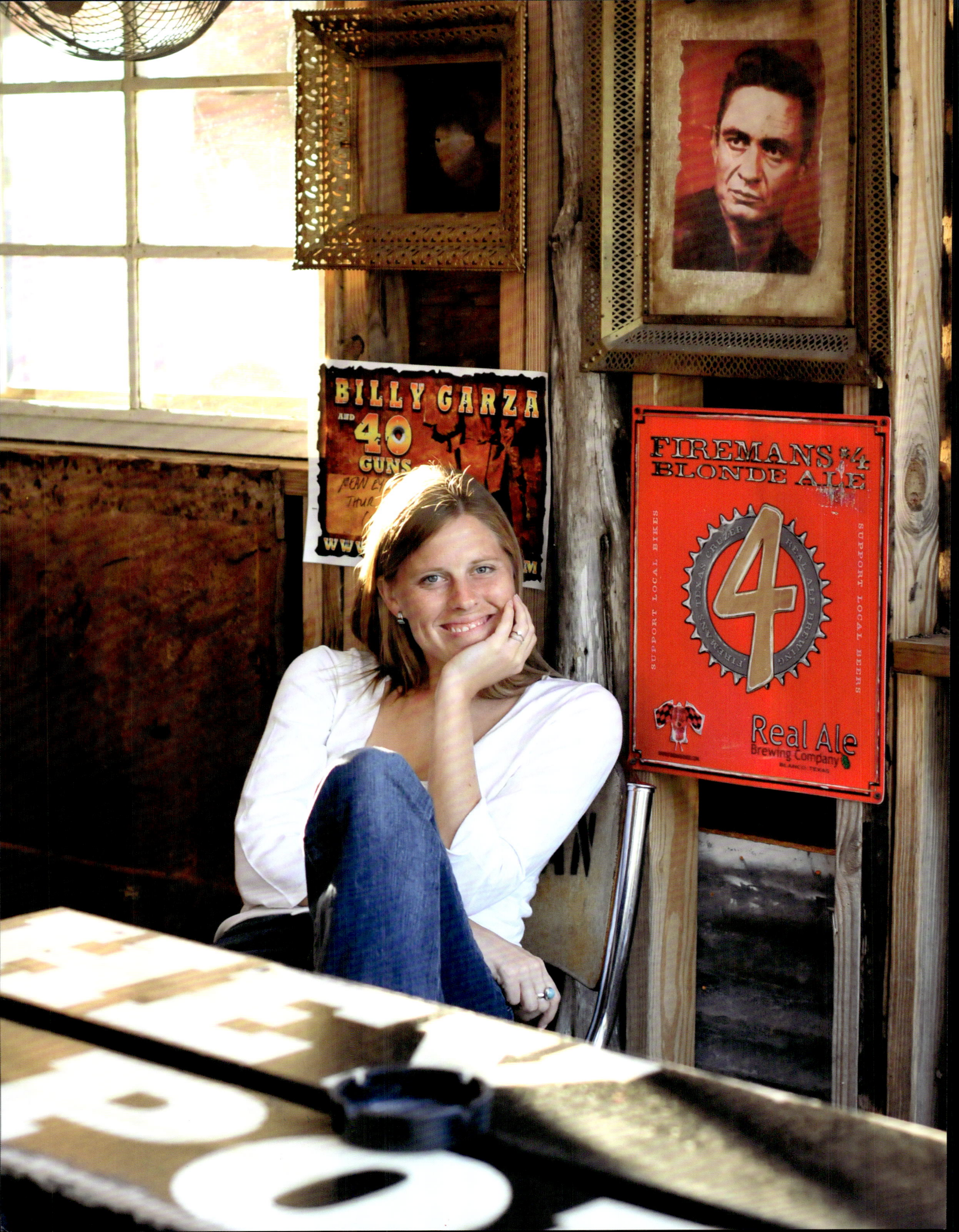

BILLY GARZA
AND
40
GUNS
FIREMANS #4
BLONDE ALE
SUPPORT LOCAL BIKES
4
SUPPORT LOCAL BEERS
Real Ale
Brewing Company

Jamie

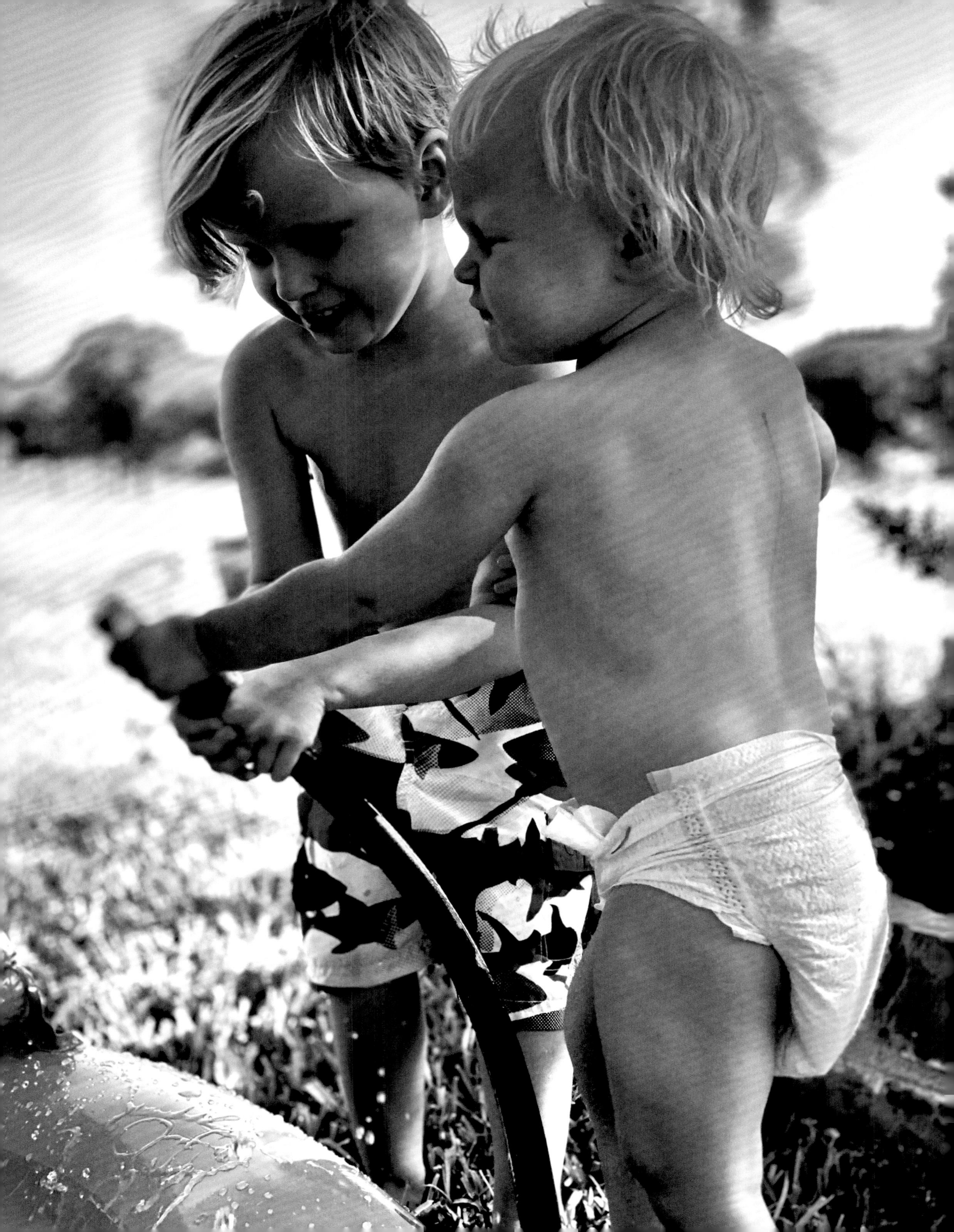

Daisy and **Maggie**

Nick Lankes and **Jamie**

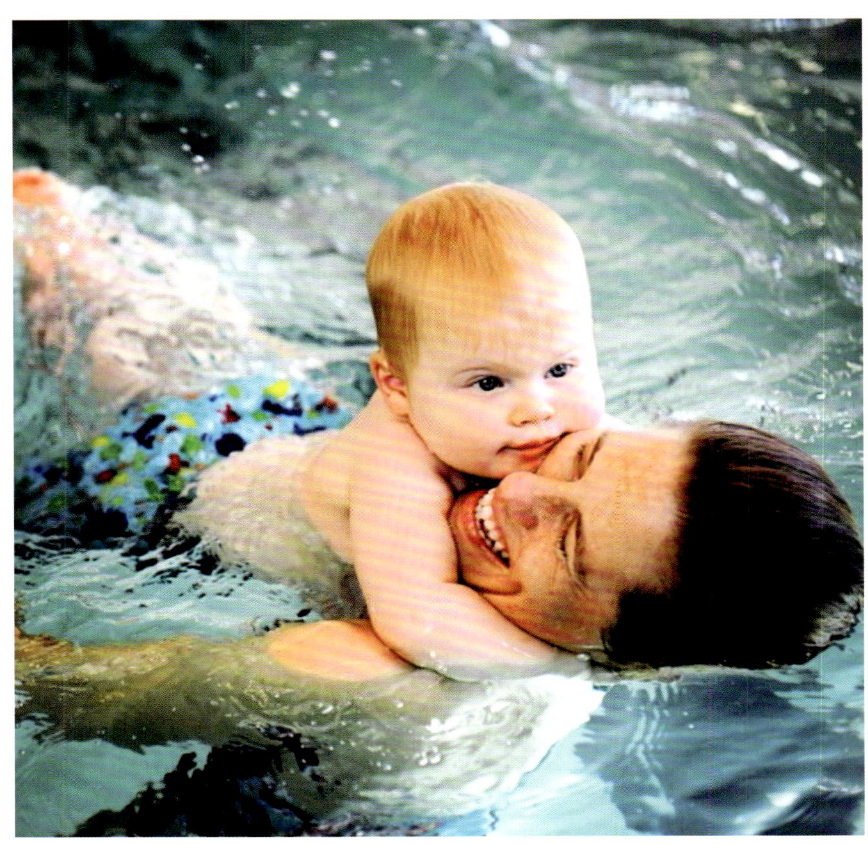

Jamie and **Nick**

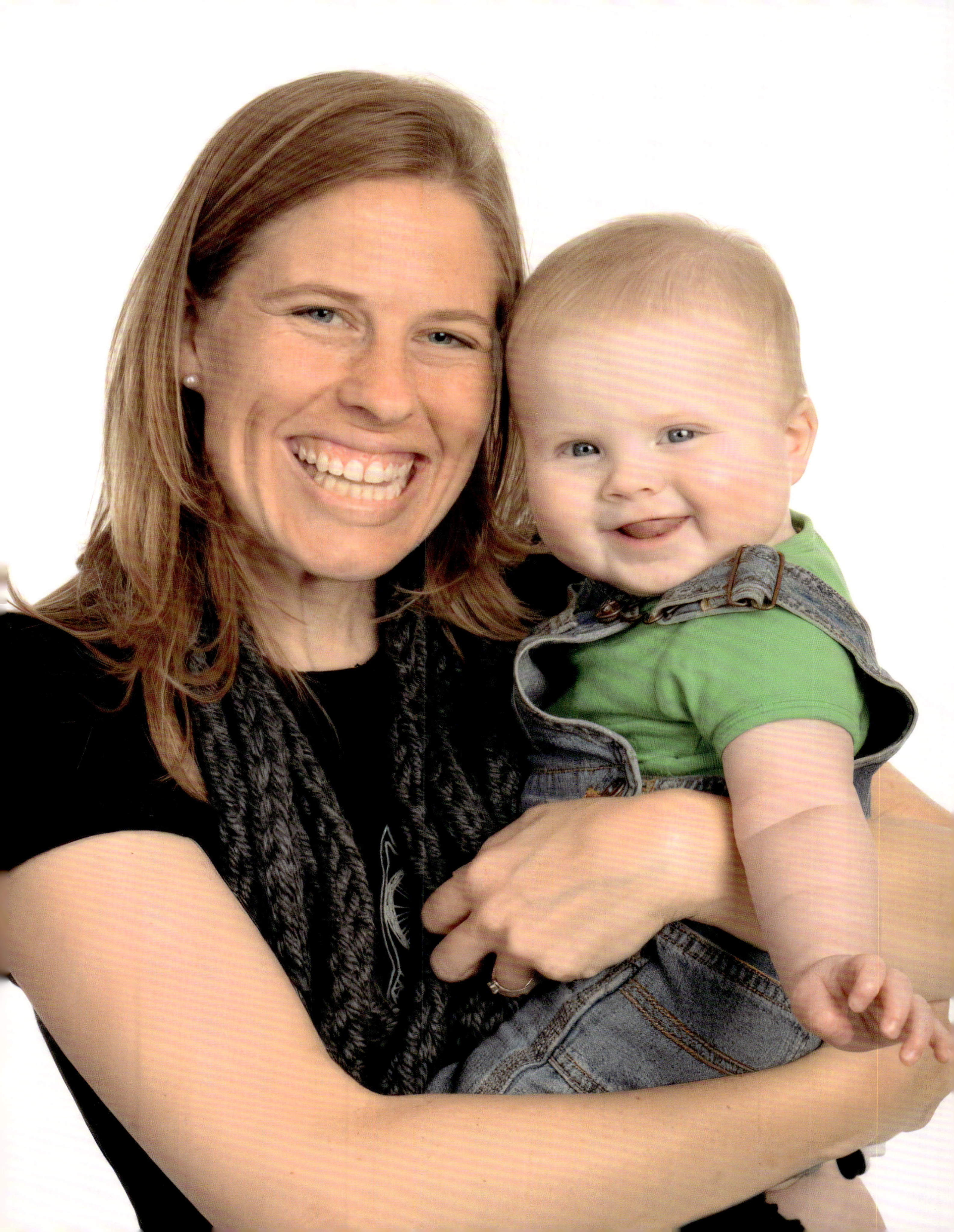

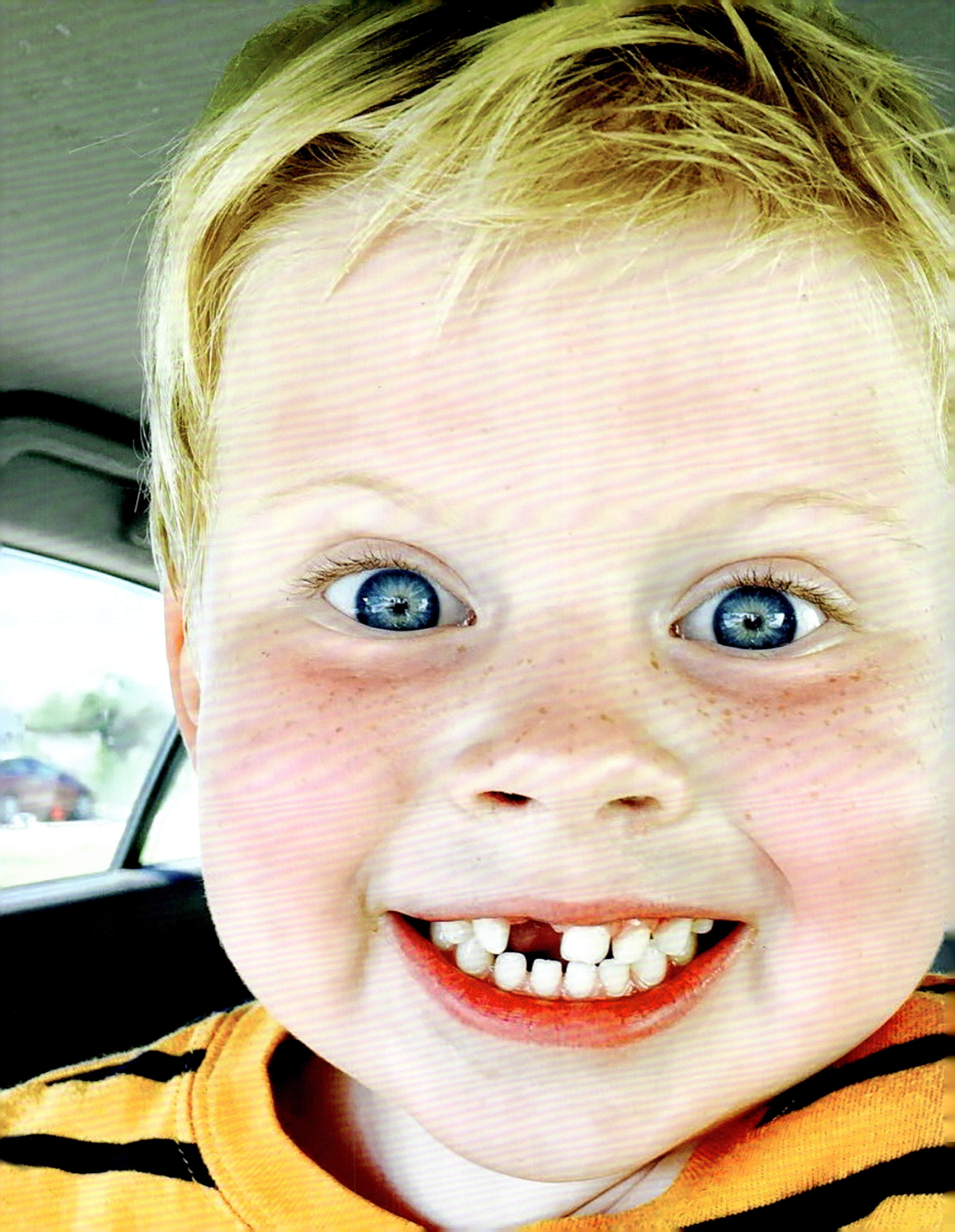

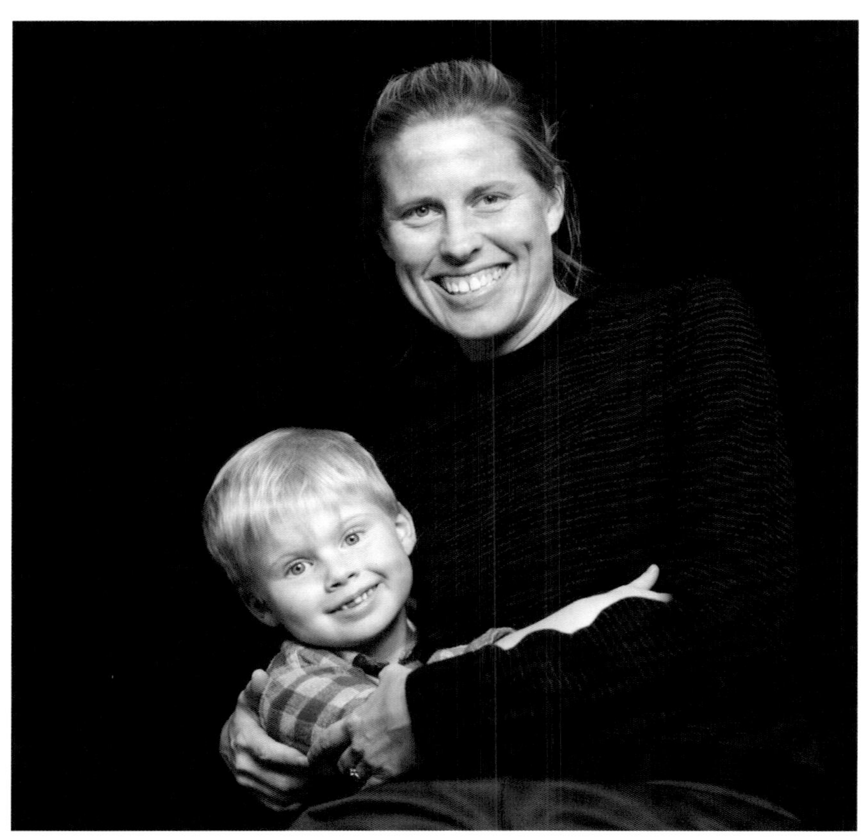

Nick and **Jamie**

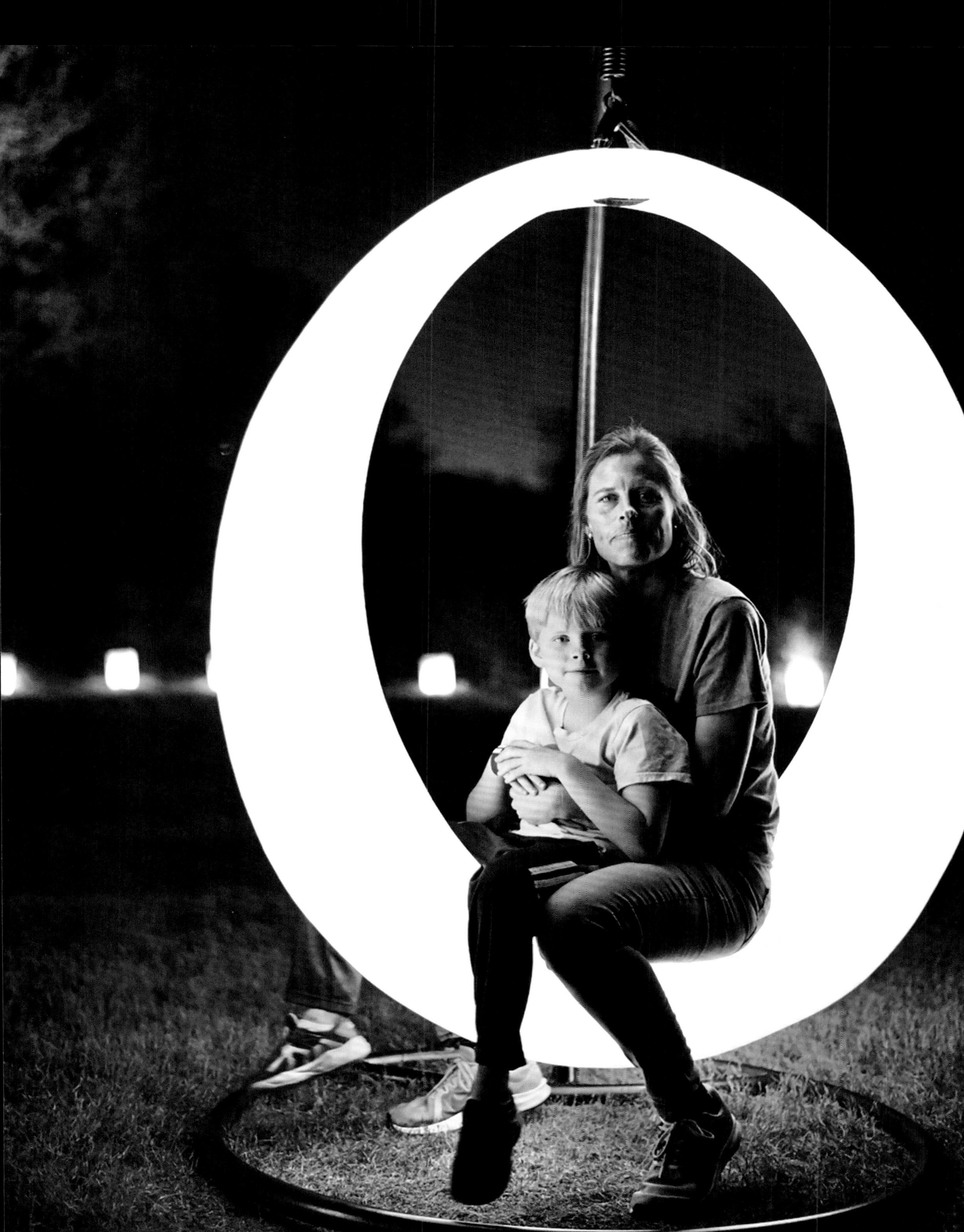

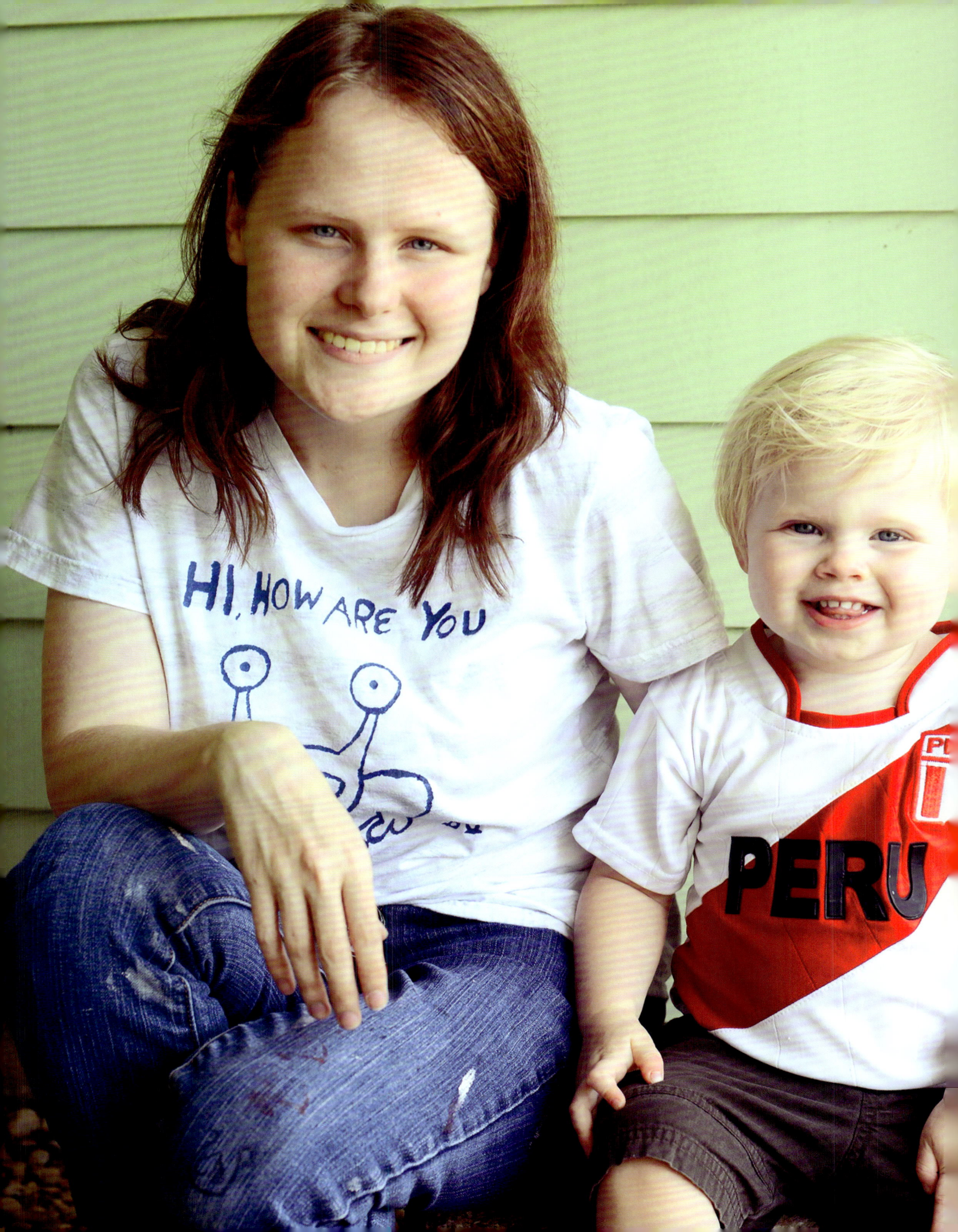
HI, HOW ARE YOU
PERU

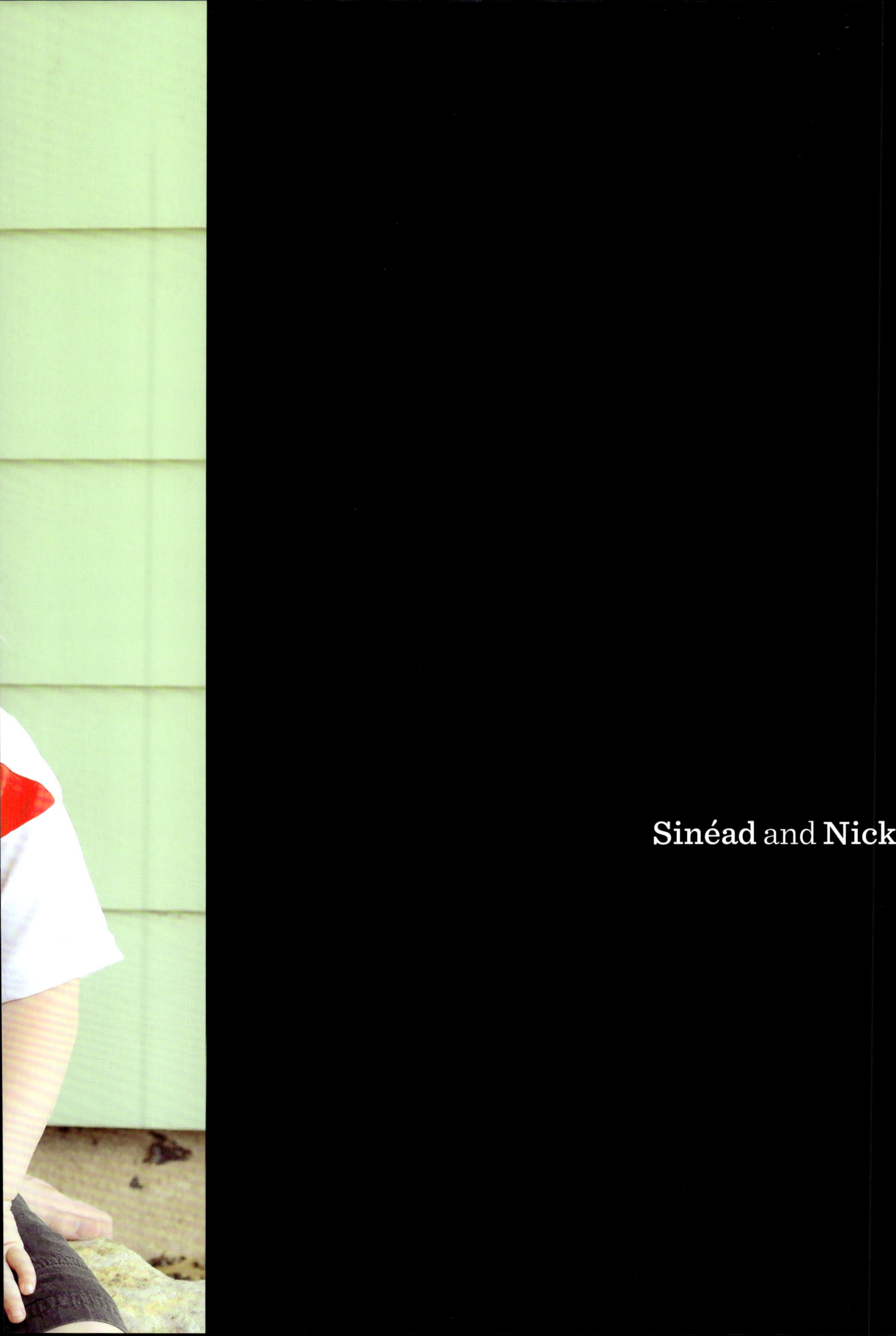

Sinéad and Nick

Nick

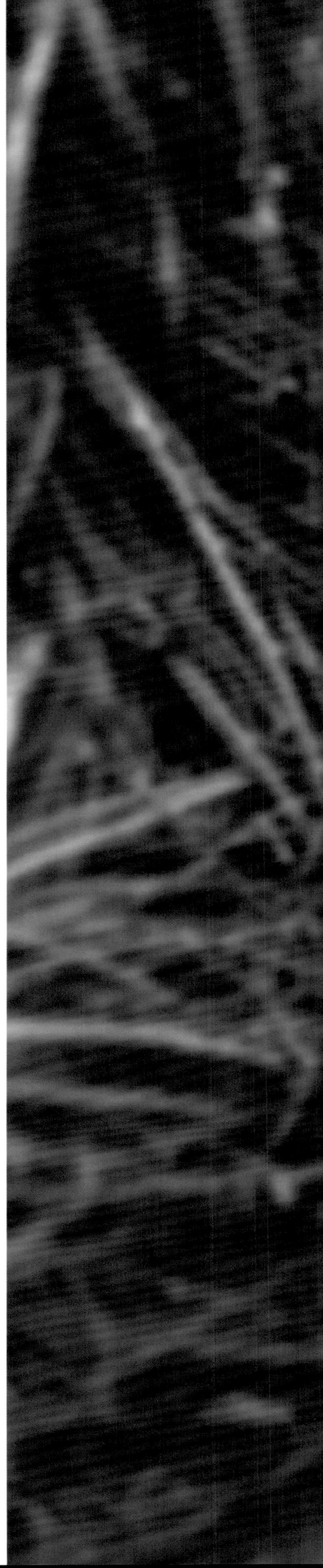

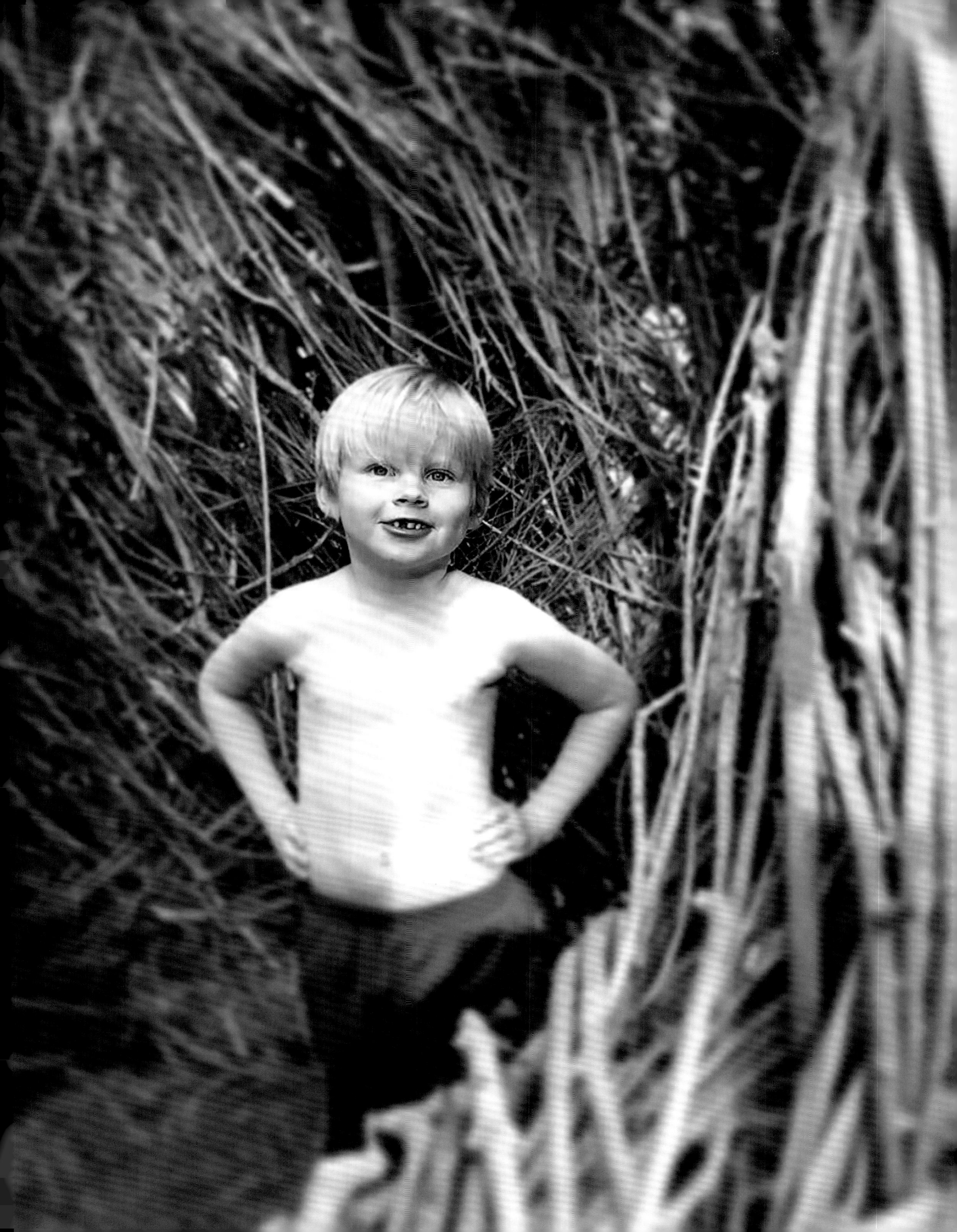

Nick

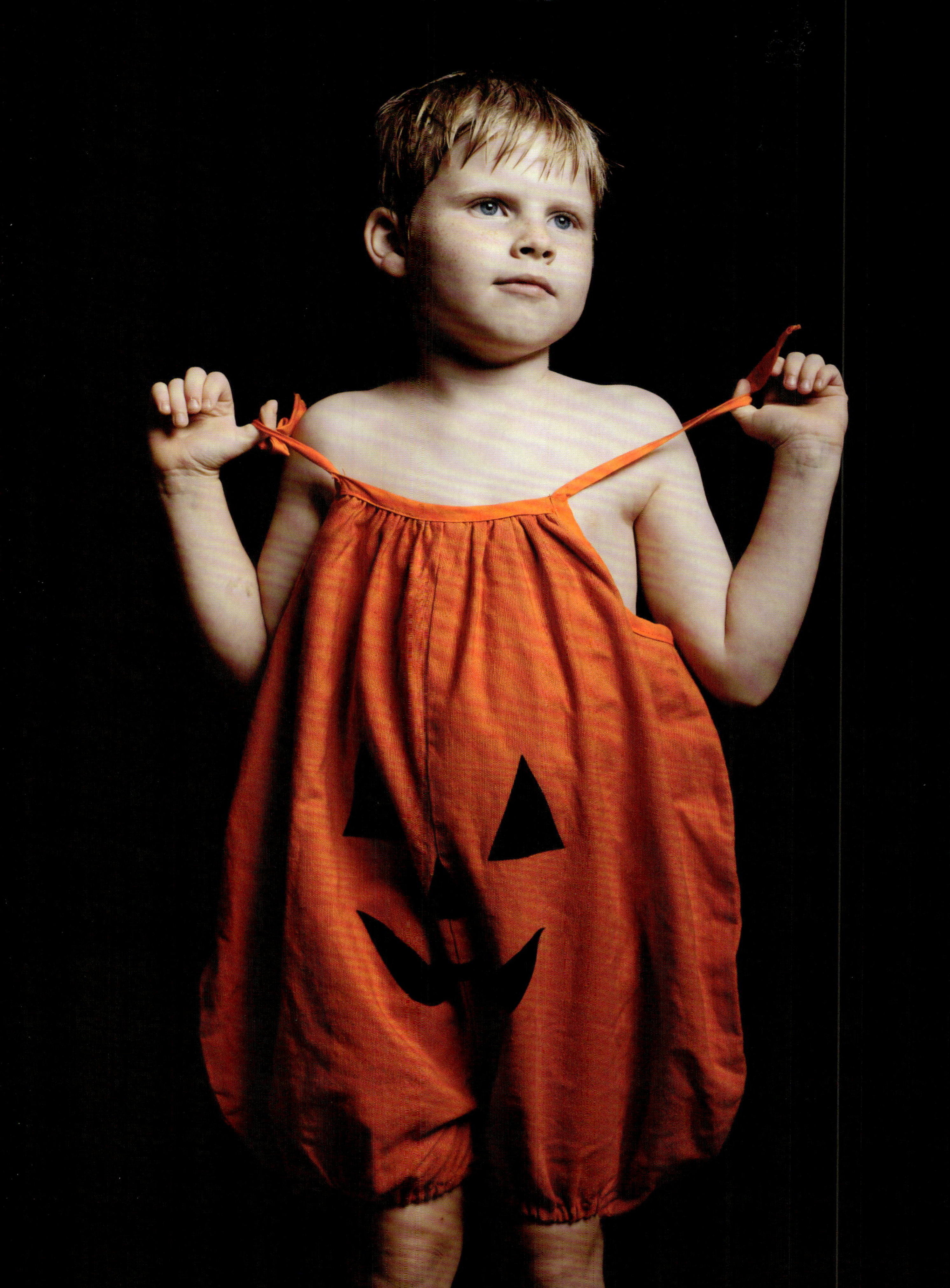

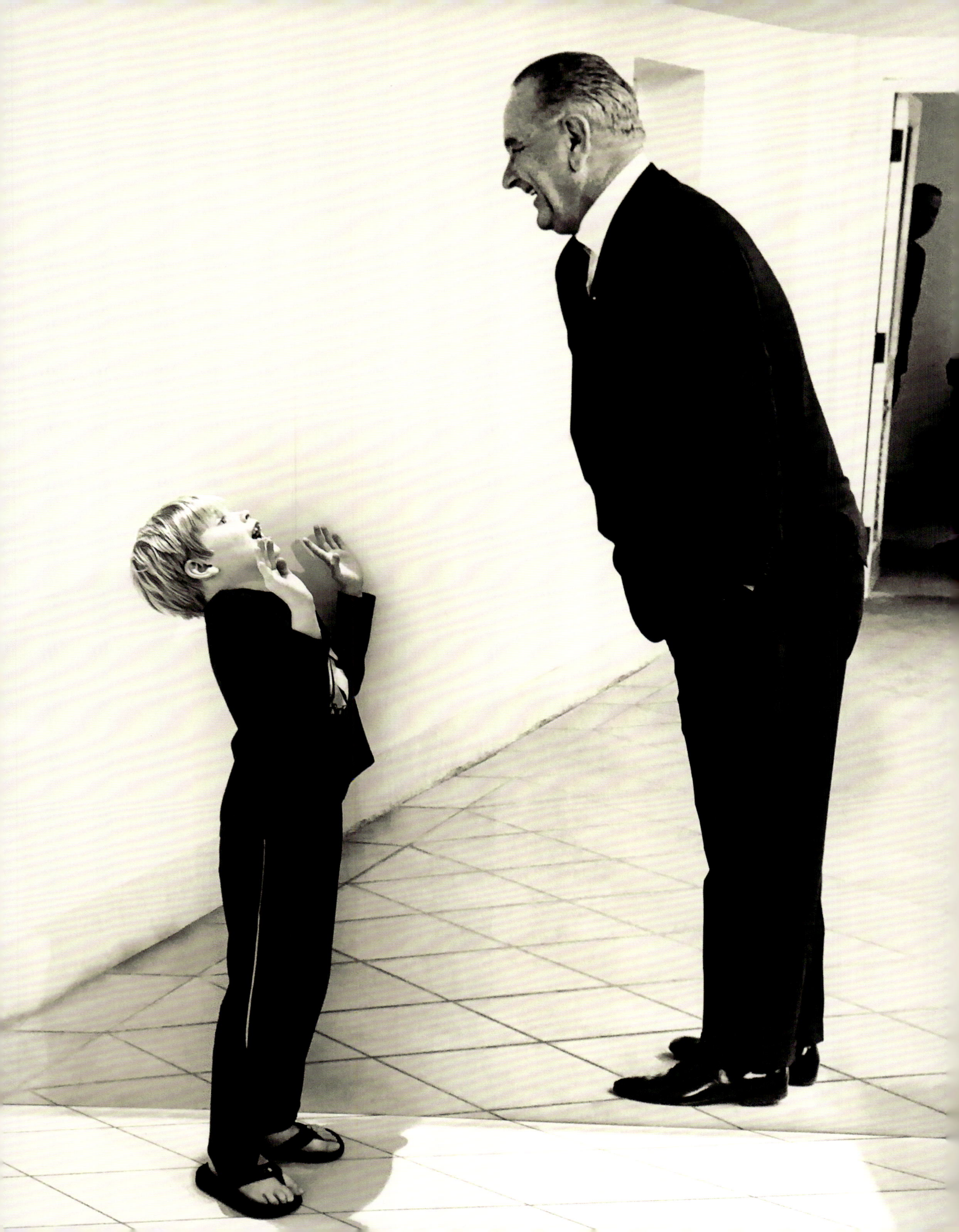

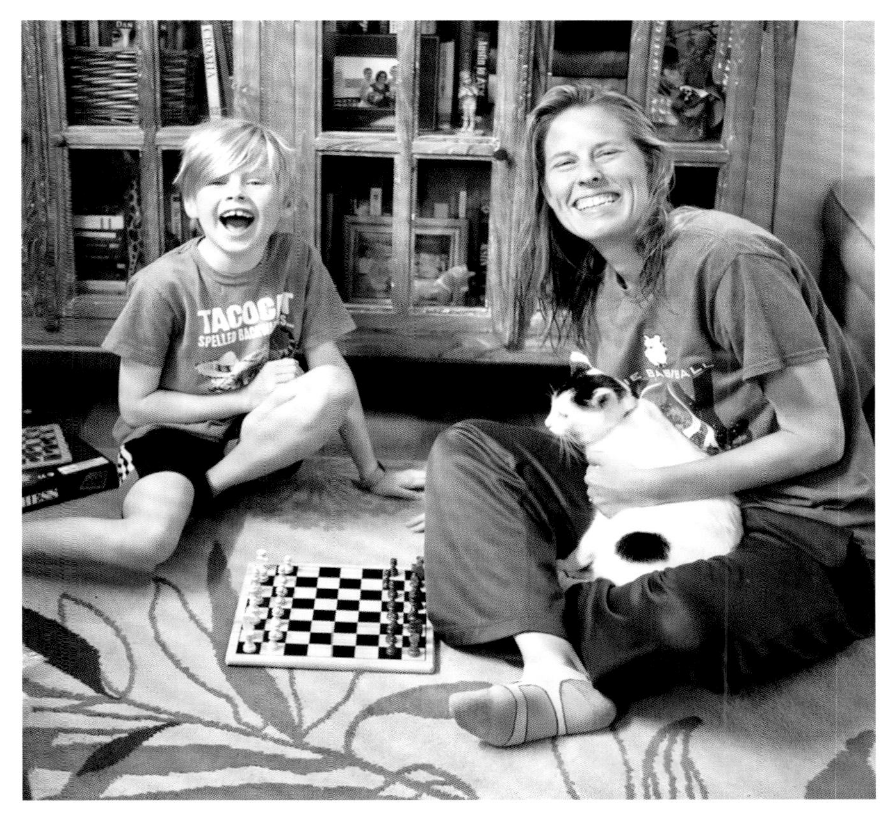

Nick and **Jamie**

Nick and LBJ

Nick

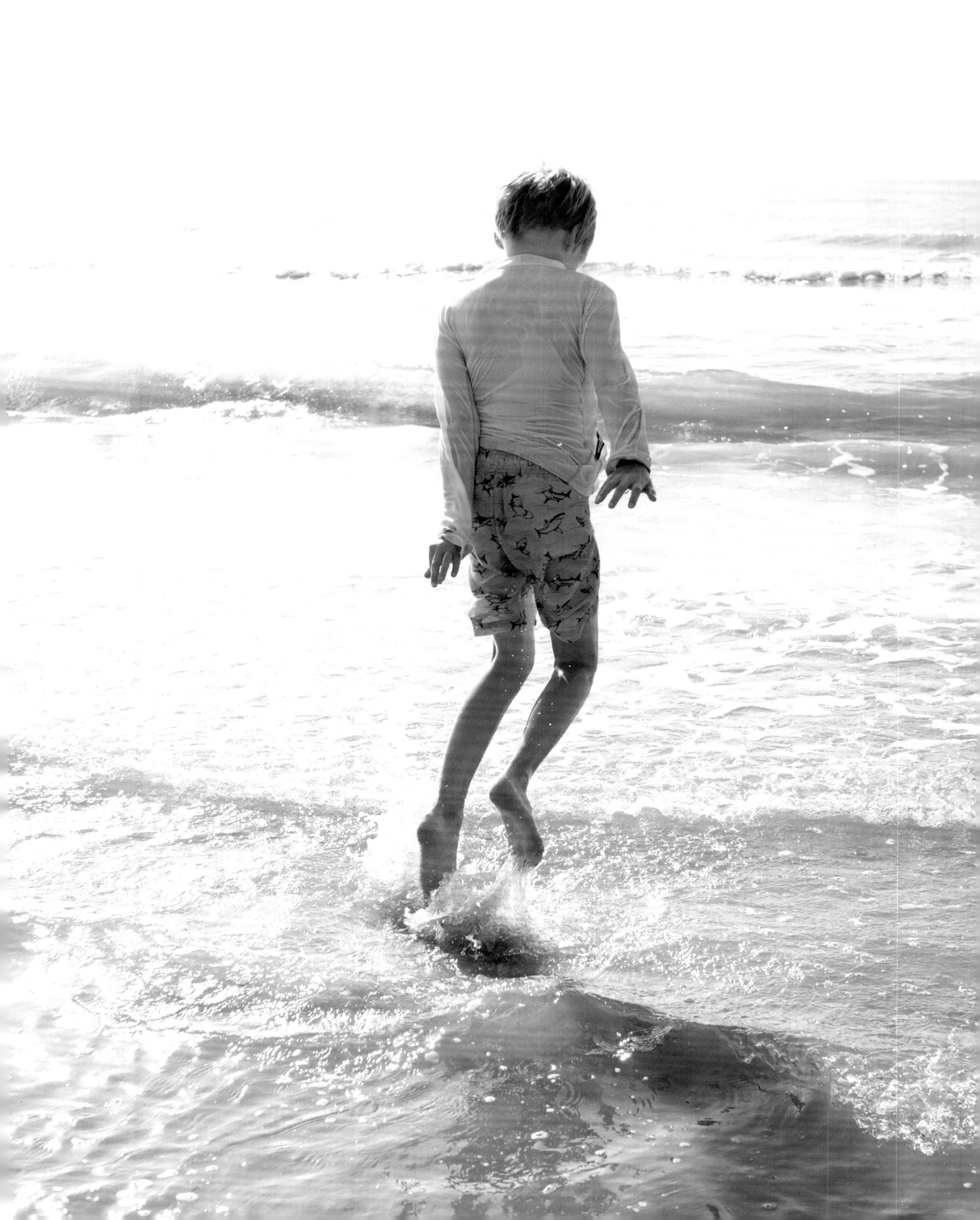

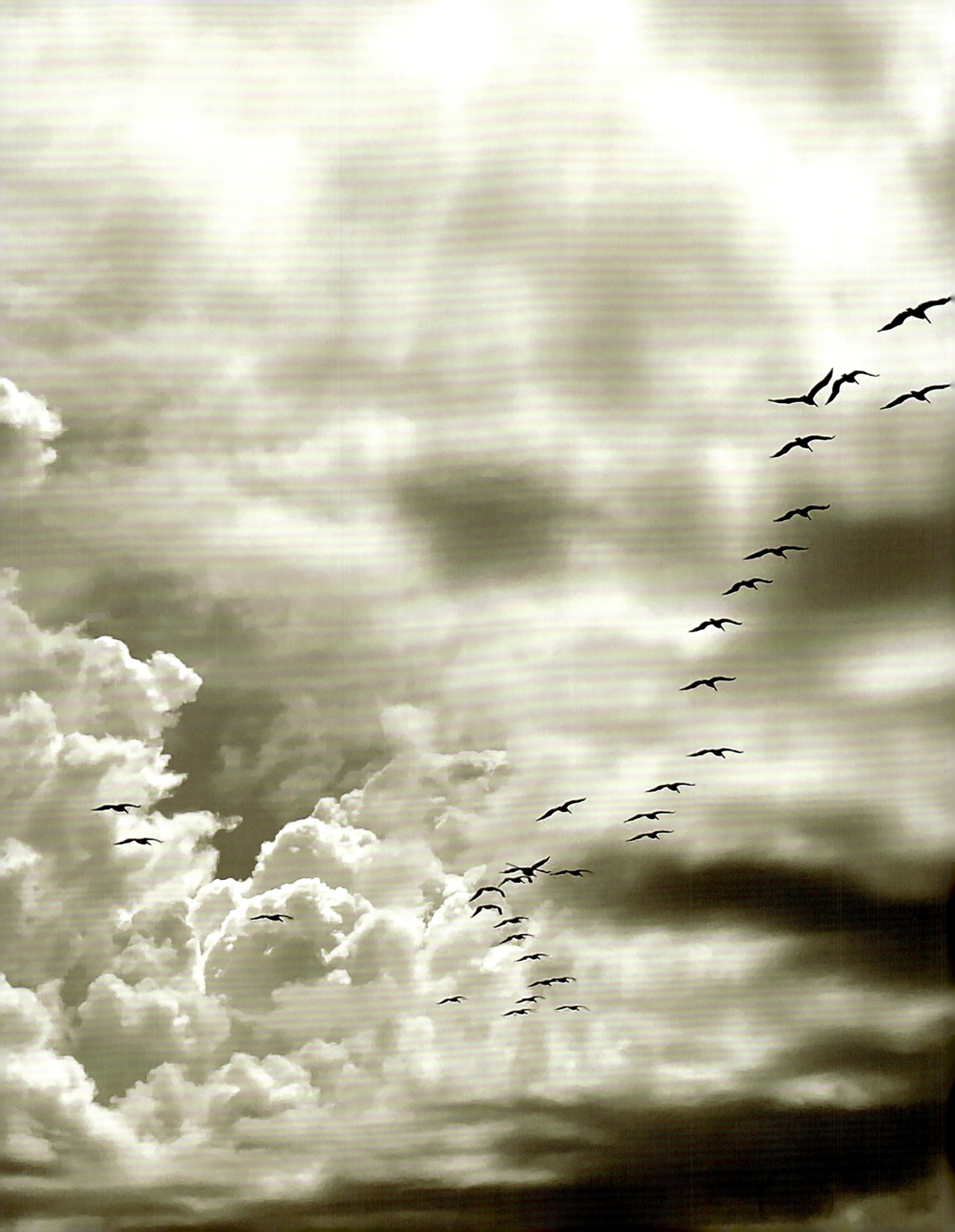

Nick

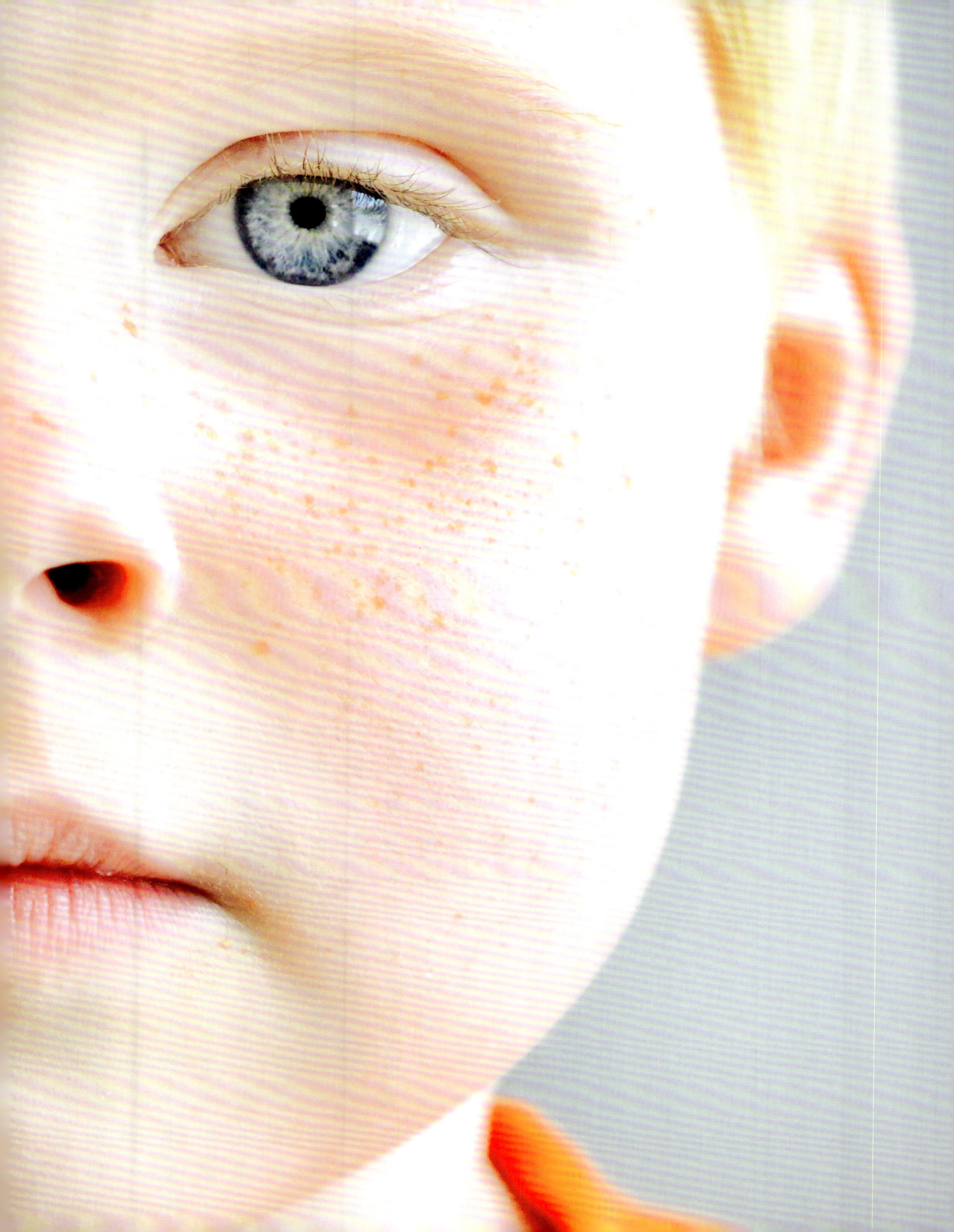

Nick

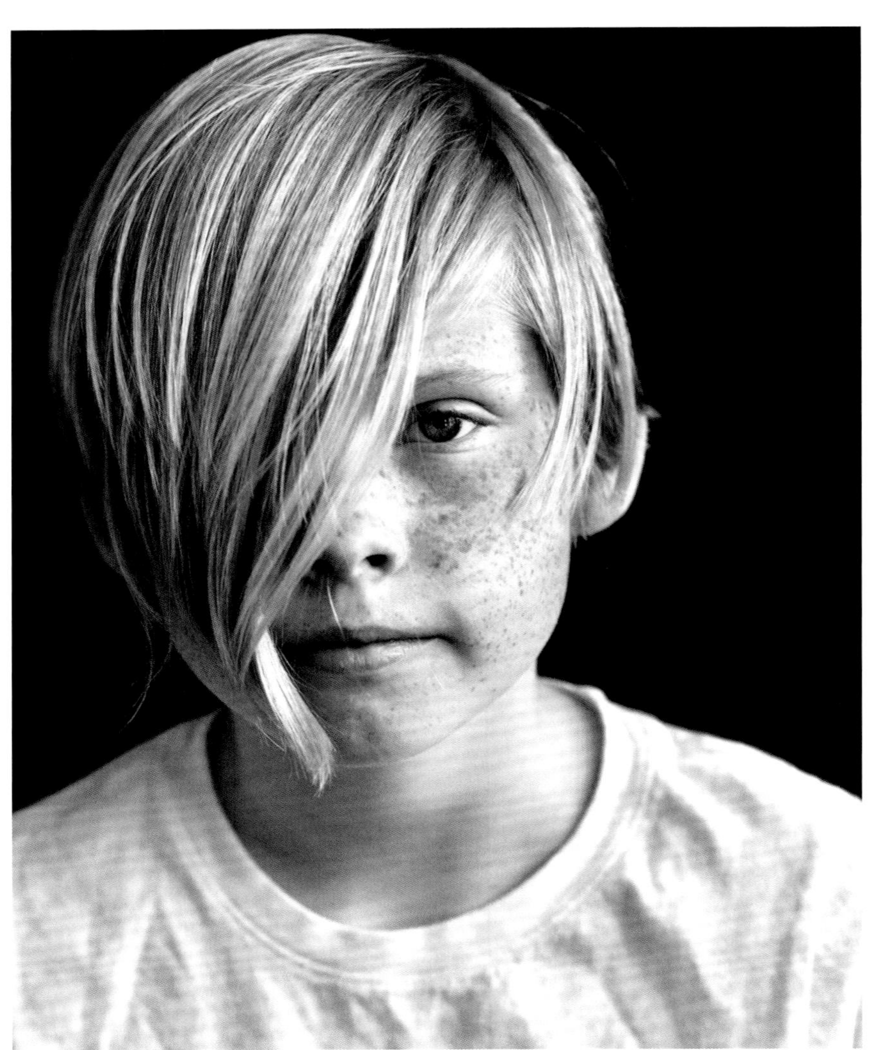

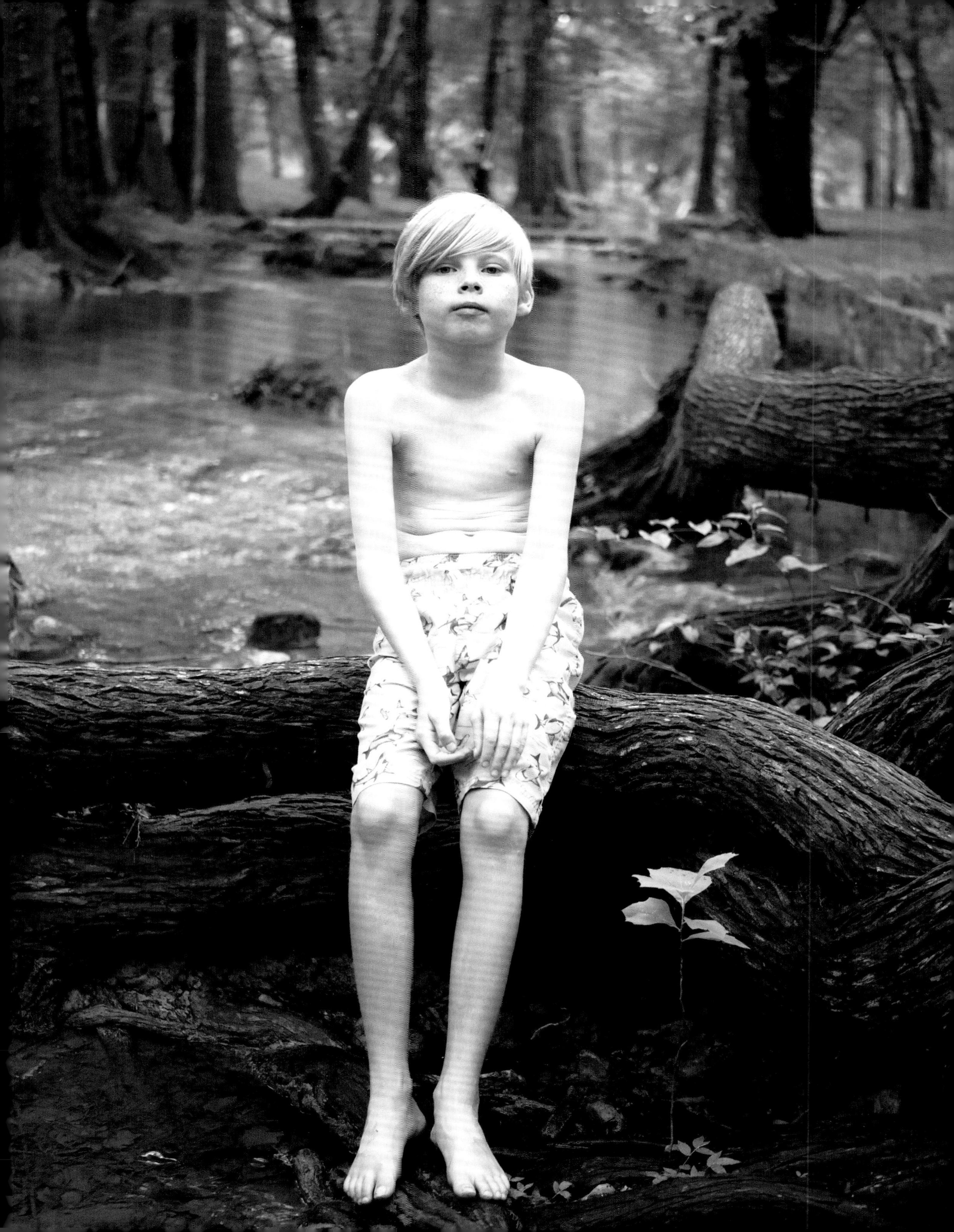

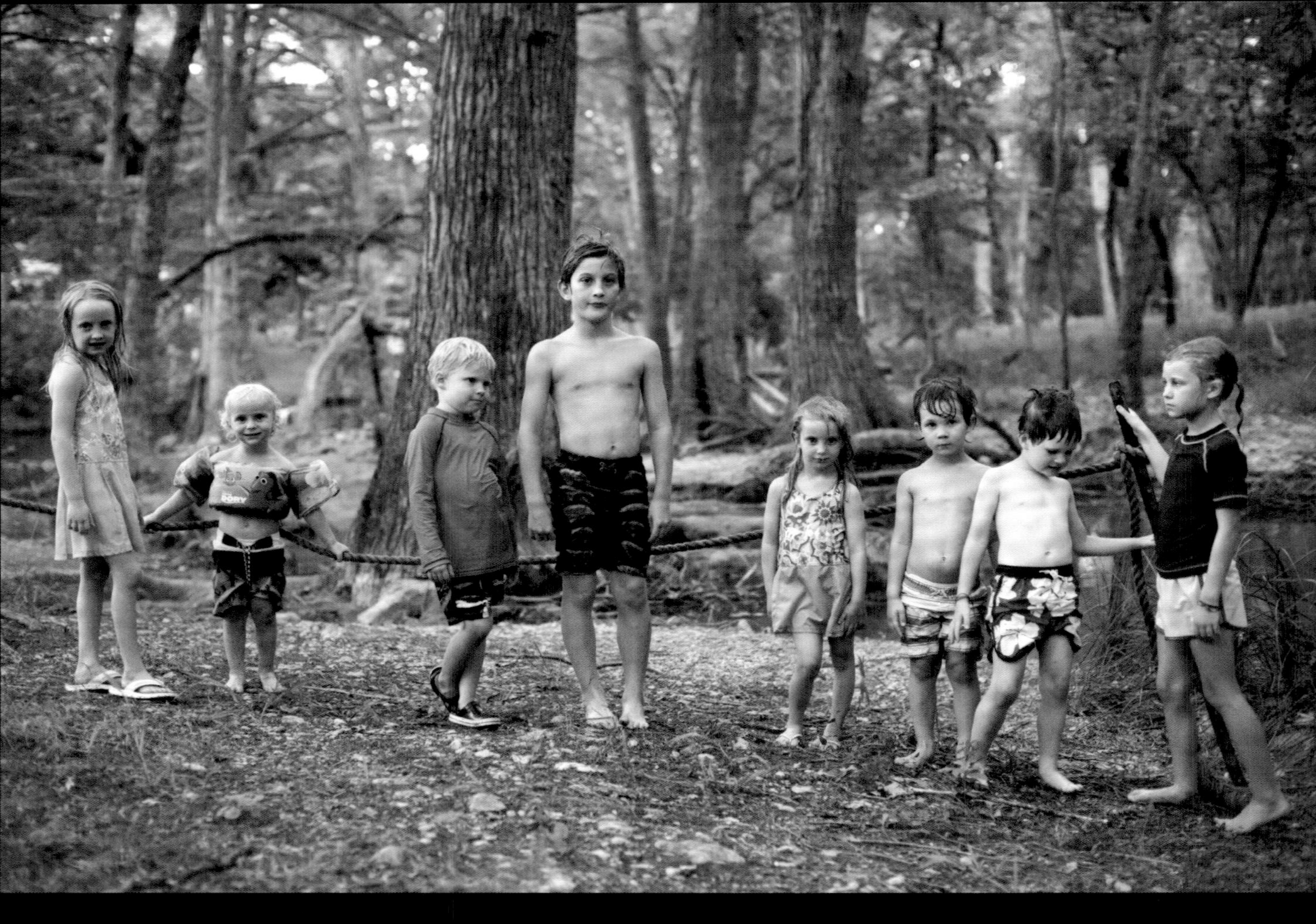

***Matt** captured children at play in 2017 with, left to right, **Lola**, **Torsten**, **Nick**, **Trent**, **Autumn**, **Penn**, **Anders**, and **Maren**. Four years later, in 2021, he wrangled them again*

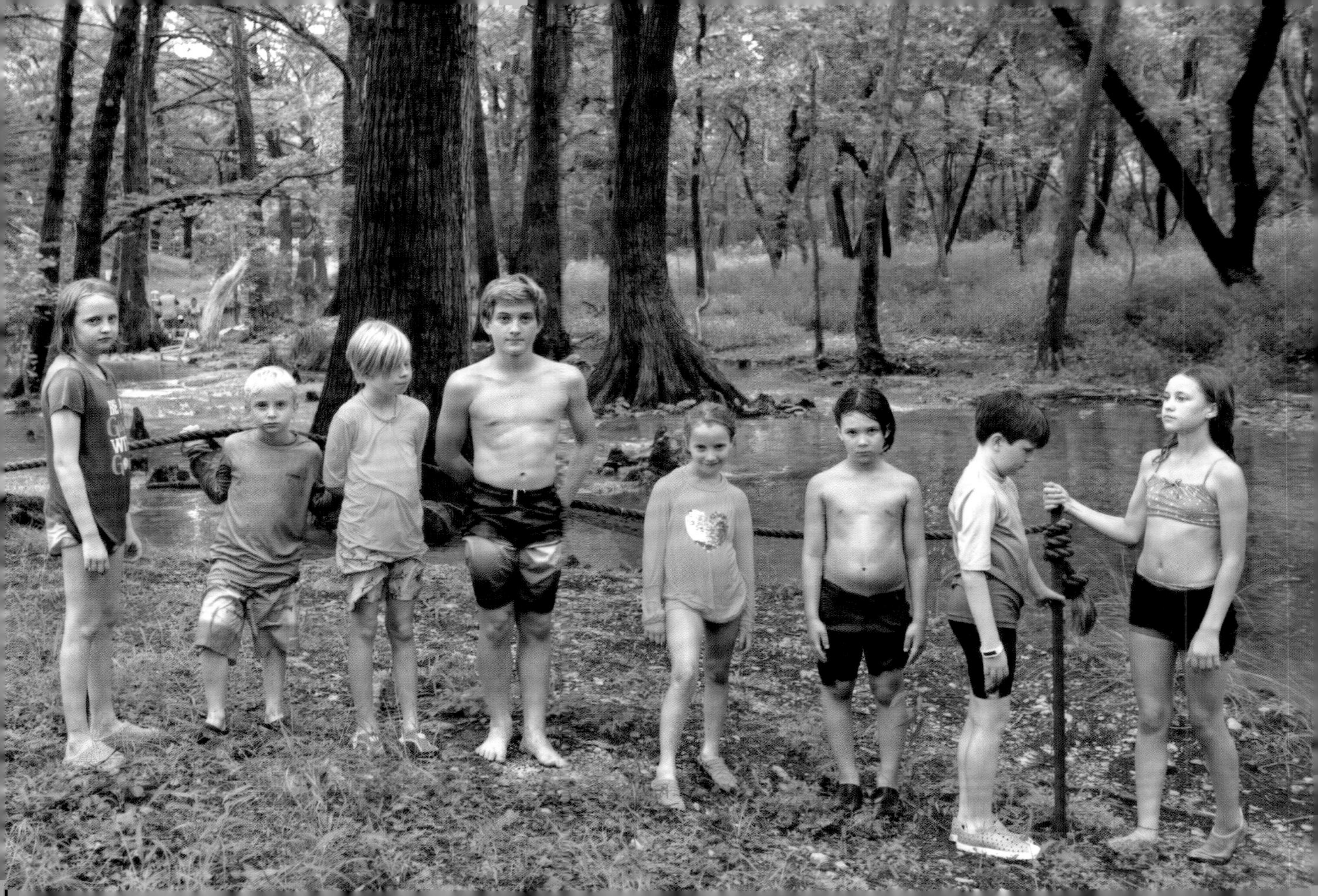

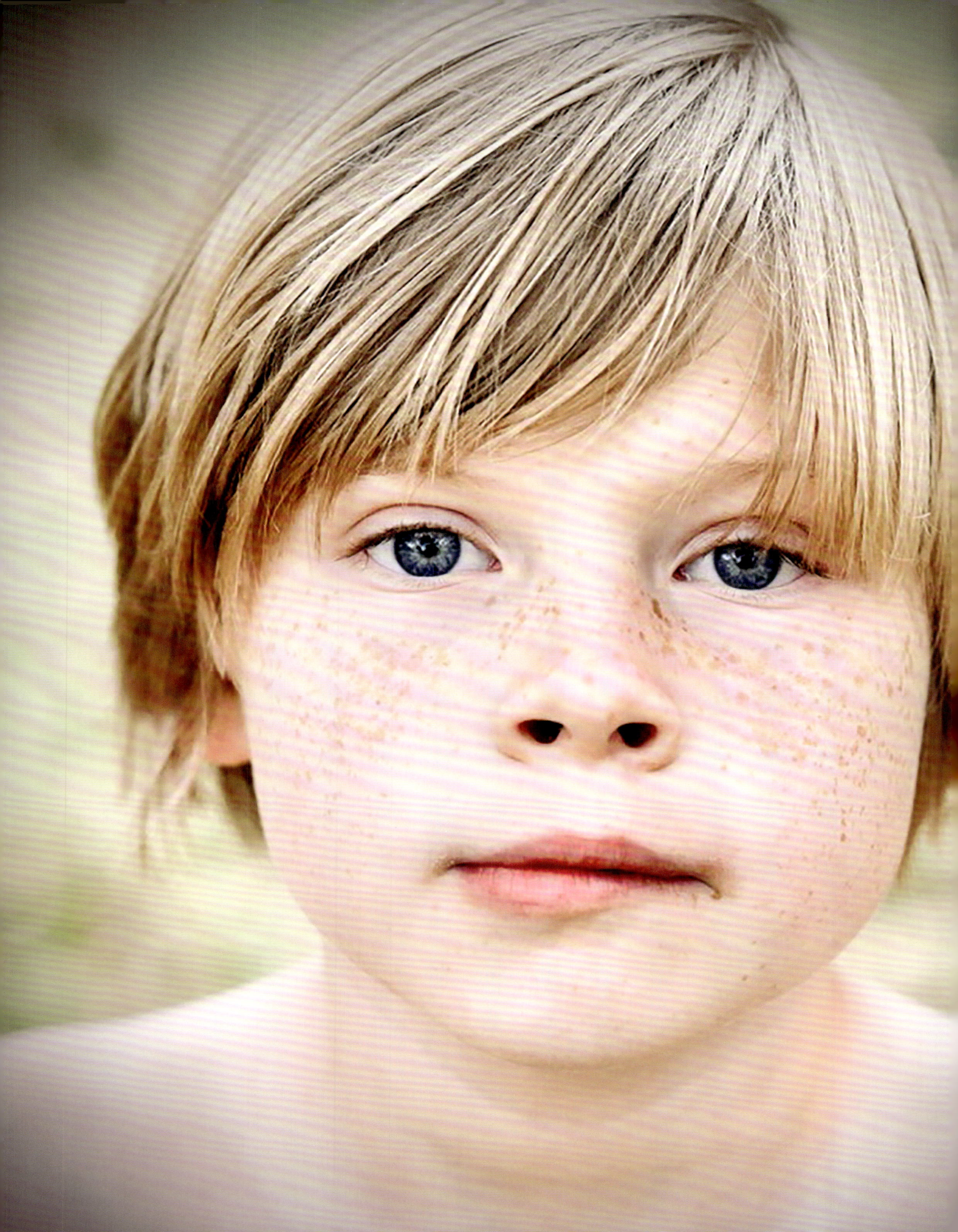

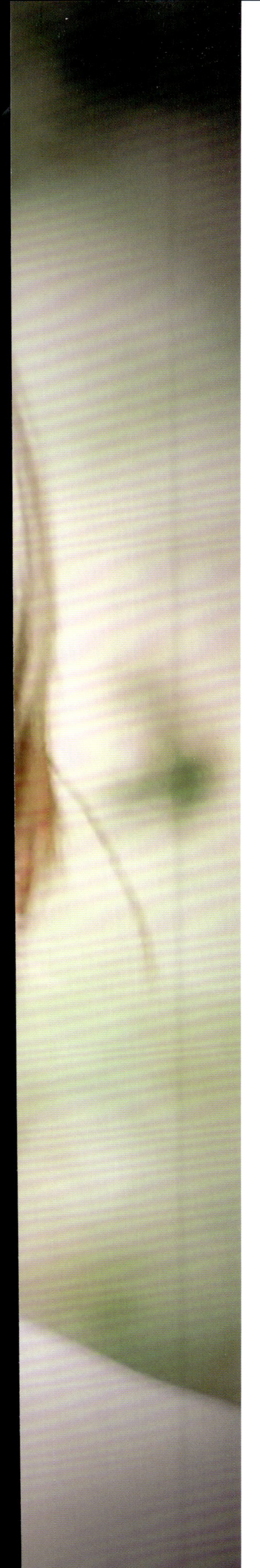

Nick

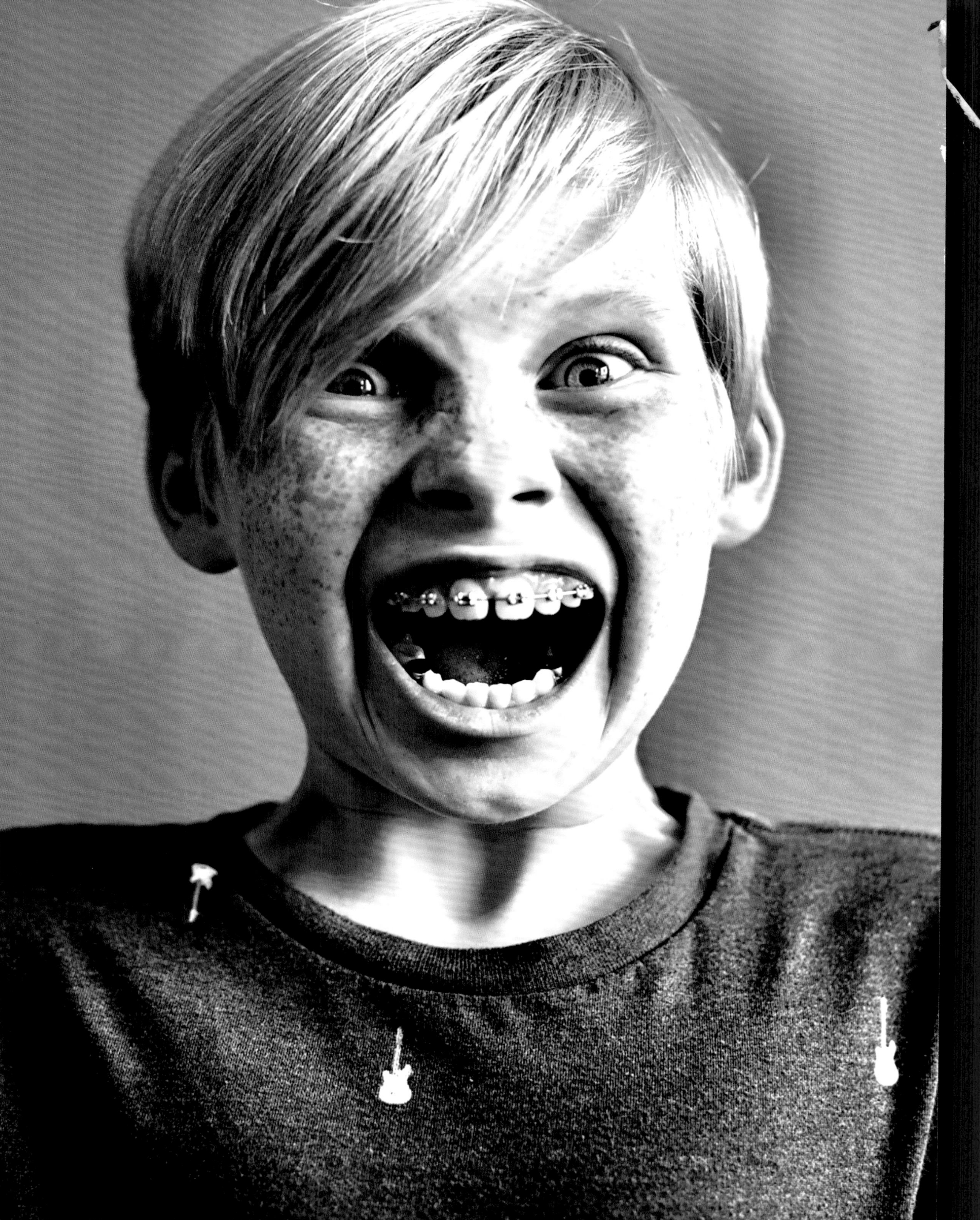

Nick

Nick

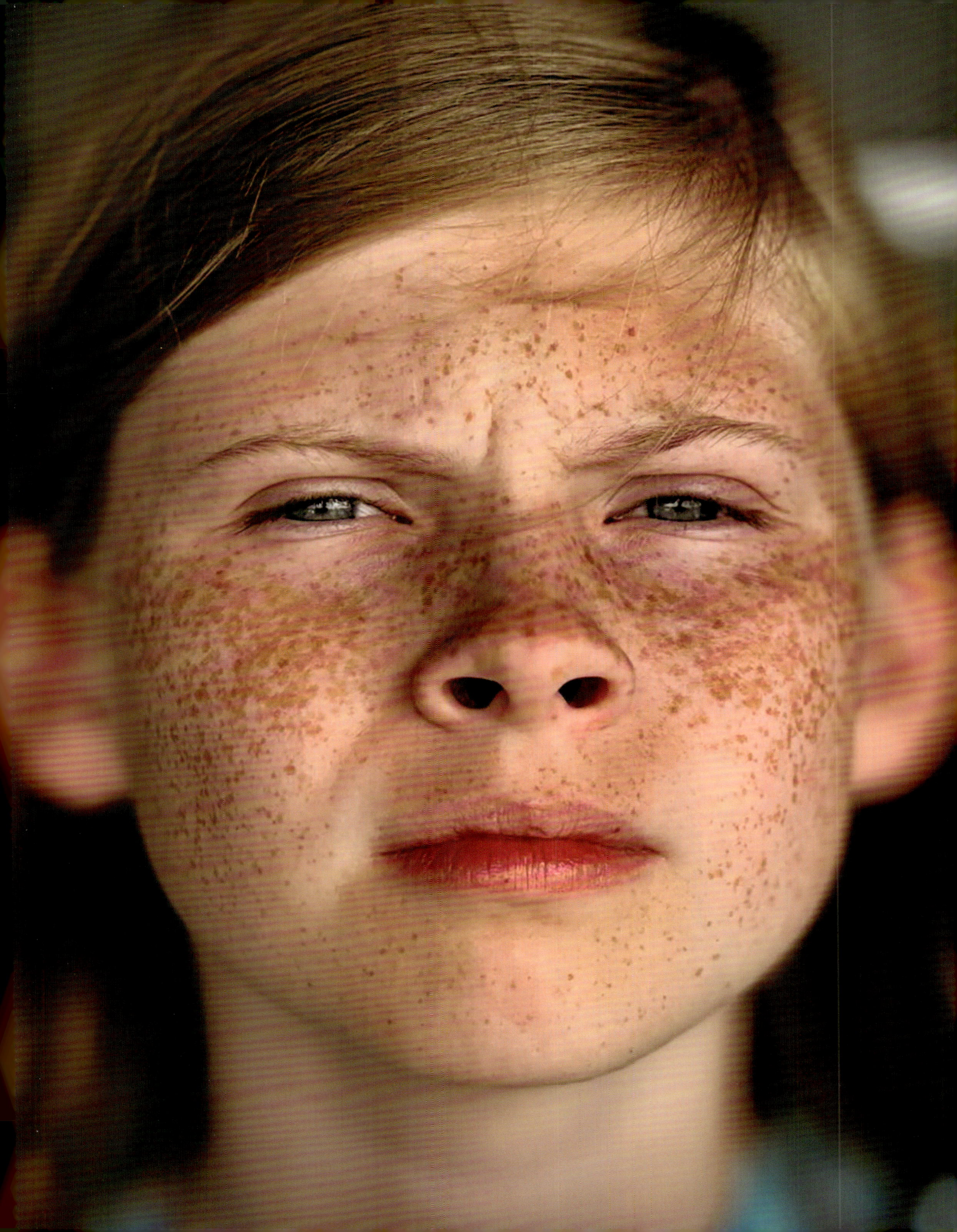

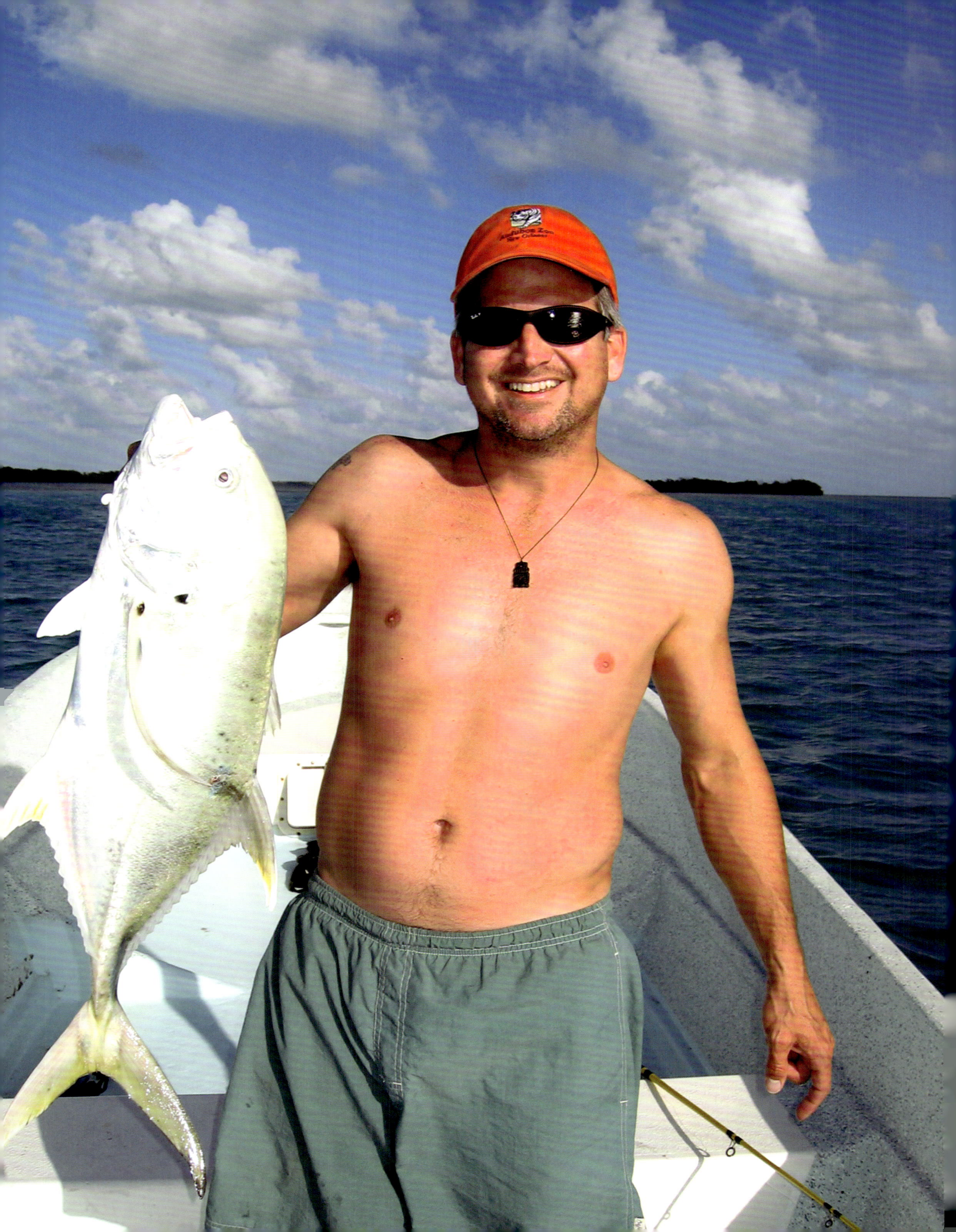

Matt and Nick

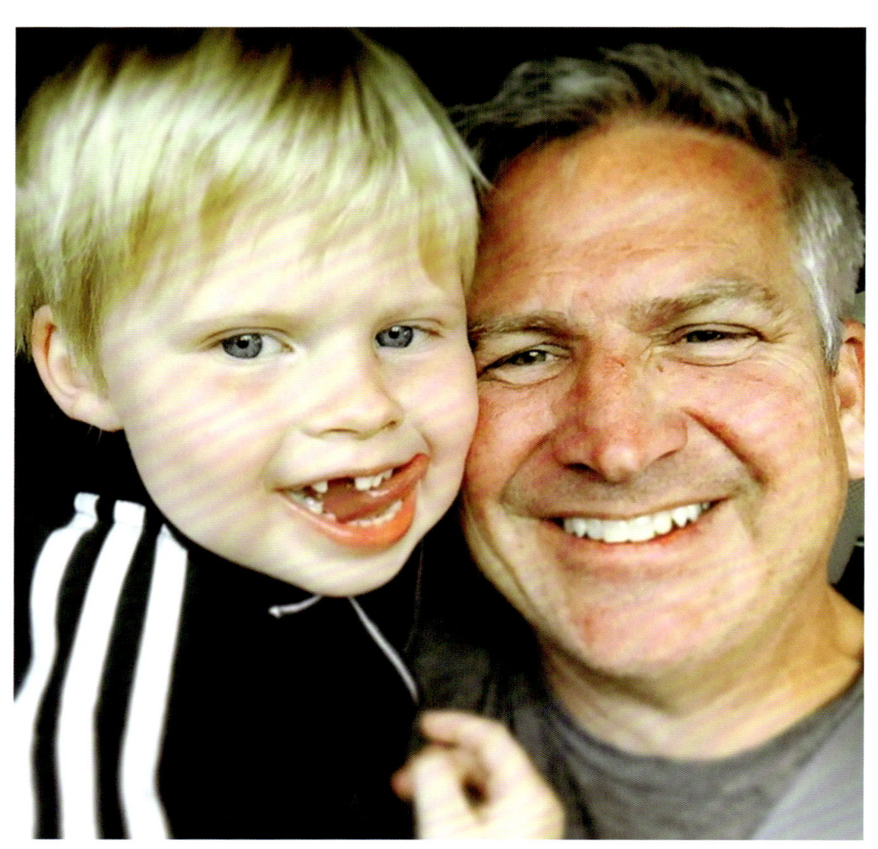

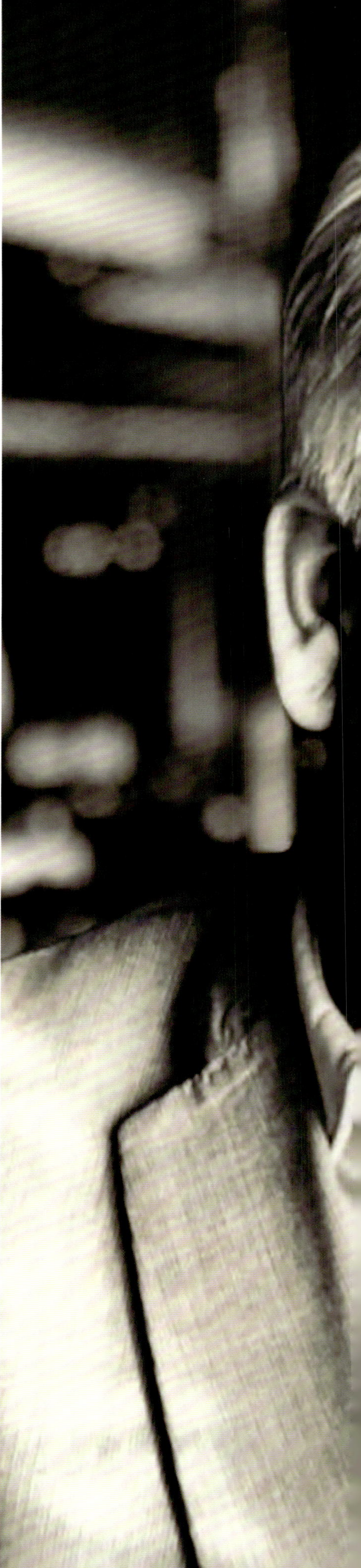

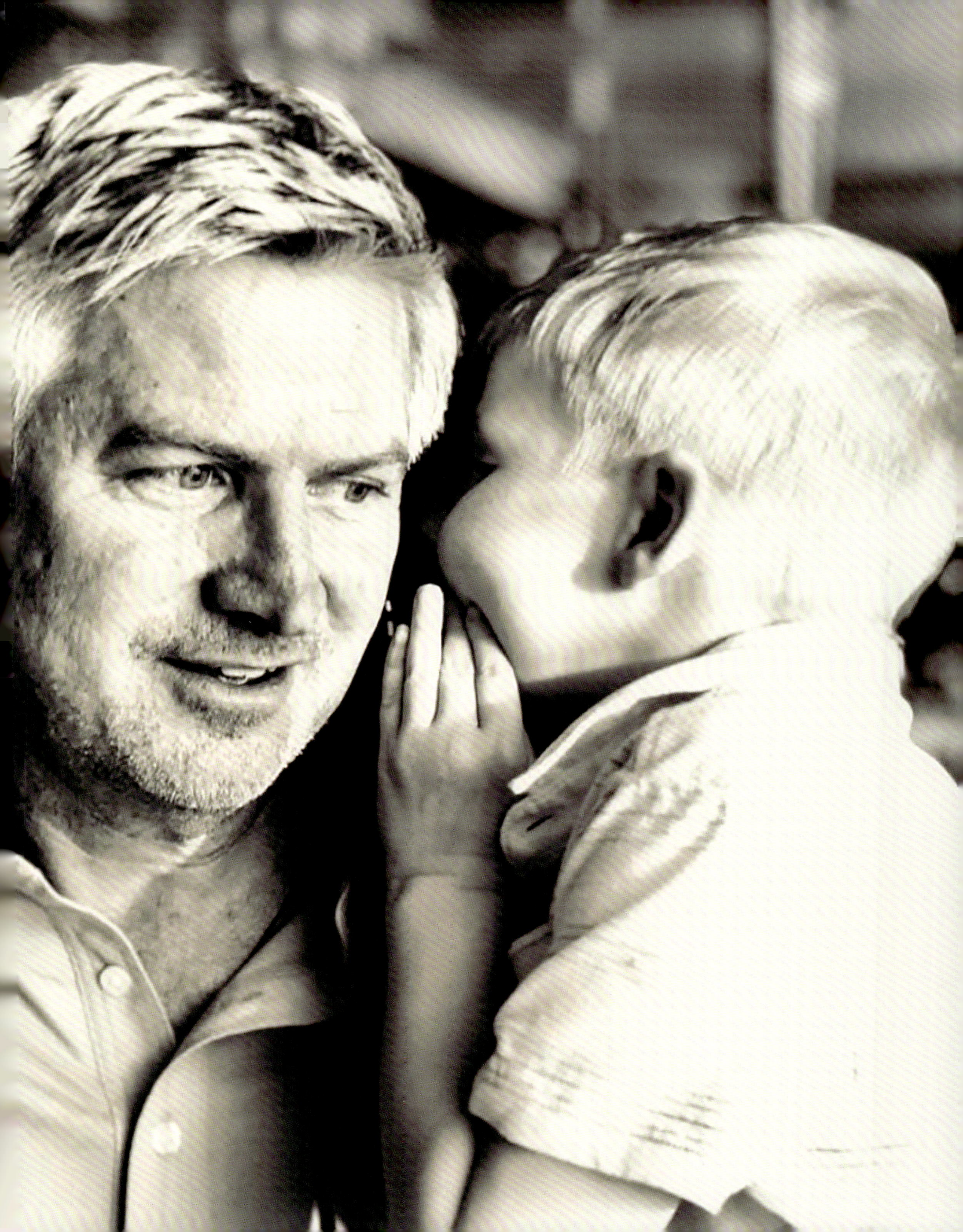

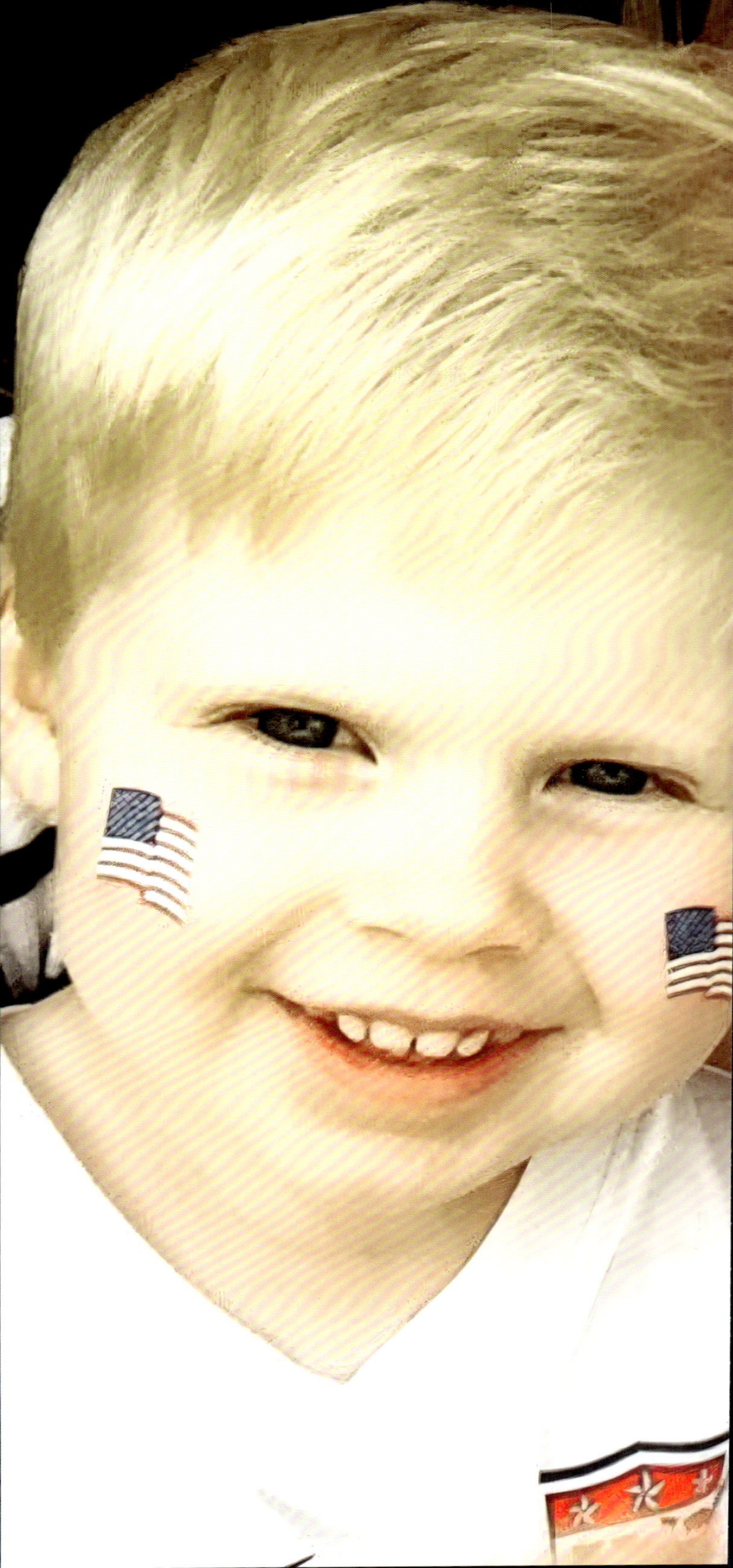

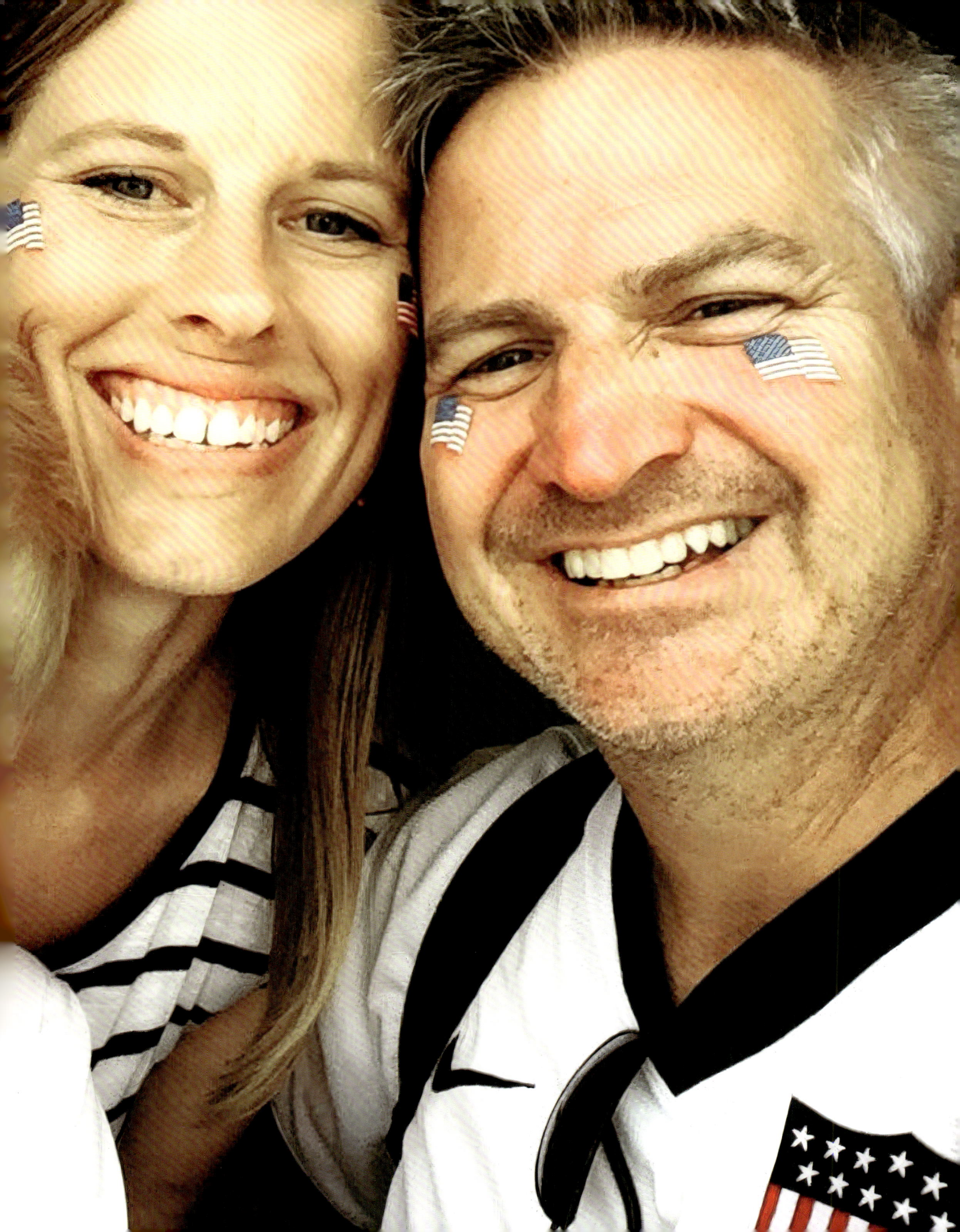

Life Through My Lens
by Matt Lankes

Seeing familiar faces year after year and watching them age in front of my lens—the subtle changes with the passage of time—is captivating for me as a photographer. We all grew older in front of and behind the camera on this film, cast and crew alike. I might win the award for the most gray!

Making the commitment to such a long project was easy, not really having a concept of the time it would require. Then after a few years I looked at the images collected so far and became excited by it all, looking forward to the final volume of work. Photographing all of the talented actors and crewmembers was a moving experience, especially working so closely with Ellar. He has always been a very sweet person and I loved that he had an interest in photography. Ellar and his mom would ask to shoot with me on occasion. We would meet somewhere in Austin and walk around for a few hours, street shooting, wandering with the wind.

One particular moment that stays with me is the movie's darkroom scene. We were filming at the same high school in Austin where I had been a student, in the exact darkroom where I first learned to develop film and make enlargements. It was a flood of memories for me and I tried to impart that importance to Ellar. I think he got it.

We are continuing to shoot his annual 4x5 black-and-white portrait. Having completed Year 13, I am looking forward to many more. Being involved with the making of *Boyhood* was an incredible adventure that I will always treasure.

Matt Lankes was the official still photographer for the film Boyhood. *Essay reprinted from the book* Boyhood: Twelve Years on Film.

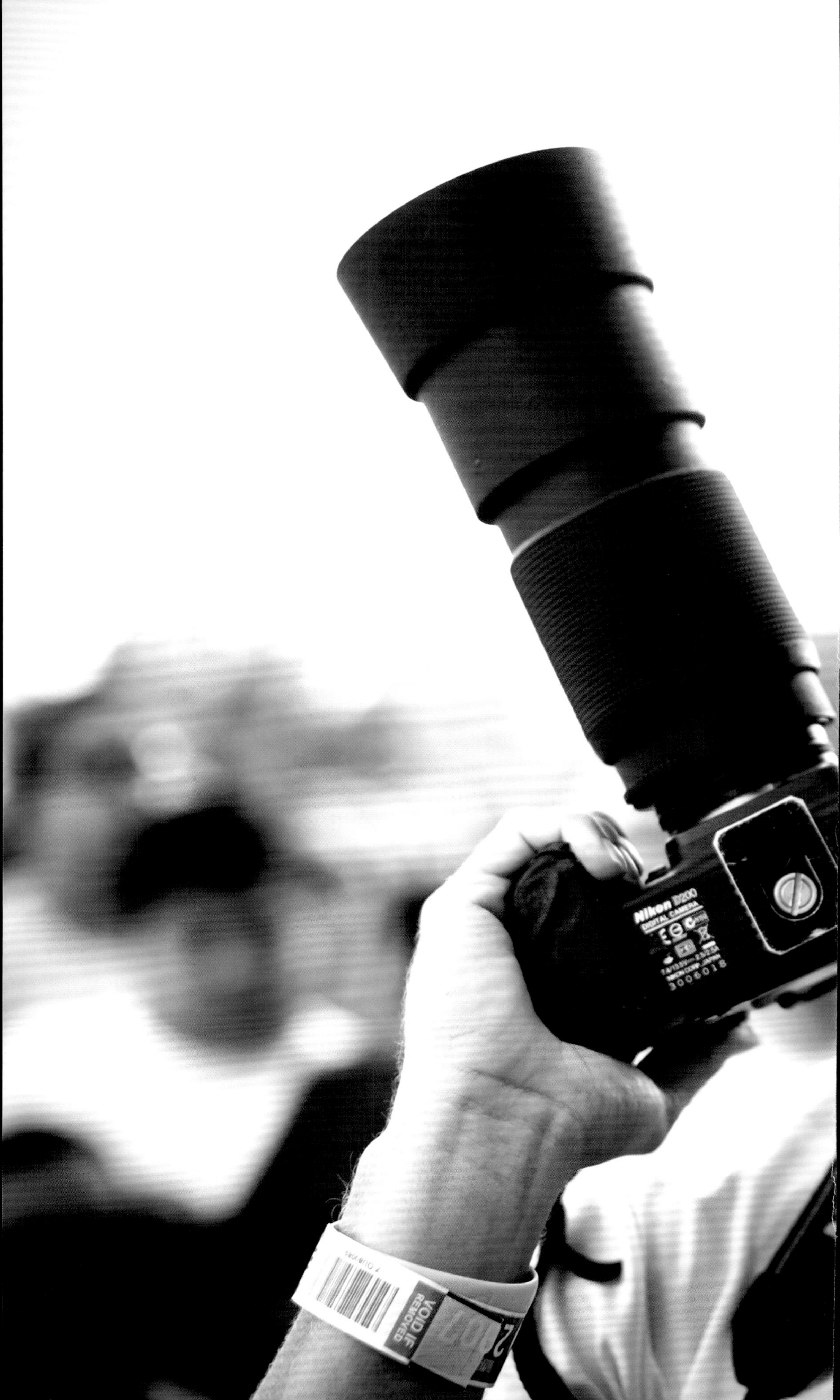

Matt

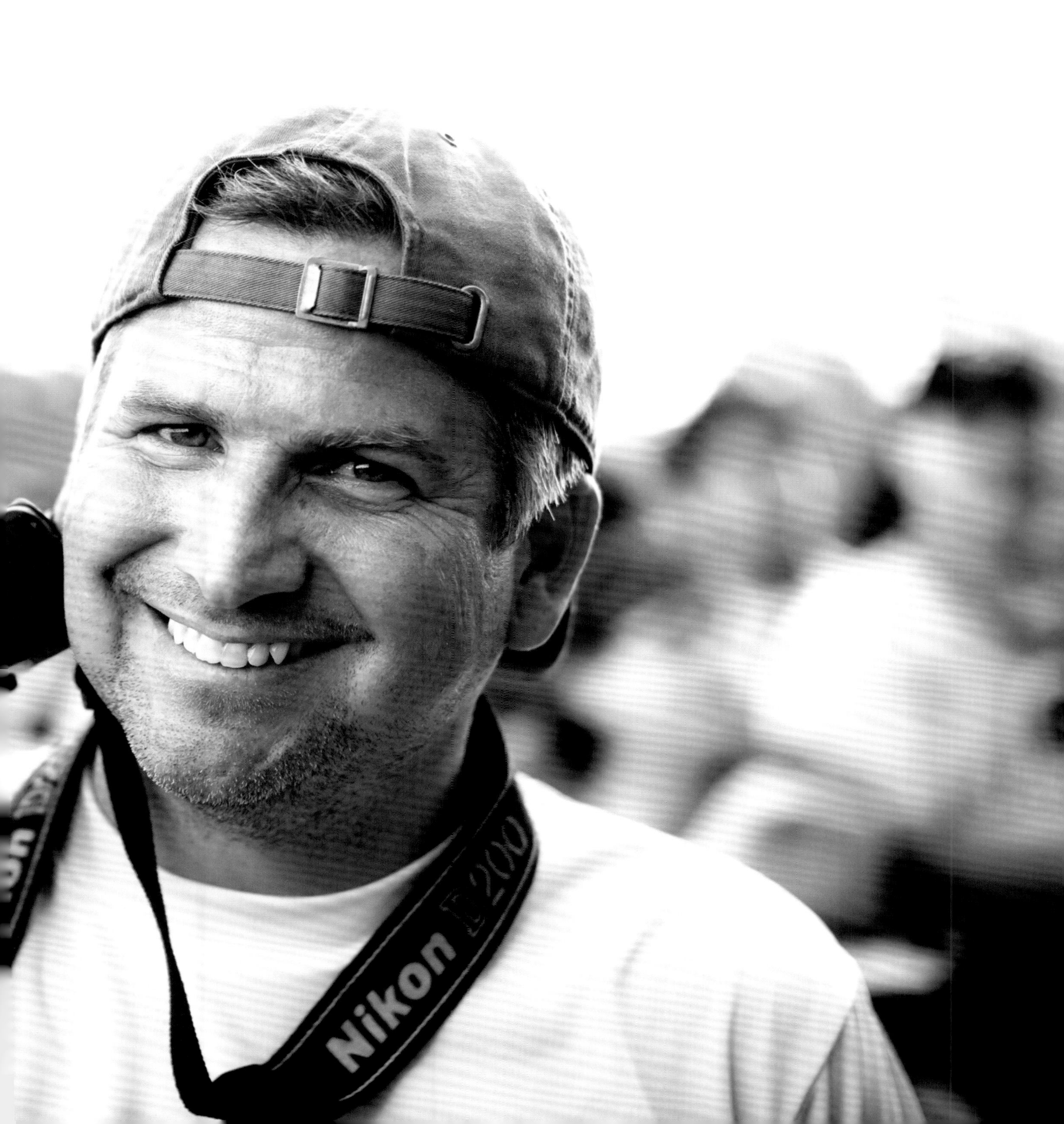
Nikon

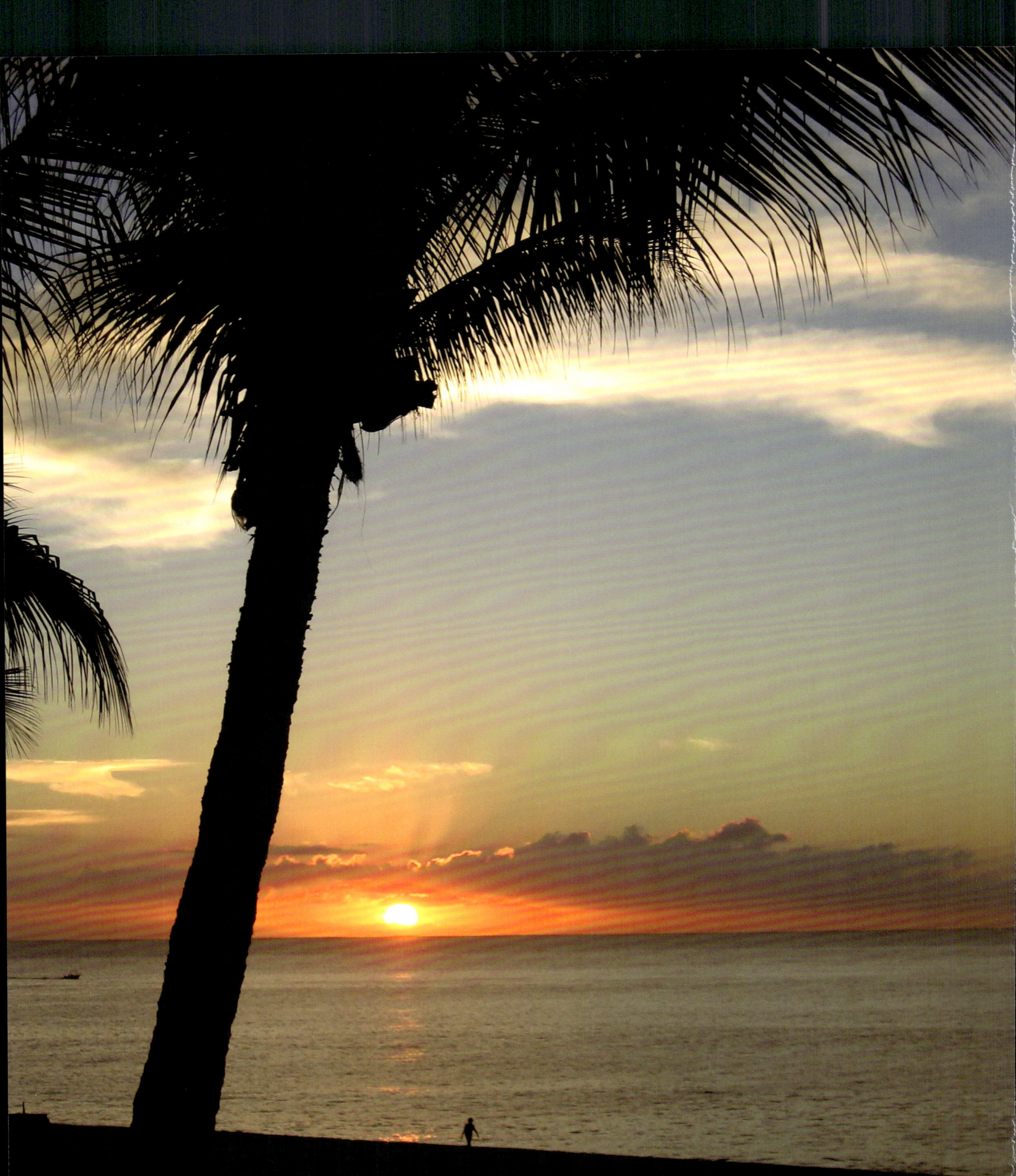

Book Project Donors

Austin Theater Alliance
Tom Amiss
Dave Anderson
Chris Cain and Still Austin
Blair Baxter
Kara Belew
Michelle Bell
Jody Westbrook Bergman
Brenda Blue
Lori and Kenny Braun
Donna and Jim Byerlotzer
Christy Carpenter
John Carver
Swell and Jake Cihal
Jodi and Eric Cole
Meg and Andy Davis
Missy and Rita Davis
Lauren Douglas
Mirsa and Walter Douglass
Kerri and Chuy Espinoza
Cari Ezell
Casey Fannin
Michaela Ferrell
Tyler Finzel
Erin Fohn
Lisl Friday
Elizabeth Gibson
The Whelan Girls
Kamille and Ryan Girton
Jace Graf
Russell Gravatt
Bobby Hale
Sara Hatfield
John D. Holmes
Hopdoddy Burger Bar
Joyce and Jim Howell
Jennifer, Calder, and Sledd Allen
Maica Jordon
Bill Kennedy
Jennifer Koch
Richard Kriese
John Langford
Rolinda and Gerald Lankes
Mandy Lawley
Sandra Leslie
Marci and Gregory Marchbanks
Kathy Mayer
Matthew Mayfield
Rob McGrath
Nancy and Wyatt McSpadden
Marcy Melanson
Jan Mirkin-Early
Moonshine Grill
Todd Mosely
Negeen Mosley
Hanalei and Merritt Myers
Anna Nagelkirk
Catherine and Chuck Nicholson
Karen and Jim Nicholson
Victoria Walker and Mark Nicholson
Elizabeth and Michael O'Brien
Cory Older
Matt Ott
Phyllis and Rick Patrick
Courtney and Charlton Perry
Turk Pipkin
Forrest Preece
Jody Pyle
Ceecy and George Robinson
Bruce Robison
Karen Rohe
Kevin Russell
Julie Hoyt Savasky
Nina and Frank Seely
Annastassia Prasanson and Raian Siao
Darden Smith
Jobell Smith
Jessica Stamp
Lana McGilvray and DJ Stout
Suzi's Chinese
Dana and Thomas Twombly
Diana Uhlaender
Virginia Visser
Robert Walden
Beth Weber
Adam Weisberg
Adrian Whipp
Catherine and David Wilkes
Amy Zeinner

First Edition 2025

Published by
Friends of Matt Lankes

All photographs by Matt Lankes and unknown photographers except for those on pages 11, Caroline Mowry; 12 (top), Jamie Lankes; 14 (middle), Laura Wilson; 200, Walter Douglass; 236, Roger DeGregori; and 238-9, Cathleen Sutherland.

Book Design by DJ Stout
and Julie Hoyt Savasky

Prepress by Jared Stevens
Prepare. Produce. Print

Printed by Martin Book
Management, Shenzen
Reliance Printing

Printed in China

Matt Thomas Lankes (1969–2025) lived a rich and meaningful life, but he left us too soon. In the summer of 2025 a group of **Matt's** friends came together to create this book of his life's work. It is a lasting tribute and a parting gift to a talented photographer and his loving family.

Special thanks to **Paul** Bardagjy, **Dana** Frank, **Catherine** Gonzales, **Jace** Graf, **Richard** Linklater, **Lana** McGilvray, **Jamie** Nicholson Lankes, **Teresa May** Nichta, **Michael** O'Brien, **Julie** Hoyt Savasky, **Nina** Seely, **Darden** Smith, **DJ** Stout, **Cathleen** Sutherland, **Natalie** Thomas, and **Savannah** Welch.